LUXURY TRAINS
of the World

LUXURY TRAINS
of the World

GEOFFREY FREEMAN ALLEN

Everest House
Publishers   New York

A Bison Book

Published by
Everest House
1133 Avenue of the Americas
New York
New York 10036

Produced by
Bison Books Limited
4 Cromwell Place
London SW7

Produced in collaboration with Colourviews
Limited

Library of Congress Catalog Number:
78-65527
ISBN Number: 0 89696 035 8

First Edition
Printed in Hong Kong

Designed by Charlton/Szyszkowski

CONTENTS

A close-up of a table in the 'Flèche d'Or'
Pullman that has been displayed, fully set
with the original crockery and cutlery in the
French Railway Museum at Mulhouse.
(Courtesy Cie Internationale des Wagons-
Lits et du Tourisme)

INTRODUCTION

Sadly I was too young and then too busy belatedly putting together a career after war service to experience American Pullman service in its prime. It is nearly forty years now since the US Government of the day laid an axe to Pullman foundations by lodging an antitrust suit in the summer of 1940. Four years later the company was directed by the District Court of Philadelphia to divest itself either of car operation or carbuilding. It chose to retain the Pullman-Standard carbuilding business. And so, after protracted negotiations, on 30 June 1947 the car operating company was sold to a consortium of 59 railroads. Under the new regime sleeping car operation continued under the historic brand name as did buffet catering within the cars, but Pullman dining was history. However dedicated the railroad service which took its place, the aura was not quite the same.

But I can vividly recall the inter-war meridian of European Pullmans. From the moment you disentangled yourself from the rest of milling humanity on a terminal platform and presented your reservation to the Pullman conductor you were suddenly, smoothly translated to VIP status. Any luggage was gently eased from your hand while you were ushered to your place. If you were known to the car staff – and a high proportion of Pullman travellers were regulars, their whims and habits diligently pigeonholed in the crew's memory – your customary drink would be elegantly served you at the precise instant you had settled your papers and eased back in your armchair, not a second before or after. Or they would know you liked thirty minutes' nap to unwind from the day's pressures before you took your aperitif; you could be sure it would arrive unasked just as you blinked and moistened your lips. If you were not, so to speak, a club member you would barely have time to adjust to the otherworldly ambience of rich wood panelling, armchairs, rose-shaded table lamps and gleaming tableware, to absorb the sensation of soft cocooning from the hubbub and harassments of run-of-the-mill rail travel, before the immaculately drilled corps of waiters would be discreetly rotating at your elbow. You felt a privileged passenger, undemonstra- tively pampered by staff who always looked and sounded as if they too felt privileged – to serve you.

To an extent the cream of Western Europe's 'Trans-Europ Express' and its more prestigious overnight sleepers preserve that ambience though not, in the economically stringent 1970s, with anything like the same prodigality of train staff. In one respect they are a generous cut above the limiteds of yesterday. Only a dedicated antiquarian, surely, could hanker for the gorgeous decor and furniture of the old-style *train de luxe* at the expense of the air-conditioned stillness and sweetness of ride which latter-day track and vehicle technology has achieved.

Give these improvements their proper weight, ally them to the skilled design for comfort of the interior of the best of modern passenger cars and the elite of today's trains can be counted as luxury vehicles amply justifying their place in this book. What they lack is individuality. Mention a famous train of the past like the 'Twentieth Century Limited,' the 'Chief,' the 'Flying Scotsman' or the 'Train Bleu' and a distinctive mental picture immediately forms. Each great train of old had its unique characteristics. These days we give trains names in a desperate effort to foster specific brand images, but more and more they take on a standardized cast in the name of economy. Only in Australia and South Africa, and in the 'Nostalgic Orient Express' re-created by an adventurous bold Swiss entrepreneur, does the individual *train de luxe* retain its special identity of unmatched accommodation and amenities.

I wish I could be certain that even today's manifestation has an infinite future. Alas, even in its present form it may not forever survive the jetliner's murder of the art of travel. Except in our own automobiles, these days we travel only to arrive. Travel is just an irritating preliminary to a change of scene, to be dismissed as quickly as technology can achieve. If Gallup were to poll opinion on the options of Concorde or the QE2 for an Atlantic crossing, would you bet on a majority vote for QE2? We have numbed ourselves to those delicious sensations of a gradually changing environment enjoyed from the comfort of a vehicle designed to maximize the pleasure.

So to hold their competitive place trains are going faster and faster. For reasons that need not detain us here, they are tending to be compressed to the body shape of a groundhugging airliner to achieve more speed. And for economy they not only become more standardized but adopt the miserably plasticized amenities of air travel. It will be a technological triumph when, in the mid-1980s, the new 160mph Paris–Sudest TGV line of French Railways whirls you from Paris to Lyons at a start-to-stop average of 132mph, but a step backward for mankind that on the journey you will grapple with lunch at your standard seat off a prepared airline-style tray dished out from an airline-style galley, not linger over an elegantly served *table d'hôte* in the distinguished diner of the 'Mistral.'

This book, then, not only salutes and re-creates the great trains of the past but pays equal tribute to the luxury trains of today while they are still with us. With that tribute goes my grateful thanks to the railroad administrations who have facilitated my experience of so many of them, and who have generously helped with information and illustration during the compilation of the story.

G. Freeman Allen
Laleham-on-Thames
August 1978

An impression of Sunday travel on the
Union Pacific Railway. (Courtesy Author's
collection)

Right around the globe the name Pullman is synonymous with high-class rail travel just as the name Stephenson is with steam rail traction. But whereas most of us have a mental image of Stephenson the man, outside North America how many could say for sure how Pullman came into their language. Pullman figures in the dictionaries of a score of the world's tongues as a symbol of luxury transportation.

Today authentic Pullmans are all but extinct as a category of railway carriage, but the name lives on as a mark of travel comfort. That is fair tribute to the American who was largely responsible for the rapid improvement of train accommodation at the end of the 19th century, ·George Mortimer Pullman.

Born in Brockton, NY, in 1831, Pullman grew up during the time of swift expansion of the US railway network in the second quarter of the century. His early career included spells of bookkeeping and cabinet-making, but it was the travelling he had to do when he took up contracting which spurred him to the enterprise that made such a mark on railroading.

Precious little had yet been done to adapt the basic railway car to the progressively longer journeys opened up by the spread and sprawl of the railroads. True, a so-called sleeping car had been devised in the late 1830s, but the early sleepers were crude affairs which were as far removed from the modern conception as a straw mattress from an ocean liner's cabin. No one had yet dreamed of meal service in trains. Pullman was· already harboring schemes for a total hotel service on wheels when in 1858 he had a trip in one of the primitive 'sleepers' which convinced him there was a rail travel market begging for bold commercial initiative.

The following year, 1859, he acquired two day coaches of the Chicago, Alton & St Louis Railroad to test his ideas. Working off the cuff without any detailed drawings and at a cost of $2000 per car, he refitted them with plush upholstered seats of which the backs could be lowered to form a continuous base for mattresses down each side of the central gangway when the car was in night use. With the beds made, curtains were drawn the length of each sleeping area on their gangway sides.

There seems to have been little pre-launch publicity to prepare customers for the new style of overnight rail travel when Pullman's first day-night convertible car made its debut between Bloomington, Illinois and Chicago on 1 September 1859. 'I had to compel the passengers to take off their boots before they got into the berths,' complained the conductor. 'There was no crowd at the station and the car, lighted by candles, moved away in solitary grandeur. I remarked to Mr Pullman that it was a fine car and he replied briefly, for he was a silent man: "It ought to be. It cost enough".'

But the outlay on these two conversions was a pittance ·set against Pullman's investment in his first all-new car. Public response to his first essay quickly confirmed Pullman's belief that travellers were ready to pay a premium for comfort, so in 1863 he recruited a small band of skilled artisans and set about the construction of a new vehicle which would fully realize his concepts. A bigger and heavier car than anything on American rails at that date, it was furnished with unimaginable richness for the railroading times with an interior finish of polished black walnut, candles set in elaborate chandeliers, pure linen bedding and marble washstands. In all it set Pullman back $20,170, five times the cost of the average railroad passenger car in the mid-1860s.

A stupid extravagance for such a rough-and-tumble travel medium grunted some critics when the car, named *Pioneer*, emerged from Pullman's Chicago workshop in 1865. Some were even fretting that the accommodation was so exotic it would be conducive to inconceivable vice. More to the practical point, however, the railroads took one look at the car and damned it as too bulky and expensive to work in their trains. That hurdle was soon

above: The 'Silver Palace' car copied from a Jackson and Sharp glass plate, *circa* 1880. (Courtesy Arthur Dubin collection)

above: The interior of the Pullman sleeper *Nimas*, built in 1883 for the New York, West Shore & Buffalo (a constituent of the later New York Central). The carpeting and upholstery were specially imported and the marquetry employed seven different types of wood. (Courtesy Arthur Dubin collection)

below: Pullman's first sleeper, the *Pioneer* of 1865. (Courtesy Author's collection)

Exterior and interior of a typical Pullman diner at the start of the final decade of the 19th century. (Courtesy Arthur Dubin collection)

cleared when, after the assassination of President Abraham Lincoln, the State of Illinois demanded that the car be included in the funeral train run over the Chicago & Alton line to Springfield on 2 May 1865. The railroad had no option but to hastily modify a few bridge and platform clearances to accommodate *Pioneer*. The prosperous future of Pullmans was thereby assured.

By 1867 Pullman had a fleet of 48 cars, either wholly owned by himself or in partnership with individual railroads under arrangements by which revenue from the cars' operation was shared. Most of the cars were built in railroad shops in those early days, when railroad managements were still skeptical about the whole enterprise. Michigan Central, for instance, was only persuaded that there were customers willing to pay two dollars for a berth in one of Pullman's expensive vehicles when it accepted Pullman's challenge and marshalled both Pullman sleepers and its own night cars in the same trains. Within a week the railroad found that travellers were flocking into the Pullmans: they were not merely showing a preference but flatly refusing to journey overnight unless they could get Pullman space. Other railroads took note and the demand for Pullmans became explosive.

The Pullman Palace Car Company as it became by incorporation in 1867, acquired its first car-building plant proper at Detroit, Michigan in 1870, but it could not cope with the business and nearly 300 more cars had to be assembled by railroad shops and other builders before Pullman established his remarkable works and surrounding town, America's

first planned industrial community, on 3600 acres of land at Lake Calumet on the southern outskirts of Chicago in 1880.

Pullman did not go unchallenged. Some railroads, like the Chicago, Milwaukee & St Paul, the Great Northern and the New Haven, persisted with their own sleeping car operations for many years. But rivals set up outside the railroad business as well. Best-known of them was New York politician and inventor Webster Wagner, who was set up in the car-building business under the wing of the railway empire which celebrated Commodore Vanderbilt was assembling in the Eastern US. Under Vanderbilt's auspices, Wagner's New York Central Sleeping Car Company had 150 of its 'palace cars' in use by 1880. Wagner himself was incinerated in one of his own cars when it was caught in a rear-end collision that led to fire in 1882 (on Friday the 13th of January, incidentally), but his business continued as the Wagner Palace Car Company until 1899, when 700 of its cars were active.

Wagner could never overtake Pullman, however. Apart from expanding his own operation and amassing enormous wealth in the process, the dynamic Pullman had been steadily buying out his competitors and imitators. Last to fall into his pocket, in fact, was the Wagner Palace Car Company in 1899, though by then George Pullman himself was dead of a heart attack, the delayed outcome of pressures exerted upon him by a very rancorous and violent railroad strike of 1894 which flared first on his own doorstep. In the early 1900s the railroads themselves gradually yielded their independent or shared sleeping car interests to the Pull-

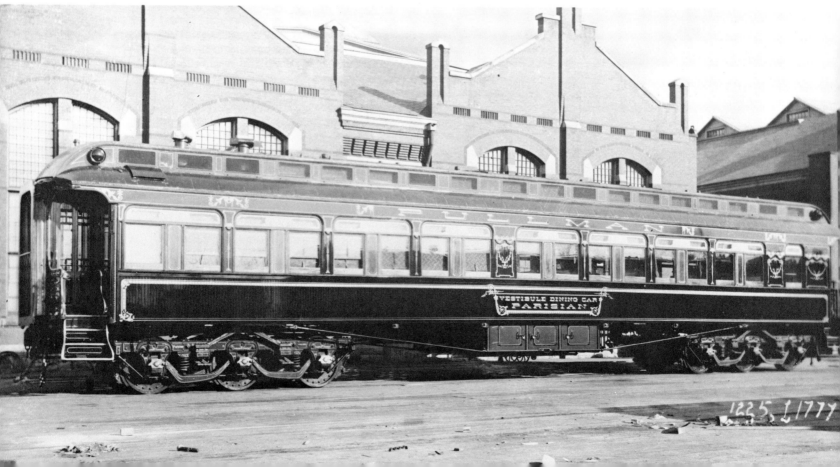

man Company, until by 1927 it had a US monopoly of the business.

From the start, of course, Pullman had made luxury day cars as well as sleepers his business. As early as 1867 he had had produced for the Great Western Railway of Canada his first 'hotel car,' the *President*, which combined sleeping space with a restaurant where you could get a dish of steak and potatoes for sixty cents or a plate of sugar-cured ham for forty cents. The following year he created for the Chicago & Alton his first full-length diner, which he named *Delmonico* after New York's famous Swiss-born restaurateur. It quickly proved such an attraction that while many railroads set up their own dining car operations Pullman added train catering to his activities and dining cars swelled what was now a spate of new parlor and sleeping cars from his plant.

By now the North American long-haul luxury train was taking clear shape. And the railroad map had extended so far that there was real need of the 'hotel on wheels.' To celebrate the availability of railroad the whole way from New England to the Pacific Coast, the Boston Board of Trade decided in the spring of 1870 to lay on for themselves and their families a sybaritic week-long land-cruise from their home city to San Francisco. No one was more alert to promotional opportunity than the public-relations-conscious George Pullman, who was frequently organizing demonstration trips in his cars the length and breadth of the rail network and readily agreed to make several brand-new cars available for this junket. One of them was fitted up with a printing press to keep the merrymakers entertained with a daily newspaper throughout the cruise, and an excerpt from the journal is worth quoting as a cameo of luxury train travel in those early Pullman days:

'The train leads off with a baggage car, the front of which has five large ice closets and a refrigerator for the storing of fruits, meat and vegetables. The balance of the car is for baggage, with the exception of a square in one corner, where stands a new quarto-medium Gordon press, upon which this paper is printed. Next comes a very handsome smoking car, which is divided into four rooms. The first is the printing office, which is supplied with black walnut cabinets fitted with the latest styles of type for newspaper and job work. . . . Adjoining this is a neatly fitted-up lobby and wine room. Next comes a large smoking room, with euchre tables, etc. The rear end of the car has a beautifully furnished hairdressing and shaving saloon. Following this come the two new hotel cars, *Arlington* and *Revere* . . . Two magnificent saloon cars, *Palmyra* and *Marquette*, come next. The train is completed by two elegant

top: Boston & Maine's 'Mt Desert Limited' of 1887 was New England's first 'limited' train. Formed of five umber-liveried and vestibuled Pullmans, it operated from Boston to the resort of Bar Harbor on Mt Desert Island, Maine. (Courtesy Arthur Dubin collection)

above: The driving of the pure-gold 'Last Spike' at Promontory, Utah on 10 May 1869 opened up the first transcontinental US route, the 'Overland,' and by 1888 the route was operating its first all-Pullman luxury train, vestibuled and electrically lit throughout, the 'Golden Gate Special.' The cars included ladies' and gentlemen's bathrooms and a barber's shop. (Courtesy Arthur Dubin collection)

commissary cars, *St Charles* and *St Cloud*. . . . The entire train is equipped with every desirable accessory that may tend in the least to promote the ease of the passengers – elaborate hangings, costly upholstery, artistic gilding and beautifully finished wood work marking every portion of their arrangements. Among the new features introduced into these cars are two well-stocked libraries, replete with choice works of fiction, history, poetry, etc, and two of the improved Burdett organs. These instruments are complete in every detail of stops, pedals, double banks of keys, etc. The cars of this train are lighted during the night in a new and novel manner, there

being under each an ingeniously constructed machine which produces from liquid hydrocarbon a gas equal in brilliancy to that made in the ordinary way.'

Nearly twenty years more were to elapse before electric lighting started to supersede gas or kerosene lamps, though steam heating from the locomotive was ridding railroad cars of their coal or wood stoves by the early 1880s. Another important development was the Pullman Company engineers' devising of the patented enclosed inter-car vestibule, first applied to the 'Pennsylvania Limited' in 1887; until then you could only get from one car of a train to another by a hazardous step from verandah to verandah over the

top center: A buffet served afternoon tea to patrons of this elegant parlor car in the B & M 'Mt Desert Limited.' (Courtesy Arthur Dubin collection)

top right: The sleeping car *Chicosa* was built for service on the Denver & Rio Grande Railway, *circa* 1888. (Courtesy Arthur Dubin collection)

above: The sumptuous interior of the 1889-built sleeper *Australia* of the Overland Route; it featured twelve Pullman sections, a drawing room and a stateroom. (Courtesy Arthur Dubin collection)

couplers. 'Ladies may now make social calls or wander at will, may even take long walks for exercise or to relieve monotony, so perfect are the arrangements and appliances,' as the publicity for another fully vestibuled luxury train of 1887, the Boston & Maine/Maine Central 'Mt Desert Limited,' put it. There is no doubt that, in the popularizing of rail as a general mode of long-distance travel this was a most important development, and much was made of it promotionally.

Pullman's early train menus were an incitement to gluttony. The range of fare was all the more remarkable when it was purveyed in one of his 'hotel cars,' because of the latter's constricted facilities; in these vehicles the meals were served from a cramped kitchen at one end of the car to tables set up at the seats in each 'section' of the convertible day-night area. Yet the 'hotel cars' plying the Chicago-Omaha leg of the Overland Route to San Francisco in the 1870s (following the ceremonial 1869 driving of the Golden Spike at Promontory Point, Utah which completed the first transcontinental route) were said to have listed no fewer than 15 seafood and fish dishes and 37 meat entrées, a prodigious selection of game amongst them.

Take a closer look at the breakfast and supper bill of fare on Pullman's 'hotel cars' operating over the Pennsylvania between New York and Chicago in the 1870s and 1880s. Besides the staples, offered in various styles, of chicken, ham, chops or titanic steaks (a Porterhouse with mushrooms on the side could be yours for just a dollar), the menu offered such exotica as English snipe, quail, golden plover and blue-winged teal: or oysters and clams, raw, stewed, boiled, fried or 'fancy roast' as you might wish, all at around 50 cents a portion. For three dollars you could wash all that down with a quart of Mumm's extra dry champagne,

then resurface for a rum omelette that would add only 40 cents more to your bill. And a fine brandy to finish? Yours to command for a mere 30 cents. 'The substantial citizenry' of the times, to quote the late Lucius Beebe, 'tucked their napkins in their collars, took a firm grip on their eating tools and put away everything on the bill from sardines and terrapin stew through to Indian pudding with hard sauce.'

Meal hours apart, life on the luxury train of the late 19th century revolved around the parlor car, with its gleaming and often marvellously ornate woodwork (that frequently applied to the car exterior too), its rich upholstery and heavy drapes, its massive freestanding armchairs with their delicate tasselled fringes and sometimes their individual footstools, its luxurious carpeting and maybe a library or a keyboard musical instrument in one corner. Some parlors incorporated a small buffet from which afternoon tea was decorously dispensed.

The really crack trains had a separate lounge for ladies and a club car for the men, where the latter could drink and smoke with a clear social conscience and heavy brass cuspidors were sited within comfortable aim of the leather armchairs. In the early days, in fact, men were debarred from drinking and smoking anywhere but in the club car. To skip beyond the time-span of this chapter, Prohibition in 1919 solved the drink question (although hard liquor was still available on trains running to and from Canada); by the time it was repealed in 1933 the cigarette had become such a natural appendage of the flapper that male segregation in club cars lost point and the vehicles gradually disappeared from the railroad scene.

The club cars were not just drinking saloons. Especially in the Eastern US the railroads were setting themselves out to impress the nabobs of commerce and the aristocracy of New England with all the trappings of a business office as well as a high-grade hotel on wheels. Some systems went to extraordinary external as well as internal extremes, none more so than the combined forces of the New York, New England and New Haven roads; not content with sumptuous velvet carpeting, white silk drapes and old-gold upholstery inside the train, they painted the car exteriors of their New York-Boston 'New England Limited' of 1891 overall white relieved only by gold lettering. Unsurprisingly, in an age of soft-coal-burning steam engines the 'White Train,' as it was bravely promoted, was so costly to keep clean that within four years it was repainted a more utilitarian shade.

Another highly colorful train, and one that adequately sums up the remarkable advance in North American luxury train travel by the end of the nineteenth century, was the new Pullman-built 'Pennsylvania Limited' launched at the start of 1898 to supersede the pioneering vesti-

buled formation of 1887 mentioned earlier. Externally this New York–Chicago train was a striking creation of Brewster green lower panels, cream the length of the windows and red above for the 'Pullman' legend, the whole generously embellished with gold filigree. Tradition has it that Pennsylvania chiefs took a fancy to the livery, which was effectively the Mexican national colors, when they were on a visit to the Pullman works and saw it applied to some palatial private cars the company was building for dictator Don Porfirio Diaz.

By now the facilities of a luxury train had been still further extended. Observation cars, for instance, were coming into vogue and the rear half of the 'Pennsylvania Limited's' last vehicle was a comfortable saloon with 5ft-deep plate-glass windows looking out over a verandah with elegantly wrought nickel and brass guardrails. Next to the saloon was a writing room, overhung by palms spreading from pretty jardinières and furnished

with secrétaire and bookcase; here a skilled stenographer was on call to take and type passengers' correspondence. The rest of the car was given over to private staterooms, each with its own lavatory, and decorated either in Oriental or Louis XVI style, with varying finishes in Circassian walnut, Tabasco mahogany, English oak, vermilion wood, rosewood or Santiago mahogany.

Next up from the rear of the train came the Pullman sleepers, featuring both the standard open-section areas and private drawing rooms with accommodation for two to five. One of the cars even boasted an incredibly ornate bridal suite with white woodwork, leaded glass, extravagant gilt ornamentation and metalwork, and lush velvet drapery. There was nothing strictly functional about the sleeper lavatories either: you stood on a ceramic tiled floor, studied yourself in bevelled mirrors and rested between operations on a padded wicker chair to admire polished woodwork that was as finely

top: In the winter of 1910 the New York, New Haven & Hartford introduced to its New York–Boston overnight service the most luxurious Pullman sleepers seen in public service. Each of the car's seven compartments had a full-length, four-foot-wide brass bedstead, a dresser, two chairs, a table, its own enclosed lavatory, an electric fan and its own heating controls. (Courtesy Arthur Dubin collection)

above: The observation lounge of the 'Oriental Limited' in a car which featured four compartments, a drawing room, a buffet and card-room, and a library as well as the lounge. Great Northern were proud of the fact that the train carried vacuum cleaners. (Courtesy Arthur Dubin collection)

right: The 1905 'Oriental Limited's' Pullman diner was supposedly styled to represent an English Inn interior with ceiling beams and leather-backed chairs. (Courtesy Arthur Dubin collection)

executed as any in the living accommodation.

Next came the diner, with elegant chairs backed and seated in embossed leather, overhung with more potted greenery and serving cuisine to challenge the finest of Chicago or New York hotels. And finally a remarkable multi-purpose car, mostly occupied by the men's saloon. To quote a contemporary description, 'it provides a buffet and all the luxury of an elegant, up-to-date club. There are daily papers, magazines and books on the tables, and facilities are at hand for those who care to play cards, chess or other games. Stock Exchange quotations are, with other items of commercial and general news, regularly supplied to the train at its stopping places. Passengers further have the advantage of a hair-dressing saloon, and there are bathrooms for ladies and gentlemen, equipped with the most approved accessories.' And finally, for this was still something of a novelty to be stressed in promotion: 'The

train is lighted by electricity, the current being obtained from a dynamo supplying the 500 lamps comprised in the installation; but in order to guard against the possibility of a breakdown, Pintsch's gas fittings can at a moment's notice be brought into use in any of the compartments. Electric reading lamps are available in the library car and in the observation car, and every section of the drawing-room sleeping cars contains two such lamps, which may be used by passengers who desire to read in their berths.' The Pennsylvania's publicity department had a right to proclaim the 'Limited' to be 'the newest and most complete Railway Train of this progressive age.'

Many moguls of industry sought something even more palatial than the private rooms of a train like the 'Pennsylvania Limited.' The commercially eager Mr Pullman was only too happy to build and sell the tycoons their own private cars, which they would pay to have attached to ordinary service trains, or in some

cases would have hauled free, so humbly grateful were railroads for such august patronage. As the luxury train acquired fresh refinements, so – on an even grander scale – did these so-called business cars. The most splendid of them ran to marble baths, hidden safes, Venetian mirrors, an open fireplace burning balsam logs (this was John Pierpont Morgan's), and even an English butler to supervise the car's private cellar and the Lucullan output of its kitchen. By the 1920s some magnates were paying as much as a quarter of a million dollars for a single vehicle.

The railroad baron Jay Gould on occasion ran his own complete train of four business cars, the staff of which included a doctor to tend Gould's fragile digestion, plus a special baggage car at the head-end that served as a byre for the milch cow which was taken on the trip to ensure a flow of milk with butterfat constituency exactly conforming to the great man's dietary regime. A French nobleman, Count Boni de Castellane, who was in-

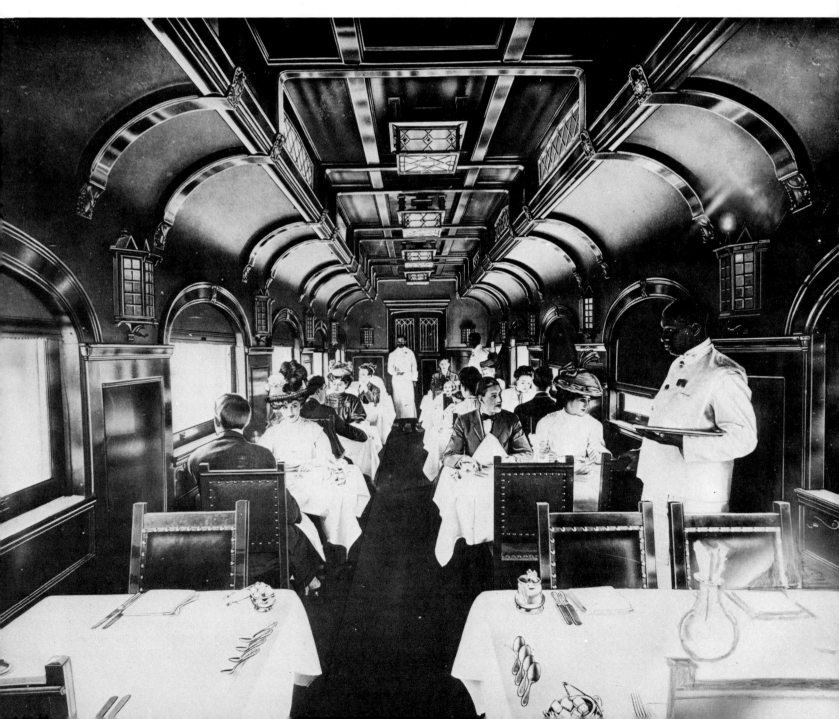

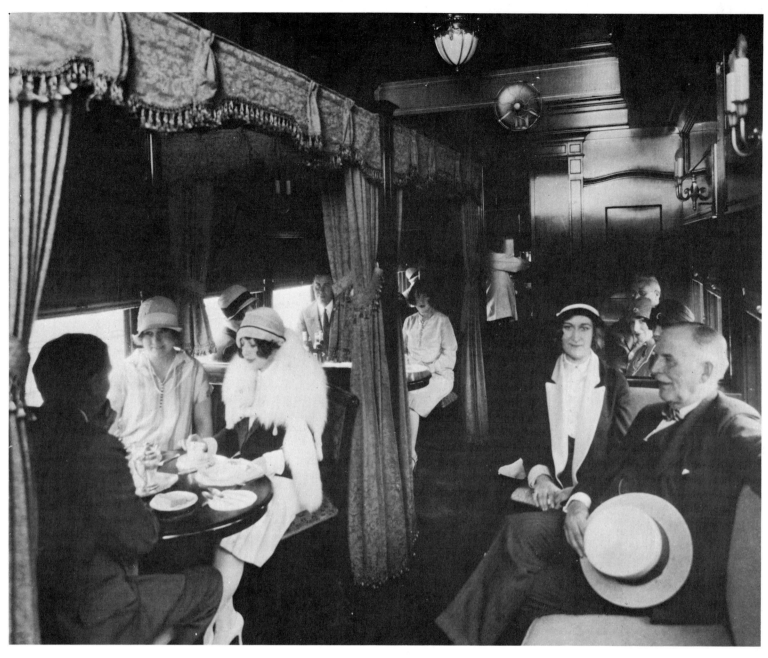

Afternoon tea service in the ladies' lounge of Chicago & Alton's 'Alton Limited.' Although not seen in this particular picture, the waitresses were arrayed in full Japanese rig. (Courtesy Arthur Dubin collection)

vited aboard Gould's train when he was courting the banker's daughter, recorded in his diary that full evening dress was *de rigueur* at dinner and that guests' private rooms teemed with butlers and valets, footmen, ladies' maids and grooms of the chambers. Of another eminent financier's wife it was said she had assured a journalist that 'The only thing that's economical about our car is the solid gold plumbing. It saves polishing, you know.'

In terms of housekeeping the Pullman operation outstripped that of any chain hotelier for scale. At the peak of the company's business in the 1930s and 1940s its stock of sheets and towels, for instance, was between $3\frac{1}{2}$ and 4 million in each case. The activity of its ten company-owned laundries was frequently worth more than three million dollars a year. It refused to rely on outside suppliers for furniture and fittings, and maintained its own workshops to turn out anything from a richly upholstered chair to a toilet seat. The company had its own printing plant,

too, from which issued a torrent, not only of working documents and publicity material, but of minutely detailed rule-books and instruction manuals for Pullman staff.

From the start Pullman determined to make the personal service in his cars a byword. Nothing, it was said, could happen in a Pullman car that was not covered by an instruction in the voluminous Pullman rulebooks, which dealt meticulously with every conceivable aspect of hospitality and service to the passenger, whether it be from conductor, porter, maid, barber or bus boy. And the tradition was jealously upheld by the car staff, to the extent that they were perenially the prime quarry for staff head-hunters from the White House as well as upper crust hotels and clubs. The Pullman porter – generally Negro, from the date the first black porter was recruited in 1870 – was justifiably the American symbol of service to the customer for decades.

As a mark of Pullman's infinite care for

detail of service, a full quotation of the Pullman service manual's elaborate step-by-step primer on the basic art of filling an order for a beer is an apt crown to this chapter:

'1. Ascertain from passenger what kind of beer is required.

2. Arrange set-up on bar tray in buffet: one cold bottle of beer, which has been wiped, standing upright; glass two-thirds full of finely chopped ice (for chilling purposes – making it a distinctive service); glass; bottle opener; and paper cocktail napkin. Attendant should carry clean glass towel on his arm with fold pointing towards his hand while rendering service.

3. Proceed to passenger with above set-up.

4. Place bar tray with set-up on table (or etc.)

5. Place paper cocktail napkin in front of passenger.

6. Present bottle of beer to passenger displaying label and cap. Return bottle to bar tray.

7. Pour ice from chilled glass into other glass.

8. Open bottle of beer with bottle opener in presence of passenger (holding bottle at an angle), pointing neck of bottle away from passenger; wipe top of bottle with clean glass towel.

9. Pour beer into glass by placing top of bottle into glass, and slide the beer down the side until beer reaches about two inches from the top – then put a collar on the beer by dropping a little in the glass which should now be upright.

10. Place glass containing beer on paper cocktail napkin.

11. Place bottle containing remainder of beer on table before passenger, with label facing him.

12. Remove bar tray with equipment not needed by passenger and return to buffet.'

The renowned New York–Boston 'Merchants Limited' of the New Haven. (Courtesy Arthur Dubin collection)

CHAPTER 2
EARLY EUROPEAN TRAINS DE LUXE

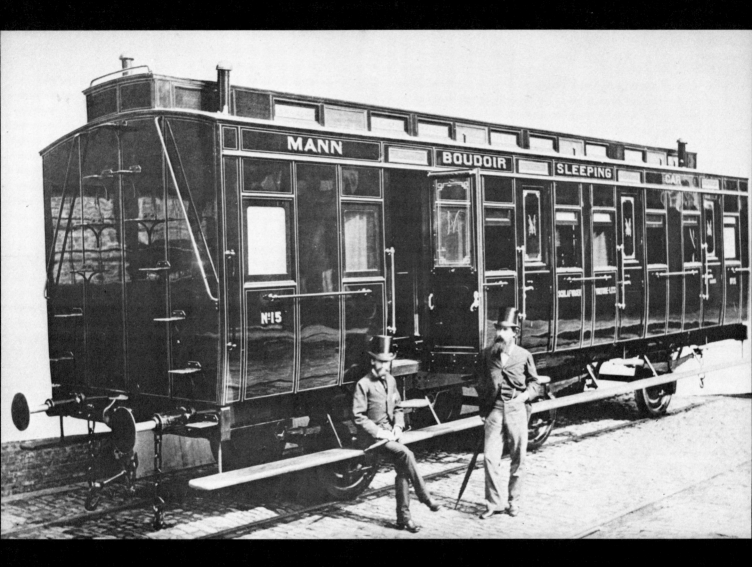

A six-wheeled Mann Boudoir sleeping car
of 1873, No 15 in the Wagons-Lits fleet.
Seated on the running board is Georges
Nagelmackers, founder of the Wagons-Lits
company; to the right is Colonel William
d'Alton Mann.   (Courtesy Cie Internationale
des Wagons-Lits et du Tourisme)

The Birth of Wagons-Lits

The first international luxury trains of Europe sprang directly from George Pullman's American model. Midwife, as it were, was an imaginative young Belgian, Georges Nagelmackers, the son of a wealthy banking family. But for his boudoir indiscretions, European rail history might have taken a different course, for it was Nagelmackers' entanglement in a risky *amour* that drove his parents to pack him off to America in 1868, when Georges was 23. There young Nagelmackers became mightily impressed with the burgeoning Pullman operation.

By 1868 European sleeping cars were not total fantasy. More than one railway had essayed some primitive development in the mid-1850s and before the 1860s had expired, the Hanoverian State Railways, for instance, were operating recognizable sleepers in their *'Courierzüge'* between Berlin and Cologne. But the international train was barely known.

The monolithic state railway systems of today's Europe were decades away in the future. In those days the Continent's rail map was a maze of individual systems within each country and it was hard enough to get those of the same nation to collaborate, let alone those divided by frontiers. The Continent's first international train, launched between Basle, Switzerland, and Rotterdam, Holland, in 1863, had only been realized through an alliance of Europe's great banking houses, who bought the cooperation of the railways involved by handouts of investment money all round.

Coming from that background, Nagelmackers marvelled at the freedom with which Pullman's sleepers ran long journeys across the territory of one US railroad after another. Europe, he was convinced, would be wide open to a similar enterprise.

Back home in Belgium early in 1870, Nagelmackers returned to the mine engineering in which he had been trained, but only for as long as was needed to work up his rail project. By April that year he was ready to publish his plan for a European sleeping car company, but immediately the Franco-Prussian war set him back. So did the frozen attitudes of some of the railway managements he approached. At one headquarters, it is said, he was magisterially put down as a jejune dreamer just for suggesting railway coaches needed lavatories.

Nevertheless, by the autumn of 1872 Nagelmackers had persuaded sufficient railways to sign short-term contracts with him to allow the foundation of a company bearing his name and the construction of his first sleeping cars. Tiny four-wheelers, they were convertible day-night coaches like Pullman's, with seat backs that lowered to form bed bases, plus an upper berth which was lowered by rope from the ceiling at night; room was found for two lavatories, one of which had a hand-basin.

The first service was launched in 1873 between Ostend and Cologne, then later extended to Berlin. Initial public response was so tepid that the enterprise looked doomed, particularly since the terms of the deals with the railways allowed the latter to discard Nagelmackers' cars at short notice. The outlook grew blacker still when Nagelmackers' own family refused to underwrite the building of the six-wheeled cars upon which the German railways were insisting.

Happily Nagelmackers found a new angel in an American military engineer, Colonel William d'Alton Mann, who had retired from the Army with a crock of gold amassed through astute patenting of every piece of equipment he devised. Intent on putting his capital into rail sleeping-cars, but realizing Pullman was already too well entrenched in his own country, Mann had come to England to look for business. He was delighted to join forces with Nagelmackers in a new company, Mann's Railway Sleeping Carriage Co, which was registered in London early in 1873.

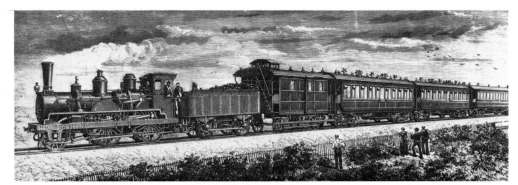

above left: An artist's impression of the inaugural 'Orient Express' of 1883, headed by a 2-4-0 of France's Est Railway on the first stage of its journey from Paris to Avricourt. (Courtesy Cie Internationale des Wagons-Lits et du Tourisme)

left: A sketch of the dining-car interior on the 1883 'Orient Express.' (Courtesy Cie Internationale des Wagons-Lits et du Tourisme)

An artist pictures the interior of an 1883 'Orient Express' sleeper showing a section made up for day use (left) and night use (right) with the lavatory in the center. (Courtesy Cie Internationale des Wagons-Lits et du Tourisme)

Although the new company's vehicles were branded 'Mann Boudoir Sleeping Cars,' Mann was content to leave the direction of the business very largely in Nagelmackers' charge. And soon the enterprise was well round its difficult corner. The first major achievement was the conclusion of a couple of contracts with two railways in France, where Nagelmackers had initially encountered particularly stubborn opposition to his concept. The second was Mann's coup in persuading the British Prince of Wales, later King Edward VII, to use one of the company's cars for a visit to Berlin and as far beyond as the Russian border on the trip's continuation to St Petersburg. The subsequent publicity, plus the newly-signed French contracts, enabled Nagelmackers to get off the ground the international service his ambition particularly cherished, from Paris to Vienna.

Nagelmackers' marketing instinct was shrewd. The Paris-Vienna operation was an immediate commercial success and at last the railways themselves started to show interest in expanding the sleeper network. By the end of 1874 the company had over 40 cars in operation and two years later Nagelmackers had enough capital and confidence to buy out Mann. On 4 December 1876, with a capital of four million Belgian francs, the concern re-emerged, registered as a company in Brussels, though with its administrative and operating base in Paris, as the *Compagnie Internationale des Wagons-Lits et des Grands Express Européens* – more popularly and succinctly known in recent decades as 'the Wagons-Lits Company' or 'the International Sleeping-Car Company.'

Until 1880, when the first eight-wheel bogie sleeper – indeed, Western Europe's first bogie passenger car of any kind – was introduced between Berlin and Frankfurt, the sleepers were still fixed-wheelbase four- or six-wheelers. There was one vital difference between Pullman's early American sleepers and the

cars operated in Europe (under a patent, naturally) in the Mann regime. The Mann Boudoir cars had their berths in separate, enclosed compartments, not in the 'sections' of an otherwise open body interior that was the pattern of the basic Pullman. Some of Mann's cars had a separate six-berth compartment for patrons' servants, who could be summoned to attend by an old-fashioned bell-pull in each of the main berths. As yet, of course, there was no vestibule connection between cars; that came in its first primitive form in 1880.

As will be described later, England was the stage for the debut of Europe's first restaurant car proper in 1879 though two years earlier the newborn Wagons-Lits company was experimenting in Germany, between Berlin and Bebra and between Bebra and Frankfurt-am-Main, with a halfway stage to full-scale train catering. Some borrowed ordinary passenger cars were fitted up with tables at which passengers could make a meal from luncheon baskets obtained before the journey. Then in 1881 the Wagons-Lits company produced its first restaurant-kitchen car, a six-wheeler, for service between Paris and the French Riviera.

The scene was set, the props in place, for the appearance of Europe's first true international luxury express.

The Orient Express

The first step was to capitalize on the popularity of the Paris–Vienna service and persuade the railways involved to experiment with a train composed entirely of sleeping cars and diners. That was done, very successfully, in October 1882 and early the following year eight railway administrations agreed to operate a similar train all the way from Paris to the Near East. At first through rail travel right to Constantinople was impossible as the Russians had successfully hamstrung completion of a direct access from Western Europe to the Turkish capital to protect their shipping business; until 1888 the 'Orient Express,' as it was

known from its birth in 1883, had to decant its passengers into a ferry at Giurgiu on the Danube south of Bucharest, the Roumanian capital. From Rustchuk, on the opposite Bulgarian bank of the river, passengers were taken on by rail to Varna and there put aboard an Austrian Lloyd liner for the last stage of their journey to Constantinople. By 1884 however rails had been laid at least as far as the Turkish border.

There was no great flourish when the 'Orient Express' made its first public run on 5 June 1883 since new vehicles ordered for the service, especially the first bogie dining car, were not yet available. It was a strictly limited-load train confined to just two sleepers, the diner and mail/luggage vans and running twice weekly. The outward one left Paris at 19.30 on a Tuesday or Friday evening and fetched up in Constantinople at 07.00 the following Saturday or Tuesday morning.

On 4 October 1883 Nagelmackers hosted a party of some 40 VIPs and journalists on a demonstration run of the 'Orient Express' with his new bogie cars. No ladies graced the guest-list. Apart from reluctance to submit them to the rigors of a five-day overland journey, nobody was quite sure such a train would not be bushwacked by brigands when it left Western European civilization behind at the Carpathians.

It was a memorable journey. Already entranced at the first sight of their sleeping berths, the journalists were next astounded at the appointments of the diner and its cuisine. The first dinner lasted until midnight. At Augsburg in Germany, consternation: the diner had run an overheated axlebox. But Nagelmackers had prepared for emergencies. A replacement was available at Munich, though it could only be one of the six-wheelers, which ran so execrably that passengers complained they could not pour or drink wine without splashing. That apart, the journalists enthused at the riding of the train: 'it runs so sweetly,' reported one,

'that you can even shave in comfort at fifty miles an hour.'

At a little station between Budapest and Temesvar a Hungarian gypsy band led by one of the best-known violinists in all Bohemia was lined up to greet the train. They came aboard, the diner's furniture was temporarily removed to the luggage van, and for the next few score miles the travellers were exquisitely serenaded with a medley of waltzes and czardas. Those musicians were a versatile bunch. They had Turkish music to salute the First Secretary of the Ottoman Embassy who was one of the trainboard guests. Then they modulated serenely, to a sequence of French songs, culminating in a spirited attack on the Marseillaise. As they came up to the anthem's chorus, the diner's kitchen door burst open and out strode the train's brawny and formidably bearded Burgundian chef, red-faced with passion, to lead the party in a strident bass-baritone. The band had been playing solidly for some two-and-a-half hours when it left the train at Temesvar.

Another surprise awaited the guests at Bucharest: the King of Rumania would like to receive the party at his summer palace. That was four hours' journey away by local railway, but they made the detour, despite the fact that unaccountably His Majesty sent no conveyance to meet them and they had to traipse on foot in a deluge of rain from the branch station at Sinaia to the royal hideaway.

The subsequent history of the 'Orient Express' is complex and need not concern this book in detail, particularly in its variations of route. It was withdrawn at the outbreak of war in 1914, then revived in 1919 but for just a year as a luxury train for exclusive use of the Triple Entente's military brass on a Paris–Vienna–Warsaw itinerary. Following completion of the Simplon Tunnel in 1906, the link with Constantinople was taken over from the spring of 1919 by the 'Simplon–Orient Express,' of which more anon, but the 'Orient Express' was back in public

business two years later. Another train was added to the 'Orient' family in 1932 with the creation of the 'Arlberg–Orient Express' from Paris to Budapest and Bucharest via Basle, Zurich, Innsbruck and Salzburg.

The Trans-Siberian Express

By the late 1890s Wagons-Lits diners and sleepers were established on a network of services criss-crossing most of Europe. Spain and Portugal had been penetrated, though because of the variation of track gauge – 5ft 6in in Iberia as against the standard 4ft 8½in in France – a through journey from Paris entailed a change of cars at the frontier. Devices for the easy exchange of bogies or the alteration of wheel gauges beneath vehicles were decades away in the future. At a very early stage in his enterprise Nagelmackers had struck up a long-lasting business arrangement with the Peninsula & Oriental Shipping Co, whose Indian mail ships sailed from Brindisi. This helped open up the Italian frontier to Wagons-Lits cars. In the early 1890s the Wagons-Lits company was running a special 'P & O Express' for the line's British voyagers from Calais via the Grande Ceinture line around Paris and Mont Cenis Tunnel to Brindisi, which was still operative between the two World Wars. Before that, in 1883, a general Calais -Nice-Rome service had been inaugurated and in the same year Nagelmackers launched a number of internal Italian services following his acquisition of an Italian subsidiary of Pullman's American company. Another development of the 1880s was a service through the Balkans from Budapest to Belgrade and Nis.

There remained the challenge of Russia. Czar Alexander III had shown some concern to improve the quality of rail travel and in the mid-1860s some tentative efforts at sleeping cars, even cars with their own bathrooms, had appeared on Russian railways. But Nagelmackers' first approaches were rebuffed. Instinctively the Russians recoiled at a concept

that simplified access to their country. But in 1882 the Czar relented and agreed to a Wagons-Lits service to St Petersburg.

At first Nagelmackers had only a Paris-St Petersburg operation in mind. Once again he was up against the problem of differing track gauges, but he was already thinking ahead of his time to a means of changing the bogies beneath his cars at the Russian frontier break of gauge. And once a means of interchanging bogies had been devised, why not maximize the use of it? Why stop the proposed train at Paris? Why not continue it southward all the way to Lisbon, with a second change of bogies at the Franco-Spanish border?

Such a 'North-South Express' might well have come about had not Bismarck and the Prussians refused to let their country's railway be used as a corridor for international communication with Russia. Until 1896 Nagelmackers had to content himself with a service from St Petersburg to Vienna (his vision of interchangeable bogies was not to be realized until 1969) and Wagons-Lits passengers on the new service had to change trains at Warsaw.

In 1898, the silver jubilee year of the Wagons-Lits company, the St Petersburg working was developed into one of the most prestigious of Europe's pre-World War I international luxury trains, the St Petersburg-Nice-Cannes express. Its passenger list frequently read like pages from a directory of the Russian and Austrian nobility of the period. Full evening dress was at least socially if not statutorily obligatory at dinner. Despite the fineness of the company's bed-linen many of the travellers, it was said, had their accompanying valets and maidservants bring along the household's own silk sheets and (probably) monogrammed pillowcases.

The other outstanding event of Nagelmackers' silver jubilee year was his conclusion of a contract with Czar Alexander III to run the 'Trans-Siberian Express.' That prompted construction of the most sumptuous vehicles in Wagons-Lits' pre-

above: The Wagons-Lits saloon, intended for the 'Trans-Siberian Express,' which was displayed at the Paris Exhibition of 1900. (Courtesy Cie Internationale des Wagons-Lits et du Tourisme)

top right: The 'Trans-Siberian Express' diner as shown in Paris in 1900. Note the roominess allowed by the wide Russian track gauge. (Courtesy Cie Internationale des Wagons-Lits et du Tourisme)

right: A corner of the smoking-room in the 'Trans-Siberian Express' saloon exhibited in Paris in 1900. (Courtesy Cie Internationale des Wagons-Lits et du Tourisme)

World War I fleet. The Czar had ordered construction of the Trans-Siberian Railway to begin in 1891. By 1898 the builders had got roughly halfway along the route that was eventually, by 1904, to extend over 5000 miles from Moscow to the Pacific port of Vladivostock. The line's first Wagons-Lits service, therefore, was the 'Siberia Express' between Moscow and Tomsk, initiated in early December 1899. The timetable allowed six nights for the journey, but that could easily be extended by the hazards of early Siberian railroading, for the route was single-track and the control of operation emphatically less than impeccable. Worse still, the first half of the line was laid with too light a rail and breakages were chronic. Derailments were frequent and all too often the operators took an age to extricate themselves from the resultant blockages of traffic.

In 1900 Paris staged a World Exhibition. Nagelmackers' company was one of the biggest exhibitors and there was no doubt about the principal attraction of its display: two remarkable lounge cars commissioned with an eye to completion of the Trans-Siberian line. One had its main saloon gorgeously finished in the style of Louis XVI, the windows hung with

rich curtains in pink silk, the plush green upholstery of the chairs set off by gilt embellishment and marvellously molded woodwork and painted ceilings that made the construction look seamless. At one end of the saloon was a piano. Elsewhere in the vehicle was an elegant hairdressing saloon, a bathroom and a gymnasium. The other vehicle was a smoking saloon in Louis XV style, finished with similar extravagance, and including in its equipment a safe for passengers' valuables. Also on view at the Paris exhibition were new sleeping cars for the Trans-Siberian, among them the first second-class sleepers that Wagons-Lits had built. The two spectacular vehicles, as it happens, never served on the 'Trans-Siberian Express.' The Louis XVI car (without its piano, eventually sold to a Frenchman) finally reached Russia rebuilt as a diner for ordinary service. After installation of a small kitchen the Louis XV-style saloon was exported, but on arrival in Russia it was reserved for private hire, though at such an exorbitant rental that it saw little revenue-earning service. A second attempt to build luxury saloons, again with a piano, for the 'Trans-Siberian,' this time in Russian workshops,

was frustrated by the outbreak of the Russo-Japanese War in 1904.

In 1903 the 'Trans-Siberian Express' could begin running the whole way from Moscow to Kharbin in Manchuria and thence into China – in fact, the Wagons-Lits company actively promoted through travel overland to Chinese cities, opening up its own hotel at Peking in 1904 (hotel operation was one of Nagelmackers' earliest diversifications and worldwide it is still today a major component of the ramified Wagons-Lits Company business). If you could stomach the rigors of the journey – Moscow to Kharbin alone stretched over nine days – you could travel overland from London to Shanghai via the 'Trans-Siberian Express' in 1903 for around £70.

At the peak of its history the 'Trans-Siberian Express' carried a train staff of 17. One of the Wagons-Lits conductors doubled as a hairdresser, another was a qualified nurse, with the makings of a modest chemist's dispensary in his charge. Should your illness be too dire for the train's medical resources then there were arrangements whereby the train staff could telegraph ahead and have a doctor awaiting the train at its

next main stop. Amongst diversions to help you while away the long journey, the train carried a library of more than a hundred books in four languages, plus a stock of chessboards and chessmen and dominoes. If you were bored with the confines of your sleeper berth (in the first-class cars, incidentally, there was a separate lavatory shared by each pair of adjoining compartments), then the diner was open continuously from 07.00 to 23.00 – and there was always the bathroom, with running hot and cold water, located in the combination baggage-and-staff car. The Trans-Siberian trip must have been a hard grind for the train crew, for whom only four beds were provided in the staff car. Still, their existence was Elysian compared to that of any dogs

passengers took with them. The animals were allowed on the train, but only if they were left chained and muzzled in the luggage van for the whole nine-day journey.

Needless to say the Revolution wrote finis to the whole Wagons-Lits operation in Russia. The company's entire stock of Russian cars, by then totalling 161, was sequestered without so much as a kopek in compensation.

The Rome Express

When we come to the 'Rome Express,' after the 'Orient Express' probably the best-known of Europe's early luxury trains, the histories of Nagelmackers and Pullman begin to intertwine. Although the advent of Pullman in Europe is dis-

cussed separately in the succeeding chapter, his influence on the creation of the 'Rome Express' cannot be overlooked.

As soon as Pullman extended his operations to Europe at the start of the 1880s he tried to interest Nagelmackers in a merger under the title of *Compagnie des Wagon-Lits et des Wagons-Salons*. But Pullman lacked the strength of hand to support his sanguine bid for a fifty-fifty partnership. By then Nagelmackers had over 100 cars in operation throughout several countries, whereas Pullman had little more than half that number in just two countries, Italy and England. The greater part of his fleet was running on British railways, where public reaction to them was initially so lukewarm that the future of the Pullman operation was as yet decidedly insecure. After protracted negotiation Nagelmackers unsurprisingly rejected Pullman's overtures and set out his stall to keep Pullman penned in the British Isles.

Within a few months it looked as if Pullman was cunningly outflanking him. Scanning his London *Times* one morning early in February 1883, Nagelmackers exploded when his eye caught a paragraph announcing a de luxe Pullman special to run, with connecting train from London, from Calais to Rome for a Fine Arts exhibition in the Italian capital. How could that be, when Nagelmackers' company had exclusive sleeping car contracts with the Nord and PLM Railways of France? Moreover the felony was compounded.

First, the special was scheduled away from London on a Friday, 23 February 1883, the normal day for the start of a journey from the British capital to make an overland connection with the P & O Line's Indian Mail sailing from Brindisi. Until

right: A close-up of a wooden-bodied sleeper built by Wagons-Lits in 1902 for the 'Rome Express.' (Courtesy Cie Internationale des Wagons-Lits et du Tourisme)

center: Before World War I the *maîtres d'hotel* of Wagons-Lits *train de luxe* diners wore the splendid rig seen here – plus, it would seem from the gentleman in the background, all warranted military honors. This photo is dated 1912. (Courtesy Cie Internationale des Wagons-Lits et du Tourisme)

bottom: The ornate toilet of a Wagons-Lits sleeping car around the turn of the century. (Courtesy Cie Internationale des Wagons-Lits et du Tourisme)

now, because of Pullman's one Continental mainland foothold in Italy, Nagelmackers had not been able to run his cars throughout to Brindisi, nor could they take the shortest route from the English Channel coast that was available following completion of the Mont Cenis Tunnel. Pullman's exclusive contracts with railways in the north of Italy compelled the Wagon-Lits train to make a circuitous journey to Bologna and there transfer its passengers to Italian Pullmans. Now here was a rival *de luxe* train billed to follow the newly-completed direct route via Paris, Dijon, Modane, the Mont Cenis and Turin to Bologna. Worse still, the British press, hitherto so ecstatic in their acclaim of Wagons-Lit service, seemed to suggest that this Calais-Rome Pullman exercise was – or should be – the opening of an unprecedented age of luxury travel between England and distant parts of Europe.

The intruding Pullman special had come about because the Pullman company had five surplus cars in England it wanted to transfer to its Italian operation. Reluctant to see them expensively freighted empty across Europe, it had come up with the idea of running a special to link up with the Rome exhibition and the upcoming travel agent Thomas Cook had been only too happy to share in the organization and marketing. That was the first move towards a close alliance between Pullman, Thomas Cook and subsequently Wagons-Lits which endured until each of the companies was affected by changed economic circumstances generally and by the new character of railroading in recent times.

Despite Nagelmackers' strenuous protest the Pullman special ran. But in so doing it actually smoothed the path for a direct Wagons-Lits service. Late in 1883 as mentioned earlier, Nagelmackers inaugurated his through train from Calais to Nice and Rome, with rapid commercial success. Within a few years, as we have also remarked, the Wagons-Lits Company took advantage of a reorganization of Italian railway companies to buy up – at formidable cost – Pullman's contracts in that country. And in 1897 the stage had been set for the launching of the 'Rome Express,' which opened its account as a once-weekly *train de luxe* on 15 November that year. This is how a contemporary journalist who rode the inaugural service recalled his experience:

'We arrived at Calais on time and were immediately boarded by the usual rush of *rouleurs* or corporation of porters. Instead of being conducted to the Customs House, there to undergo the usual *visite*, which means having a salad made of the contents of one's bags, with a guarantee mark of – say honesty – impressed on the fronts of your best dress shirts by the dirty thumbs of the *douanier*, we were conducted between a double row of *douaniers* direct to the 'Rome Express,' standing spick-and-span, ready to receive us into its warm corridors.

'It was composed of two sleeping cars, one restaurant car and two mail and baggage cars. The sleeping cars had berths for 20 passengers each [the writer must have been befuddled by an unpleasant Channel crossing: the original 'Rome Express' sleepers actually incorporated one four-berth and seven two-berth compartments]. The restaurant car, to which was also attached a smoking saloon, had places at table for 42 passengers.

'Most of the passengers went to their compartments and divested themselves of their heavy coats, wraps and hats. One old friend of mine, the well-known editor of a London newspaper, put on a pair of old and very easy-looking dancing pumps. Not the least of the many advantages of a *train de luxe* is that one can make oneself as comfortable as in one's own home, the temperature of the train being kept at about 68 degrees Fahrenheit. We saw ourselves all together for the first time when we sat down to lunch. We were eighteen and we soon became friends. It is astonishing what a well-cooked and well-served meal will do in that respect. Our menu was as follows:

Hors d'oeuvres variés
Filets de sole au vin blanc
Côtelettes de mouton à la Mont Cenis
Petits pois à l'Anglaise
Galantine de volaille
Langue écarlate
Fromage Fruits
Café et Liqueurs

'Simple and wholesome. *The peas had been brought from Brindisi, ex-Corfu* [author's italics, not the 1897 writer's – such was the trouble taken to serve fresh peas in November!] by the homecoming 'Peninsular Express,' which had arrived at Calais the day before. The pears at dessert were the finest I have ever eaten and the grapes were Chasselas – the real thing. This lunch cost – not, of course, including wines and liqueurs – exactly four shillings! We sat an hour over our coffee and cigars, nearly coaxed to sleep by the soft gliding motion of the car.... We arrived in Paris at 4.35 [at the Gare du Nord] and left again at 4.50, having picked up some dozen passengers, amongst them an attaché of

the British Embassy in Rome, a celebrated opera singer and his charming wife, who were going to Turin en route for Milan; and some members of the Imperial House of Russia going to Aix-les-Bains.

'At five o'clock we took a cup of tea while passing over the Grande Ceinture. [The Grande Ceinture is the peripheral route in Central Paris which provides a link between the Gare du Nord and the Gare de Lyon in Paris.] Dinner was served soon after passing the Forest of Fontainebleau:

Hors d'oeuvres
Consommé à la Duchesse
Barbue sauce Hollandaise
Aloyau de boeuf rôti
Haricots verts
Poulet de grains Salades
Soufflé à la Rome Express
Glaces Fromages Dessert
Café. Liqueurs

'A good, well-served meal costing only five shillings and sixpence, washed down with a bottle of light Bordeaux and a bottle of dry Imperial '84.... Our baritone eventually joined us in the smoking-room for a rubber of whist, which we lubricated with whisky and soda.... We got out for a walk along the platform at Mâcon whilst the engine was being changed; but the air was chilly and we soon withdrew to our cosy cars and retired to bed. I had been told by our very polite conductor (an Englishman, by the way) that I need not get up at the frontier – that the Italian Customs officers would merely pass through the cars as a matter of form without waking us.... I knew the Italian Customs of old and was somewhat doubtful that things would go so easily as my friend the conductor seemed to think. But man proposes and the Sleeping Car Company disposes. I slept so soundly that I did not wake until I was touched on the shoulder by

left: One sleeping-car of the 'Simplon Express' was run from Venice to Calais. Between Paris and Calais it had a train working to itself apart from a *fourgon* and a van. In this 1908 picture Nord Railway Atlantic No 2,645 is in charge. (Courtesy Cie Internationale des Wagons-Lits et du Tourisme)

below left: A typical early 20th century European *train de luxe* comprising two luggage vans or *fourgons*, enclosing a diner and two sleeping cars; this is the 'Simplon Express' established by the Wagons-Lits company between Milan and Paris in 1906 soon after completion of the Simplon tunnel, and photographed in 1907 pausing at Iselle on the southern side of the tunnel with a Swiss 2-8-0 in charge. (Courtesy Cie Internationale des Wagons-Lits et du Tourisme)

below: The through Moscow–Paris Wagons-Lits sleepers of the 'Nord Express' photographed in 1910. (Courtesy Cie Internationale des Wagons-Lits et du Tourisme)

the waiter, who wanted to know if I would prefer coffee, tea or chocolate with my toast, and telling me in the same breath that we should be in Turin in half an hour. In less than five minutes a nice white serviette was spread on the little table in my compartment alongside my bed, and I was served with a delicious cup of *café au lait*, some toast and a *brioche*. . . . The conductor brought me the *Gazette Piemontese* and other papers.'

Speed was no hallmark of the Italian Railways in those days – in fact, they were about the most pedestrian in Western Europe until, under Fascism, the key trunk routes had their service standards dramatically transformed in the 1930s – and it was not until 22.25 on the day after departure from London that our 1897 'Rome Express' traveller touched down in the Italian capital. Even so, he was entranced with his experience. His summing-up, moreover, indicates the breadth of activity into which the Wagons-Lits

concern had already expanded by the end of the 19th century:

'The International Sleeping Car Company does not aim to encourage sleep. . . . Its cars are comfortable, luxurious and perhaps productive of drowsiness, but its business is to snatch an idle man from the degrading influence of London club life, shoot him across the Channel, and take him in fast trains over miles of country to any corner of Europe he may wish to visit. It will send the tourist anywhere with comfort and dispatch, rescue him from madness by smoothing out the intricacies of Continental routes, check his luggage, engage rooms for him in one of its own palatial hotels on the Nile, or some of the beauty spots of Europe in which it has built veritable palaces, secure an airy corner of a caravanserai in Turkey, or find him a dwelling in the romantic fastnesses of romantic Bosnia.'

The company's London manager conveniently summarized for the Victorian

writer – and for us – the remarkable growth and development of the Wagon-Lits railway activity up to the close of the century:

'We have 550 cars travelling daily over 90,000 miles of lines and our capital is over 30 million francs. We commenced in 1877 with 58 cars, which daily covered 8000 miles, our capital at that time being 4 million francs. Last year we carried in our cars over 2 million passengers. . . .

'Our staff is international, every European country being represented. No member of our outside staff speaks less than three languages, whilst it is not uncommon to find several who speak six or eight. . . .

'We build nearly all our own cars and a large number of ordinary carriages for the various railway companies. We also built the French Presidential train and other royal carriages, amongst them being those of the Emperor of Russia. Our principal works are at St Denis, whilst we have other very large ones at St Ouen and at Valenciennes, with others in Germany and in Russia.

'All the important capitals of Europe are linked by our services of cars or *trains de luxe*, with the exception of London, which became isolated from our system by the suppression by the English railway companies of the Club Train Service [as recounted in the succeeding section of this chapter] a circumstance which was, in the opinion of many, the first retrograde movement ever made in the railway world.

'Of our principal limited *trains de luxe*, the "Orient Express," daily between Paris and Vienna and three times weekly to Constantinople, leaves London at 09.00 and arrives at Constantinople at 11.45 of the third day, or, allowing for the difference between Greenwich and Oriental time, in about $72\frac{1}{2}$ hours from London – a distance of $2144\frac{1}{2}$ miles, in great part over single track and bad at that. Then we have the "Peninsular Express" via Calais and Mont Cenis to Brindisi, Egypt and the

East, leaving London every Friday evening at 21.00. Our best-known train to pleasure-seeking people is the "Mediterranean Express" *train de luxe* between London, Paris, the Riviera and Ventimiglia, but which runs from November to April only. The "Sud Express" is a *train de luxe* between London, Madrid and Lisbon, carrying passengers and the mails for South Africa, South America, etc. Then there is the new "Ostend and Vienna Express," a daily *train de luxe* with connections to Constantinople, and a daily "Vienna-Riviera Express." The "Nord Express" is another most important train, running from Paris and London (that is, from Ostend or Calais) direct to St Petersburg. The distance is $1727\frac{3}{4}$ miles and the journey is accomplished in 50 hours. Last June we commenced running the "Gibraltar Express." The distance is $1644\frac{1}{2}$ miles and is covered in 57 hours.'

So much for the development of luxury travel on the European mainland by the close of the 19th century.

As for the 'Rome Express,' it is the only one of the pre-1900 European mainland

trains de luxe we have described in detail which survives today more or less intact, though in status it is a very poor relation to the trains of the same name up to 1939. Suspended during World War I because of the proximity of the Calais-Paris main line to the battlefronts and the heavy military traffic over the frequently single-track Alpine links between France and Italy, it was one of the first international luxury trains to be reinstated, though at first only thrice weekly and on a still more lethargic timing of $30\frac{1}{2}$ hours from Paris to Rome. With the aristocratic 'Train Bleu,' a post-war innovation given its due in Chapter 5, the 'Rome Express' shared the distinction of acquiring, in 1923, the first single-berth Wagons-Lits sleepers. Initially these were wooden-bodied vehicles, with eight single and four double compartments, painted in the company's now long-familiar standard livery of royal blue, instead of the varnished teak style it had employed in its early years. Two years later came the first all-steel Wagons-Lits sleepers.

There is no need here to itemize the variations of route and frequency in the later history of the 'Rome Express,'

except to remark that in 1920–21 it briefly carried through coaches for Taranto and Brindisi, and that in the summer of 1924 came the important addition of through sleepers from Boulogne to Rome and Florence; in the winter of 1930 these Channel coast sleepers were extended four times weekly all the way to Syracuse and Palermo in Sicily. The 'Rome Express' made the first surrender of prestige in late 1931, when it admitted second-class passengers; they were accommodated in the double-berth compartments, while first-class fare guaranteed you a single-berth compartment. But in the mid-1930s the 'Rome Express' was still an exclusively sleeping car express, generally comprising from Paris six sleepers, a diner and two *fourgons*, or luggage-brakevans. One of the *fourgons* incorporated a shower for passengers' use. The schedule was by now a bit more invigorating, but an 11.00 departure from London's Victoria to connect with the 'Rome Express' leaving Paris' Gare de Lyon at 20.20 that evening still landed you in Rome no earlier than 19.05 the following evening.

Today's 'Rome Express,' pulling out of the Gare de Lyon at 20.39, makes Rome by 12.24 next day thanks to modern electric traction and all the other trappings of modern railway operation. But nowadays it is a mixture of sleepers, couchette cars and ordinary day cars. If you are not hungry for speed, and if you are prepared to closet yourself in your sleeper compartment the whole way, the 'Rome Express' is still a pleasing experience. Its sleeping cars are all of the latest type and its timecard awakes you to one of European railways' most scenically striking stretches of route, as the train hugs the beetling coastline along the Italian Riviera from Genoa to Pisa. Quit your berth for a meal in the diner, however, and you will face a daunting obstacle course the length of the train through couchette and day coach corridors crammed with the baggage, bundles and probably bodies as well of migrant Italian workers and their families overcrowding the less pricey areas of the train.

The elite Paris-Rome train these days is the 'Palatino,' a post World-War II development we shall come to in Chapter 8. That is a whole day faster than the 'Rome Express' of 1897, reaching the Italian capital in a little over 13½ hours' rail travel time from Paris, as early as 9.15 the morning after leaving the French capital at 19.36.

Britain's First Luxury Trains

Britain looked a ready-made market for a Nagelmackers or a Pullman at the start of the 1870s. The first bogie coach had yet to be seen – it was to come early in that decade – and the universal four- or six-wheelers were innocent of corridors, vestibules, radiator heating and of any interior lighting save an archaic oil lamp in the roof, or the pioneering use of coal gas on two or three lines. As for refreshment and other human needs, you either took a luncheon basket with you and did your best to control the body's subsequent pressures until the train's next stop, or you combined intake and output at one or more of the meal stops that were built into the longer express train schedules. Some of the station restaurants – Swindon and York, for instance – were respected throughout the country for the service and cuisine they dispensed at this period.

Better was on offer for the affluent family. As the decade progressed a number of railways built family saloons, which would be attached to practically any regular service train for a family's exclusive use against purchase of an appropriate total of first- and second-class fares. By the 1880s it was commonplace to find two or three of them marshalled into the principal night trains from London to Scotland. The usual layout was a saloon for the family with comfortable armchairs for the parents, a lavatory, and a second-class compartment for the family retainers. Before the century's end some elaborately ornate vehicles – by then on bogies, of course – had been conceived, by the Manchester, Sheffield & Lincolnshire (later the Great Central) in particular.

The decor of the main family room in an MS & L car was an extraordinary confection in neo-Grecian style, with lincrusta fashioned to simulate stonework in panelling and roof embellishments studded with quasi-cameo reliefs of Greek goddesses. Furnishing was lavish, with individual armchairs and a *chaise-longue* as well as a traditional three-seater bench armchair against one end-wall of the room, all in handsomely figured plush. What is more the vehicle even had the makings of an armchair observation saloon at one end, beyond the servants' room. As time went on, the family saloons were also hired for special parties and staff outings; on the latter, Hamilton Ellis has recounted, the observation room was invariably the preserve of the firm's hierarchy, 'who would summon youthful colleagues to join them for a few minutes of benevolent unbending and a glass of beer.' Some of the MS & L family saloons, incidentally, survived as special-purpose

left: A contemporary artist's impression of the first dining car to be operated on a British railway by the Great Northern in 1879. (Courtesy British Rail)

above: In the earliest days there was no vestibuled connection between coaches. Passengers in the six-wheeled coaches of this London Kings Cross–Manchester express, leaving London behind Great Northern 2-4-0 No 752, had no way of stepping into the big twelve-wheeled, clerestory-roofed diner (third vehicle) when the train was on the move. This kitchen-diner was built in 1885 by the Manchester Sheffield & Lincolnshire Railway for the Kings Cross–Sheffield and Manchester expresses it ran jointly with the GNR. (Courtesy Locomotive & General Railway Photographs)

YORK. ANTWERP. ROTTERDAM & HAMBURG VIA HARWICH.

GER   DININC SALOON   16

vehicles until World War II.

Pullman made his bid for a British dominion with his American-style sleepers and parlor cars in 1874, as described in detail in the next chapter, but the first British sleeping car essays had emerged the previous year. All took their inspiration from the family saloon, since at first it seemed inconceivable that any but families or very intimate acquaintances would think it prudent to share such a vehicle, let alone one of its sections, with strangers.

First to take the rails was a North British Railway six-wheeler, run on alternate nights between London Kings Cross and Glasgow, which had two three-berth compartments connected by a corridor with flanking lavatory and wc, plus a second-class servants' compartment and a roomy luggage locker. For its furniture this and one or two other early non-Pullman sleepers employed the *lits-salon* arrangement adopted for some early Continental European sleepers. Each compartment, just over 8ft long between partitions, had three high-backed armchairs against one wall. To turn the chair into a bed, you pulled outward a handle at the top of the high panel forming the seat back. The panel came forward and downward, folding the chair double, and on the back of the chair was revealed a species of mattress. On that you laid your

top left and right: The interior and exterior of the six-wheeled kitchen-diner built in 1891 by the Great Eastern Railway for its York–Harwich Continental boat train. Note the impressive destination board wording. (Courtesy British Rail)

above: The 14.00 London Euston–Glasgow on the eve of World War I, displaying the elegant twelve-wheeled coaches built for the midday service by the LNWR. Double-heading the train up Camden bank out of the London terminus are the 'Precursor' class 4-4-0 No 1737 *Viscount* and the 'Prince of Wales' class 4-6-0 No 979 *W M Thackeray*. (Courtesy Author's collection)

bedding – which you had to bring with you; no linen was supplied by the railway in those early days, except on the Midland Pullman sleepers.

Subsequent primitive sleeping cars of the 1870s persisted with the open-section, multi-berth layout, with males and females segregated in their separate sections. In their earliest essay, employing the *lits-salon* layout, the Great Western exploited the extra body-width allowed by their broad gauge to cram *four* two-feet-wide beds in parallel against the end-partition of the seven-berth men's section! Unsurprisingly the customers revolted at the sheer indecency of it and the two vehicles, which were operated between London and Penzance, were soon rebuilt as more salubrious family saloons. It was, however, the Great Western too which in 1881 premiered the pattern of the modern British sleeper's separate compartments, five double-berth and two single-berth, nicely furnished in morocco leather with elegant lincrusta and gilt moldings to the woodwork. The 1881 Great Western car was still devoid of bed linen, but no supplement was levied for its use – which was, by the way, exclusively for first-class passengers. That was so in Britain until the London & North Eastern Railway pioneered second-class sleepers, and with them upper and lower berths, in 1928.

From 1880 onwards the advance in comfort was quite rapid. More and more railways took to the bogie coach (though there were a few significant recalcitrants for much of the decade, notably the Great Northern and the London North Western); compartments were made more roomy; oil was superseded by gas lighting, fed from cylinders mounted beneath the frames, and by the first electric lighting devices on the London Brighton & South Coast and the Midland; and increasingly coaches were equipped with lavatories, though some railways took time to accept that second- and third-class travellers deserved this relief as much as first-class passengers. A few of the more penurious systems were reluctant to see revenue-earning space surrendered and for a time cut their losses by fixing tip-up seats to the outside of the lavatory doors – an arrangement that scarcely endeared train travel to delicate Victorian womenfolk.

The Great Northern Railway had unveiled the country's first side-corridor coach layout in 1881, but it was the Great Western which in 1891 produced Britain's first train fully vestibuled and gangwayed throughout, which was put on the London Paddington-Birkenhead service the following year. It was one of the first, also, to be steam-heated by piping from the locomotive; until then only a minority of coaches had heating from their own stoves and the hire of a footwarmer was as essential a prelude to a winter's rail journey as buying a ticket. Prime object of the vestibuling was to give passengers free access to the separate men's and women's lavatories in the train-set and to allow the guard to patrol the train; he could be summoned in emergency by a bell-push in every compartment. There was no diner in the train.

The Great Northern Railway had tried the country's first dining car – a Pullman – between London and Leeds in September 1879, but it was almost the end of the century before diners became a recognized component of long-haul British expresses. For one thing, sensitive Victorian gentlefolk demurred at the idea of dining in full view of the 'plebs' at the lineside or more particularly on the platform wherever the train might pause. For another, as already observed, many of the station dining rooms at the traditional meal stops rated good food-guide mention (had there been such a publication in those days) and many railways sold quite delectable luncheon baskets at their principal stations. Chester, for instance, offered passing 'Irish Mail' travellers a choice of what it tagged the 'Aristocratic' or the 'Democratic' basket. For five shillings the 'Aristocratic' basket gave you a pint of claret or a half-pint of sherry, chicken, ham and tongue, cheese, bread, butter and condiment. The 'Democratic,' at half the price, opened up to disclose a

pint bottle of ale or stout, a cut or two from humbler joints of meat, or a meat pie and bread and cheese. High- or low-born, many passengers preferred to tuck into this provender in the seclusion of their compartments. That being so, argued some railways, why throw up the substantial profit from station catering for the risky business of a train restaurant service? The North Eastern Railway, for instance, was still unconvinced on that score as late as 1900, seven years after the three rival Anglo-Scottish routes had applied both first- and third-class diners to their principal trains in the internecine competition which transformed the quality of rail service between England and Scotland in the last two decades of the 19th century.

One should add, however, that the distinction of introducing Britain's first multi-class diner belongs to the Great Eastern Railway, which in 1891 had built for its York-Harwich boat train a quaint three-car, vestibuled set of six-wheelers.

The center vehicle was a combined oil-fired kitchen and 18-seater first-and-second class diner, the other two were second- and third-class compartment coaches, the latter including the country's first third-class dining compartment. An unexplained oddity of this set was that third-class ladies travelling alone must have been thought either unlikely or else unseemly company in the dining compartment, since their compartment at one end of the third-class coach was blocked off from the corridor by their own lavatory and another adjoining which served the remainder of the coach.

The comparative shortness of intercity journeys in Britain discouraged development of the elaborately equipped 'hotels on wheels' Pullman and Nagelmackers were creating for the much longer hauls in North America or across the European mainland. Nevertheless, within the standard categories of day coach, dining car and sleeping car, Britain had some handsomely luxurious ordinary coaches as well as Pullmans to display by the outbreak of World War I. Brand-leader, unquestionably, was the London & North Western Railway, with the Midland a challenging runner-up.

The *ne plus ultra* in British non-Pullman luxury train design up to World War I was the midday 'Anglo-Scottish Express' via the West Coast Route between London Euston and Glasgow. Inaugurated in 1889, it had first acquired distinction in the summer of 1893 when, after the East and West Coast partnerships had followed the Midland's competitive lead and eliminated second-class from their front-rank Anglo-Scottish trains, it was equipped as the first express between London and Scotland to run with first- and third-class coaches interconnected by corridor and vestibules from end to end. That earned it the popular name of 'The Corridor,' which stuck for years even after the express had been officially named the 'Midday Scot' in 1927. First- and third-class passengers had their separate dining cars athwart the kitchen, and within a few months the 'Corridor' notched up another entry in the annals, becoming the first British train to include two separate dining sections when a composite-class restaurant-kitchen car was inserted in its Edinburgh portion as well as the diners in the main Glasgow part of the train.

The original 'Corridor' coaching stock of the 1890s was handsome enough for its time, with its ample two-a-side seating in the first-class, but it was totally eclipsed by the stately twelve-wheeled vehicles with which the train was re-equipped in the summer of 1908. They were derived from designs the London & North Western had produced the year before for its American boat traffic from Liverpool. The LNWR was very jealous of this business. Liverpool was still England's main transatlantic port and the Midland Railway, with its part-ownership of the recently-opened Central station in the city and its espousal of Pullmans, seemed to be bidding for the heavy inflow of American travellers. But neither railway had a station close to the docks and the steamship companies were getting restive at the discomforts of the road link between their quaysides and the rail terminals in the city. Although Southampton was still in its diapers as a deep-sea port, the LNWR was shocked when the thoroughly disgruntled Inman company, then operating the world's two biggest passenger liners, switched its base to the south coast port. In a great hurry the LNWR created a passenger line to the dockside and there erected a new ocean liner terminal, Riverside station. Next it built for the onward journey to London some luxury train-sets, the 'American Specials,' which were ready by 1907.

Apart from a luggage-brake at each end and a kitchen car in the center, all of which were eight-wheelers, every car in the eight-coach 'American Special' set was a twelve-wheeler. The designers were out to impress Americans with the style to which Pullman was accustoming them in their own country and so, unusually for British coaches at the time, the passenger cars had entrance doors at the corridor ends only. Two of the five twelve-wheelers in the set were diners, one first-, the other composite second- and third-class, and two of the remaining three cars were first-class of really palatial character. Despite their size, $65\frac{1}{2}$ft long and 9ft wide, each first-class car had only six compartments. In only one of them were there four compartments of the orthodox kind, with fixed – but superbly comfortable and upholstered – seating. The rest had loose armchairs, supple-

mented in one extra-large compartment in each vehicle by a sofa and occasional table.

The following year a fleet of equally elegant twelve-wheelers was built for the 14.00 Euston-Glasgow 'Corridor' and its balancing up service from Scotland. The drawing-room layout of some 'American Special' first-class accommodation was not repeated, but the 'Corridor' compartments in both classes were decidedly roomy for the times (so were the lavatories), besides being handsomely furnished, with a great deal of effulgent brass ornamentation and curtained windows in the first-class. One small detail worthy of remark is that these were possibly the first British coaches with separate reading lights in the compartments.

Before we move on to Pullman's establishment in Britain, Nagelmackers' abortive stab at a foothold across the English Channel must be recorded. The International Exhibition to be held in Paris in 1889 looked just the bait to entice the gentry of London into luxury service to the French capital. And the London Chatham & Dover Railway was happy to play host. It was already in merger talks with its arch-rival, the South Eastern, and the two companies were in fact pooling their passenger receipts across the Channel. But any marriage would be a shot-gun wedding enforced by financial stringency so far as their respective chairmen, John Staats Forbes and Sir Edward Watkin, were concerned. Consequently Forbes had no scruples about blacking his neighbor's eye.

So the Wagons-Lits company had a train of four saloons and two *fourgons*, built in Belgium and shipped to England, the whole vividly liveried in green instead of the then customary varnished teak, and a companion train was prepared for a connecting service from Calais to Paris. Unlike Wagons-Lits' European mainland day cars of the period, these British coaches were laid out as open armchair saloons. Meals were served to the passengers at their seats from a kitchen in one of the *fourgons*, which also embodied a smoking room to observe the decencies of the period. Forbes even went to the length of ordering a new cross-Channel ship, the *Calais-Douvres*, to round off the through service.

Presumably because a supplementary fare of 16 shillings was charged to ride in such luxury, and the British were as yet unaccustomed to fare surcharges, the LCDR service was immediately dubbed the 'Club Train.' However, it had no admission limitations of the kind that characterized the later 'Club Trains' in the North of England, which developed from 1895 when a group of businessmen persuaded the Lancashire & Yorkshire Railway to provide them with exclusive

accommodation on their morning and evening commuter trains between Blackpool and Manchester. The L & YR responded with an armchair saloon incorporating a small pantry from which an attendant dispensed refreshment, re-

served for the use of the first-class season-ticket-holding gentlemen. Other residential areas took a fancy to the idea and soon 'Club Trains' were running morning and evening into and out of Manchester from North Wales and Windermere as well as Blackpool, whence there were eventually third- as well as first-class 'Clubs.' The Midland had one, too, between Morecambe and Bradford. As late as 1935 the LMS was building a new arm-chair saloon with kitchenette for com-

Inside a twelve-wheeled diner built in 1893 for the London St Pancras–Glasgow service jointly operated by the Midland and Glasgow & South Western Railways. (Courtesy British Rail)

muter 'club' use, but the concept died with the outbreak of World War II.

To revert to the so-called 'Club Train' of 1889, South Eastern's Watkin was apoplectic at his enemy's breach of the agreements between them. In short order he had Nagelmackers build a similar train to feed the Paris service from his own route.

The official title of the combined service, the two British trains and the French train from Calais to Paris, was the 'Paris Limited Mail.' As time went on there were days when the mail was practically all they carried. One deterrent, already experienced by Pullman, was English antipathy to supplementary fares. Another was inept scheduling. Both British trains left London around tea-time and pulled into Dover within five minutes of each other; that meant passengers did not reach Paris until about midnight – and all too often it was in the small hours, as an inferior boat was frequently substituted for the *Calais-Douvres*. Even though it had signed a twelve-year contract with the Wagons-Lits company, the LCDR tried to abandon the desperately unremunerative operation in 1892, but was dissuaded for a while by a French threat to retaliate by hobbling the operation of LCDR steamers across the Channel. By October 1893 the English financier newly appointed as Vice-President of the Wagons-Lits company, Davison Dalziel,

found himself occupying the Paris-Calais train in solitary state and then – according to some accounts – besieged at Dover by LCDR and SER staff, each desperate to corral just one passenger for their train on to London.

Both trains were abandoned before 1893 was out, the Wagons-Lits cars eventually finding their way on to boat trains from Le Havre and Cherbourg to Paris, but meantime South Eastern's Watkin had decided to try luxury trains elsewhere on his system. Determined not to get involved with Pullman, he bought from one of Pullman's American rivals, the Gilbert Car Manufacturing Co of Troy, USA. Like the first British Pullmans, the six Gilbert vehicles were shipped in parts from the US and assembled in England, at the South Eastern's Ashford works.

Thumbing a competitive nose at his other neighbor, Watkin demonstrated his new purchases to a press party between Charing Cross and Hastings in March, 1892. Four of the Gilbert cars were open saloons with an extravagance of seating space previously inconceivable in Britain. The main saloon had no more than 17 seats, all swivelling armchairs, and there were only seven more in the smoking compartment. Decor, both inside and out, vied with the most ornate in contemporary American style. The fifth car was a buffet and the sixth, initially, a shell used as a luggage room. The only

shortcoming was that use of Pullman's patent inter-car vestibule was barred, so that the cars went into service with a forbidding inter-vehicle walkway over two metal plates above the drawgear. At first, the Gilbert cars saw little use as a complete train even though the South Eastern decked out two ordinary four-wheel brakes to run with them, because of their extremely uneconomic seat/weight ratio and they were marshalled singly or paired in London-Dover boat trains and London-Hastings services.

Nevertheless with the neighboring Brighton company apparently making a success of Pullmans, the South Eastern decided to buy another luxury train, this time from the British builders, Metropolitan Carriage & Wagon. At the same time the South Eastern changed tack and prepared to open its luxury trains to all three classes – and without supplement. This was an extraordinary move, considering the abysmal third-class accommodation on ordinary South Eastern trains, a byword for squalor throughout the South of England.

The Gilbert cars were rebuilt and in December 1896 put into service as a complete train, a commuter service for the elite, up from Hastings to London in the morning and back in the afternoon at a civilized 15.40 that suited the formal closing hour of the City's finance houses. The following September the new British-

top left: A typical Midland Railway express at the close of the last century. (Courtesy Locomotive & General Railway Photographs)

above: The South Eastern Railway's 'Hastings Car Train' of the 1890s with its American-built Gilbert cars behind a class F 4-4-0. (Courtesy Locomotive & General Railway Photographs)

left: The British-built luxury cars which the South Eastern Railway bought from Metropolitan Carriage & Wagon were applied to a 'Folkestone Vestibule Limited' service in September 1897. A year or two later the train was photographed behind an SER class B 4-4-0. (Courtesy Locomotive & General Railway Photographs)

built cars were introduced as a companion service between the Kent Coast and London, the 'Folkestone Vestibuled Limited.'

Inside and out, the Folkestone cars were even more flamboyantly styled than the Hastings train. Third-class passengers goggled at the unheard-of felicity, at their humble level, of two-and-one well-upholstered seating athwart the center gangway of their saloons. The second-class layout was the same, but here you paid for more florid decor and a smoking compartment instead of the ladies' section that occupied the same space in the

third-class car. As for the first-class cars, they were sumptuous, with a mix of sofas, fixed and swivelling armchairs, and elegant curtains draped over the wide windows. The ladies' lavatory of the first-class parlor car was practically a saloon on its own, with its relaxing sofa as well as two free-standing chairs.

Sir Edward Watkin, among the most picaresque and ambitious of Britain's 19th century railway moguls, with eleven railway directorships (including one in the US) to his name, had retired in 1894, to the relief of the shareholders in every concern he fronted. In 1898, after several

false starts, the LCDR and SER at last agreed a working fusion which gave birth to the South Eastern & Chatham Railway. The Watkin-inspired resistance to Pullmans faded away and within a few years of the new century's opening the British Pullman company had a contract to operate its cars on the Channel ports boat trains. After World War I dereliction at Blackheath, the SECR's luxury Hastings and Folkestone cars were taken over in 1918 by the Pullman Company and rebuilt in the British Pullman style.

CHAPTER 3
PULLMAN CROSSES THE ATLANTIC

One of the Midland Railway's American-
built Pullmans with open verandah ends is
the leading coach of this train heading north
through the London suburb of Mill Hill
behind a Johnson 4-2-2 about 1900.
(Courtesy Locomotive & General Railway
Photographs)

Inspiration for the rapid advance in British rail travel comfort in the last quarter of the 19th century came from James Allport, General Manager of the Midland Railway from 1853. The miserable mid-century passenger environment appalled him. At the close of the 1860s Midland coaches were still exclusively hard-riding boxes on four wheels, offering three compartments in first class, two in second, but cramming five wooden-seated thirds, only half partitioned from each other, into the gaunt bodywork. There was no room for luggage inside: that had to be hoisted up on to the almost flat roof.

It was not just the cattle-truck character of third-class accommodation which disgusted Allport. In those days third-class passengers were excluded from the faster and more conveniently timed trains in the timetable. As Allport himself once described it: 'I have felt saddened to see third-class passengers shunted on to a siding in cold and bitter weather – a train containing amongst others lightly-clad women and children – for the convenience of allowing the more comfortable and warmly-clad passengers to pass them. I have even known third-class trains to be shunted into a siding to allow express goods to pass.'

A man of iron resolution – some commemorate him as the Bismarck of mid-19th century British railway politics – Allport had to wage a twenty-year struggle with reaction before he conclusively changed the face of the British express train. From the start of 1875 the Midland became a two-class passenger railway, first and third. The wretched wooden thirds were consigned to the breakers' yards as fast as they could be superseded by new vehicles; seconds were converted to thirds, which would henceforward have compartments at least 6ft wide and upholstered seating as a matter of course (to the outraged consternation of the Midland's rivals, who soon had to follow suit – some of them were not even treating

second-class customers so well); and third-class passengers would be admitted to the better trains. The following winter the Midland turned out the first of its graceful, clerestory-roofed twelve-wheelers, elegantly furnished in both classes. These were paragons of comfort for the period, even though as yet they were unvestibuled, were lit by oil lamps and lacked lavatories and heating other than by footwarmer. In later years these coaches were updated with steam heating and gas lighting, and even at the century's end a respected critic purred that they still rode 'like a dream.'

Although Allport's memorial is primarily his easement of the common rail traveller's lot, his was also the initiative which imported Pullmans to Britain. Granted special leave of absence by his Board in 1872 he followed Nagelmackers to the USA and covered some 6000 miles in Pullman's parlor and sleeping cars. What he saw and experienced captivated Allport far more than the early European essays of Nagelmackers and Colonel William d'Alton Mann and on his return in 1873 he persuaded the Midland directors to receive George Pullman, who was presented to the Midland's shareholders at their next half-yearly meeting on 15 February 1873. Reaction to Pullman's sales-talk and display of models and diagrams was somewhat skeptical, but the astute Pullman disarmed misgivings by undertaking at his own risk to build cars to the British loading gauge, ship them to England and meet their costs of operation. Allport was insistent on a homogeneous train formation, so agreement to Pullman's operation of his own supplementary-fare dining, parlor or sleeping cars was made conditional on Pullman construction for Midland purchase of similar-outline vehicles with orthodox accommodation in all classes; these were to run, free of surcharge, alongside the Pullmans.

The first British Pullmans were shipped 'knocked down' from Pullman's Detroit

works and assembled at Derby early in 1874. Built entirely of wood, right down to their bogies, they were patently of American parentage, with their clerestory roofs and open-end verandahs railed off with wrought-iron guards and gates. Inside, the first two sleepers, *Midland* and *Excelsior*, both had the typical early American 'Pullman section' arrangement, with longitudinally-fixed upper berths that were folded back against the roof between windows and clerestory· during the day, and berths below that were convertible to seating bays for day travel, though *Midland* had a unique ground-floor arrangement in which the lower berths became sofas with their backs to the car's outer wall. Each had a stateroom and separate male and female lavatories. It was the third car, *Victoria*, a parlor with 17 fully rotatable and even partly-reclining armchairs plus two private rooms, that really heralded Pullman's British dawn however (and so gratified Pullman that he adopted the model for his American operations in 1875).

below left: The London Brighton & South Coast Railway's 'Sunday Pullman Limited' headed by class B2 4-4-0 No 320 *Rastrick* in the South London suburb of Balham, *circa* 1899. This was the first British Pullman train to be vestibuled throughout. At each end of the train is a six-wheeled so-called 'Pullman Pup' built by the LBSCR to carry the dynamo to power the train's electric lighting (and also to serve as a luggage van). Pullman livery at this time was overall umber. (Courtesy Author's collection)

below: The new 'Southern Belle' of 1908, in umber and cream livery, passes South Croydon behind LBSCR class 13 4-4-2 tank No 22. (Courtesy Author's collection)

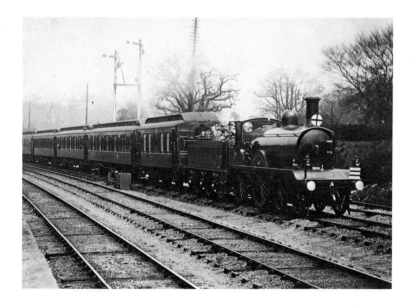

The electric multiple unit 'Brighton Belle' Pullman of Britain's Southern Railway leaves Brighton in the last years of its British Rail service. The service was ended in 1972. (Courtesy B A Haresnape)

In March 1874 Pullman entertained the press to a run from London St Pancras to Bedford and back in a train of these first three cars. Pens scurried through extravagant prose at the sumptuousness of the plush armchairs, the gas-lighting (a wondrous improvement on the noxious oil-lamps which as yet only the Lancashire & Yorkshire Railway had begun to supersede) and even at the luxury of trainboard lavatories, hitherto reserved to family and invalid saloons. But inspiration faltered as Pullman stuffed the party with a spread of poultry, game and sweetmeats taken on board at St Pancras, then floated the guests in generous libations of champagne, liqueurs and brandy. Through the final haze of cigar smoke some may have clung to sufficient consciousness to record that this was the first formal meal to be served (though not yet cooked) on a British train. One writer could only stagger back to Fleet Street and breathe heavily to his readers that he had disembarked at St Pancras with 'nothing left to desire.'

The fare-paying public was not so easily beguiled. On 1 June 1874 the Midland inaugurated an all-Pullman style train between St Pancras and Bradford, down by night and up by day, formed of first- and second-class sleepers, luxury parlor and Pullman-style day coaches, Midland-owned, for ordinary passengers. This was a memorable event on several counts. The practice was not encouraged on safety grounds, but for the first time an intrepid passenger could walk the length of a British train on the move by stepping between Pullman verandahs. It was the first British train to put lavatories at everyone's disposal, third class included. And it was the first train in the country to be reasonably heated throughout by radiators fed in each car from a small coke-fired boiler, the Baker heater, much in vogue in the USA at the time. A conductor and a domestic servant were on hand to minister to the Pullman patrons.

Momentous all this may have been, but at first the public was unimpressed. Incredibly, it spurned the Pullman-style ordinary-fare day cars. One can only imagine that conservative distaste for the vehicles' American-style reversible-back seating was so powerful that it dulled senses to the cars' infinitely superior heating – let alone their healthy sanitation. These cars were soon discarded. Gradually, however, Yorkshire businessmen took to the parlors and sleepers to the extent that when the Midland gained access to Liverpool in the spring of 1875 it was emboldened to put on another Pullman train, a day service.

By the end of 1875 the Midland was running 36 Pullmans, 11 of them sleepers, on a variety of services. From the opening of the arduous Settle-Carlisle route across

the Pennine hills on 1 May 1876 Pullmans featured in the Anglo-Scottish services which the Midland operated jointly with the Glasgow & South Western and North British Railways. Scottish railwaymen on these two routes were still apt to call every through St Pancras train a 'Pullman' well into the mid-twentieth century, decades after the Midland had given up Pullman service. The Midland bought up the cars in 1888 and not only kept them on the same workings but went back to American builders for Pullman-style replacements in 1900. These later cars survived well into the 1920s; even the early cars lingered on into this century, some as excursion saloons, others as picturesque trailers on one or two of the Midland's rural branches.

By the time the Midland had projected its Pullman services into Scotland – and as early as 1878, incidentally, history records the first private-charter operation of a Pullman train for a Scottish land cruise which wandered as far north as Wick – the company had its foot in the South of England railway door. Opening up with cars from the Midland, the London Brighton & South Coast Railway had introduced drawing-room Pullmans to some of its Brighton trains from late October 1875. And in 1880 the London & South Western Railway toyed with a Pullman on its Waterloo-Exeter service, but the venture was ill-supported and short-

top left: A parlor car of the 1908 'Southern Belle.' Note the elegant marquetry of the woodwork. (Courtesy Author's collection)

above: Inside *Princess Patricia*, one of the last three LBSCR Pullmans to be assembled at the railway's Brighton works from parts built by Pullman in the USA. It was put into traffic in 1906. This is the smoking saloon which was finished in red leather and oak. (Courtesy Charles Long collection)

above: 1920s 'Southern Belle.'
(Courtesy Author's collection)

above: This Baker Street–Aylesbury train,
headed by one of the first series of
Metropolitan electric locomotives (1904–
1906).   (Courtesy Real Photographs)

left: The lounge of the 1906 Pullman *Princess Patricia*.   (Courtesy Charles Long collection)

lived. The LSWR had better luck on its London Waterloo-Bournemouth route, where it inaugurated Pullman service in 1890 and eventually gilded the four principal day trains each way with a Pullman drawing-room car for the indulgence of its first-class traffic. The Pullmans were taken off from 1905 onwards, after the Bournemouth line had acquired its first corridor restaurant car trains, but from the 1930s the route became one of Britain's best-known Pullman courses when the Southern Railway handed it a daily all-Pullman train, the 'Bournemouth Belle.'

Better-known still, in much of Western Europe as well as in Britain and from a much earlier date, was the all-Pullman train between London Victoria and Brighton which the neighboring London Brighton & South Coast Railway had firmly established by the early 1900s. It started tentatively in December 1881 twice each way daily, with four cars that attracted attention as much for a technical refinement as for their extravagant appointments – the buffet, the ladies' boudoir, the compartment for servants of the travelling gentry and, of course, the elegant armchair seating. For this 'Pullman Limited Express' was the first in Europe to sport electric lighting throughout (though with traditional oil-lamps retained as an additional insurance). The Brighton line's Locomotive Superintendent, William

Stroudley, was trying out the system devised by the Frenchman Fauré, wherein a gargantuan 32-cell battery was mounted on a shelf under the car floor and fed a dozen incandescent bulbs within the vehicle. The batteries could cope with only six hours' supply and were charged before each return trip to the coast by a steam-driven dynamo specially installed at Victoria for the purpose. If the 'Limited' was significantly delayed on its journeys, of course, the lighting was liable to fade to dimly religious pallor by the time the return working came in sight of the London suburbs.

Like the Midland Pullmans, the Brighton's first 'Limited' generated indifferent business. To some extent this was probably aversion to the concept of supplementary-fare travel, but the LBSCR also made a marketing misjudgment by running the train once each way on Sundays as well as twice daily on weekdays. This incitement to hedonism on the Sabbath so outraged many Victorians that they felt unctuously bound to boycott the 'Limited' on weekdays as well. Within two months the Brighton management shamefacedly withdrew the Sunday working. Before long it was also compelled to adulterate the weekday trains with orthodox first-class compartment coaches.

Towards the end of the Victorian era, however, society was cautiously unlacing and at the end of 1888 the LBSCR was

emboldened to revive Sunday Pullman service – this time, moreover, with an all-Pullman train running on Sundays only, the London-Brighton 'Sunday Pullman Limited.' The equipment was brand-new, American-built cars shipped across the Atlantic in parts and assembled at the British railway's Brighton works, and all with Pullman's newly-patented inter-car vestibules, the first to be seen in Britain. Now the moving train generated its own electricity for lighting. In the interim Stroudley had devised a belt drive from the carriage wheels to a dynamo which he housed in a six-wheeled vehicle styled like a Pullman to match the rest of the train – hence its popular designation as a 'Pullman Pup.' The 'Pup' doubled as a luggage van.

This time the public did not rebuff the Brighton. Renamed the 'Brighton Limited' early in 1899, the train steadily built up its clientele and encouraged the railway to reconsider daily operation. Meanwhile the deaths of Nagelmackers and Pullman were setting the stage for expansion of Western European Pullman operations. In 1906 Lord Davison Dalziel, the English financier whom Nagelmackers had personally nominated to take over chairmanship of the Wagons-Lits company, moved to buy the British Pullman Palace Car Company from the trustees of George Pullman's estate and completed the purchase in 1907. At first the Pullman company was Dalziel's personal fief, but in 1915 it was transmuted into the Pullman Car Company. From now on the European association of Wagons-Lits and Pullman services was intimate.

The 'Brighton Limited' was the obvious choice for Dalziel's first step to enlarge the Pullman bridgehead and the LBSCR readily agreed to redevelop it as a daily train. A palatial new set of seven twelve-wheeled cars was ordered from the builders Metropolitan Amalgamated Carriage & Wagon Co of Lancaster, the first Pullmans to be constructed wholly in Britain and the first to adopt elliptical roofs instead of the characteristic Pullman clerestoried style. Externally they were finished in the latterly familiar Pullman livery of cream above the waistline, umber below, though this had supplanted the previous overall umber livery on the Brighton's last three US-built cars a year or two earlier.

Fully re-equipped and first-class throughout, the all-Pullman train was reborn on 1 November 1908 as the 'Southern Belle.' For the first time British Pullman patrons now had their meals cooked on board. And in car *Grosvenor* they could drape themselves around a bar, though the decorum of the day counselled Pullman to publicize it more discreetly as a 'buffet.' Should you misguidedly believe that extravagance in advertising copy is a hothouse plant of latter-day Madison Avenue or Mayfair public relations, try some of the saccharine prose from a fully-bound, full-color brochure promoting the 'Belle' which the Pullman company was circulating in 1910:

'A "chain of vestibuled luxury" tersely and truthfully describes the new Pullman train which now runs daily between London and Brighton, accomplishing the journey in 60 minutes. This train-de-luxe has been built by the Pullman Car Company at very great expense. . . . Ingenuity and skill have contributed to the improvement of details wherever the slightest change or the adoption of a new device could conduce to the perfection of appointment and convenience, so that the "Southern Belle" of today is the newest, most complete and up-to-date train in the world.

'Upon entering the "Southern Belle" we leave London behind and the noise and worry and ugliness of its work-a-day life. The train is still stationary, but we have come into a place of enchantment, and of beauty and exquisite comfort. The spirit of a cultured man or woman is uplifted at once by this palace of elegance and refinement. It has an immediate appeal to the eye. It has a delightful effect upon one's senses. It is all very restful and soothing in its influence upon the mind and the body.

'It is always amusing and instructive to watch some pretty well-dressed woman making her choice of seat for this short journey. She gives a little cry of delight upon entering the first carriage. Perhaps she enters the *Grosvenor* car – each one has a different name – and her eyes are filled with admiration as she looks at the beautiful mahogany panelling inlaid with satinwood, at the delicate molding of the frieze and cornices, at the fluted pillars, at the carpet with its soft shade of green with the *fleur de lys* pattern, at the damask silk blinds, and at the cosy chairs and settees in a restful shade of green morocco.

' "How perfectly lovely! It's as cosy as our drawing room, Dick."

'Perhaps "Dick," who may be her husband' [I have manfully resisted the temptation to italicize that guarded qualification] 'nods assent, or shows his knowledge of domestic architecture by observing that this is in the Adams style, beloved by eighteenth-century connoisseurs.

'But his young wife is bent upon exploration, and pulling him by the cuff explains that she could not settle down without knowing what lies beyond. She flits into the *Cleopatra* car and says "Isn't this beautiful, Dick?" She strokes the smooth panelling of Indian satinwood, inlaid with gray sycamore, and delicate tulip-wood. She puts up her pretty inquisitive face and sees how the domed ceiling of purest white is decorated with beautiful moldings. Her woman's heart is surely captured by the velvet tapestries of the chairs and lounges, in shades of blue with delicate tracery of gold, and she points out to "Dick" how the soft carpet of deep rose color gives a lovely glow to the whole compartment. . . .

'As the train speeds on its way there is the music of light laughter in the carriages, coffee cups are tinkling and the sun is gleaming in the liqueur glasses. Every now and again when the train rushes through a short tunnel, the carriages are made brilliant and even more beautiful by the little electric lights which glow from the ceilings and the standard lamps on the table – a soft suffused light which enriches the color harmonies of these parlor carriages. Men are smoking cigarettes or cigars, but the cars are perfectly ventilated and the air is always fresh. This

fresh air, too, is warmed and on the coldest day there is no danger to delicate lungs or throats.'

All this sybaritic existence was yours for a Pullman surcharge of no more than a shilling on the ordinary first-class fare. The Edwardians revelled in the 'Belle' and in a very short time the LBSCR had to double the daily service each way and triple it on Sundays.

The next railway to acquire Pullmans was the unlikeliest of customers, London's Metropolitan Railway. The Metropolitan deal was the by-product of Dalziel's abortive bid for business on the Great Central, the overly ambitious company which had driven the last main line from the provinces into London in 1899 and was battling its longer-established rivals with a flashy service of short, swiftly-timed trains, each one – a proud GC boast, this – garnished with refreshment cars. In 1909 Dalziel had coaxed the GC Board into approval in principle of a service of all-Pullman trains under a 15-year contract whereunder, unusually, Pullman would not charge their passengers a supplement but take ten percent of the trains' gross revenue. Another innovation was to be Pullman observation cars at the tail of each train. Early in 1910 the GC Board reneged on the agreement, deciding that if it were going to run luxury trains it would prefer to build and own its own vehicles. Meanwhile the Metropolitan, which shared tracks into London with the GCR from the high-class dormitory towns northwest of the capital, had paled at the prospect of GC Pullman trains skimming the cream of its City-bound commuter traffic. A hurried path was beaten to Dalziel's door and a contract signed in June 1910, even though the GC's Pullman threat had evaporated five months earlier.

The Metropolitan's two Pullmans, *Mayflower* and *Galatea*, were inserted from June 1910 in two locomotive-hauled train-sets operating on peak rush-hour trains, up in the morning and down in the evening, from the outer suburban towns of Aylesbury and Chesham to the Metropolitan's in-town center at Baker Street, then over the underground Inner Circle to the heart of the City at Aldgate or Liverpool Street. Not only were these Europe's first electrically-hauled Pullman trains: they were then and, I think, have been ever since, the only underground commuter trains in the world to mitigate the usual miseries of rush-hour travel with the prospect of breakfast or tea (cooked on paraffin Primus stoves, by the way) in armchair comfort. Up to 1914 moreover they offered returning London theatergoers supper on a late-night, 23.35 service from Baker Street to Aylesbury. The luxury was limited to the 19-passenger capacity of each car's seating, as inter-car vestibuled accommodation was barred on London underground trains; you could not walk into and out of the Pullman en route. Although the Pullmans were withdrawn during World War I, they were reintroduced after it and surprisingly survived the absorption of the Metropolitan by the all-embracing London Passenger Transport Board to continue operation until 1939. They did not reappear after World War II.

Despite the Great Central fiasco Britain did see its first Pullman observation car before the 1920s were out. In 1914 Lord Dalziel signed a contract with the Caledonian Railway for exclusive catering service on the latter's trains. Ten new cars, all but one twelve-wheelers, were built to serve as diners, without supple-

mentary charge, on the Caledonian's front-rank trains from Glasgow to Aberdeen, Edinburgh and Perth (at various times some were also applied as supplementary-fare extras for first-class commuters on trains between Glasgow and Crieff or Moffat). The solitary eight-wheeler, delivered in 1914 but not introduced to the richly scenic Glasgow-Oban route until 1923, was the observation saloon *Maid of Morven*, a highly distinctive car, regally furnished with movable armchairs and especially memorable for its gracefully rounded and completely glazed rear-end.

At the outbreak of World War I Pullmans had yet to establish much of a foothold in mainland Europe, for reasons already discussed. Thus, when the private Dalziel regime became the Pullman Car Company on 30 September 1915 its interests centered on the 74 cars active in Britain. Immediately peace returned, however, the company set about expanding its operations on both sides of the English Channel, as will be told in Chapter Five.

left and center: Exterior and interior of the Caledonian Railway's Pullman observation car *Maid of Morven*. (Courtesy British Rail)

below: The South Eastern & Chatham Railway's Pullmans were the last in Britain to retain overall umber livery. This is the 'Thanet Pullman Limited,' a Sunday all-Pullman train between London Victoria and Ramsgate Harbour which the SECR introduced in 1921, headed by class E1 4-4-0 No 504. (Courtesy Author's collection)

CHAPTER 4
AMERICA ENTERS THE 'TWENTIETH CENTURY' AGE

The observation lounge of the 1948 'Twentieth Century Limited' as it leans to a curve at Garrison, NY. (Courtesy Author's collection)

Arguably the best-known and most hallowed of all North American luxury trains, New York Central's 'Twentieth Century Limited,' took the rails for the first time between New York and Chicago on 15 June 1902. It was the concept of a remarkable patent medicine salesman-turned-railroader, George H Daniels, who ran the New York Central's passenger business from 1889 to 1907.

Daniels was a dynamo with a mid-20th century marketing flair decades ahead of its time. Had he achieved little else he would always be respected as the pioneer of that traditional American facility, the free 'redcap' baggage service for rail passengers, which alone scored the NYC a host of prestige points with the travelling public. His consuming passion, however, was to establish a daily service of unprecedented speed and luxury on the railroad's prime New York-Chicago route.

The 1893 staging of the Columbian Exhibition in Chicago was a golden opportunity for Daniels to field-test his ideas. Armed with a handsome train specially built for the exercise by the Wagner Palace Car Company, Daniels put on for the summer and autumn duration of the fair an 'Exposition Flyer' which linked New York and Chicago in 20 hours for the 980-mile journey, an incredible transit time for the period. The 'Flyer' was a commercial triumph, and the persevering Daniels was at last authorized to launch an all-year-round de luxe train between New York and Chicago in November 1897.

Two beautiful seven-car trains were constructed by the Wagner company for

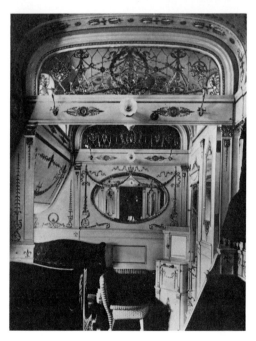

this service, the 'Lake Shore Limited,' which was to be a pathfinder for the 'Twentieth Century Limited.' Three cars in each set were sleepers, one of them through from Boston to Chicago, and a club car, parlor car, diner and observation car completed the formation. Businessmen in the club car had their own buffet for service of wine and cigars to soothe away any anxieties set off by the stock market quotations fed into the car at intermediate stops, where the station staff received them by wire for the 'Limited's' special benefit. Bored with smoke-room smut perhaps, they could take refuge in the barber's shop at the other end of the car or beyond that in the white-

tiled bathroom. The ladies in the parlor car had their own buffet as well as a library and part of the car could be curtained off to create a private sitting-room. Yet another buffet was at the sleeper occupants' disposal – and all these buffets, incidentally, were in addition to the opulent full diner, awesome in its carved oak finish, where more heavy curtaining provided for creation at will of two small private dining areas effectively sealed off from the main saloon. And talking of privacy, partitions between two adjoining staterooms in the sleeping accommodation could be folded aside to enlarge the pair into a really capacious bridal suite. Finally there was the end car, combining eight staterooms with the observation lounge, the static furniture of which included a second library and a human appointment, a stenographer.

Staffing, both male and female, was on a scale to match the train's facilities. And the Wagner company was scarcely less meticulous than Pullman in ordering the behavior of its train servants. Consider these extracts from its 1898 staff manual:

Personal appearance: Avoid putting hand in pockets in tails of uniform overcoats in cold weather giving employee a decidedly loafering appearance, as well as spreading the tail of the coats and getting them out of shape.

Collars and cuffs: White linen only – celluloid are prohibited.

Maids: Will wear the prescribed uniform while on duty, and must at all times carry sufficient linen for the round trip. They will also have the following equipment: Book of Rules,

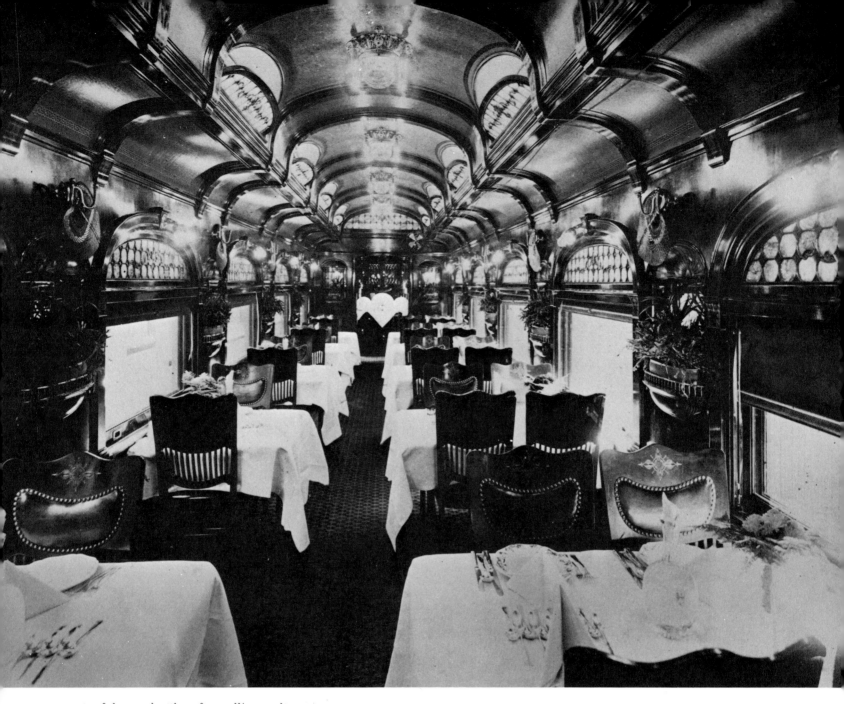

set of keys, bottle of smelling salts, liquid camphor, black and white thread, package of needles and box of assorted pins for ladies' use. Maids must be extremely careful to maintain a proper deportment while on duty. Under no circumstances will they allow any familiarity on the part of the crew or passengers, and they should at all times avoid even the appearance of it. No excuse will be accepted for any violation of this rule.'

The 'Lake Shore Limited's' New York-Chicago timecard specified 24 hours from city to city. That was not good enough for Daniels. As the 20th century dawned he pressed for and secured agreement to go for a 20-hour timing. And with inspired genius he coined the aptest of all titles for a train opening a new epoch in fast, luxury travel – 'Twentieth Century Limited.'

The first, five-car 'Century' ran each way on 15 June 1902. It was decidedly a 'Limited,' for that short formation only accommodated 42 passengers, and des-

pite the extra fare charged to ride it (the 'Century' was one of the few crack trains in North America to command a supplement for pure speed and comfort irrespective of sleeper and other charges: others included the Pennsylvania 'Broadway Limited,' the Santa Fe 'Chiefs' and the New Haven 'Merchants Limited' and 'Yankee Clipper.') Daniels' inaugural 'Century' must have been hard put to meet running costs out of revenue. A good many were convinced the enterprise was not technically viable either. 'Surely,' sniffed the London *Times*, 'it is only an experiment. . . . Can so high a rate of speed be maintained daily without injury to the engine, the rails and the coaches? The operators will soon find that they are wasting fortunes in keeping their property in condition and then, loving money better than notoriety, the 20-hour project will be abandoned.'

It was not. In fact even with steam traction it was steadily trimmed, until ultimately a 16-hour transit was attained in the diesel age. In those early steam days the

Central must have thrown economic sense out of the window to ensure the 'Century's' prestige. Not only were operating staff ordered to give her priority over all other traffic, but frequently standby engines were held in steam with a crew close at hand along the route to cover any locomotive failure. And for many years passengers were guaranteed the refund of a dollar on their fare for every hour the 'Century' was late.

The standard of living on the early 'Century' staggered visiting Europeans, as yet in the infancy of Wagons-Lits and Pullman development on their own continent. The range of accommodation and the lavish staffing of the train with porters, maids, valets, barber and stenographer were an unprecedented travel experience. So was dinner in the diner. The stately decor of heavily molded mahogany, leaded upper lights to the windows, pot plants on the walls between them, flowers on every table and the specially commissioned high-quality linen, crockery and silverware would

catch their breath before they picked up the menu. But then the menu itself – were they really on a train? Here is what it offered, *table d'hôte*, on an average night in 1904:

Blue Points on Half Shell

Consommé Julienne   Cream of Tomato

Olives   Salted Almonds   Celery

---

*Boiled Chicken
Halibut, Vin Blanc
Potatoes Naturel*

---

*Small patties of Capon Financière
Apple Fritters Glacé au Kirsch*

Prime Ribs of Beef Au Jus

---

*Boiled Potatoes   Mashed Potatoes
Baked Sweet Potatoes
Boiled Onions   Green Peas
String Beans*

Punch Crême de Menthe

---

*Roast Young Goose with Dressing,
Apple Sauce*

---

*Lettuce, Mayonnaise or French
Dressing*

---

*Banana Custard, Orange Cream Sauce
Assorted Cake   Fruit in Season
Ice Cream*

---

*Canadian Club Cheese
Roquefort Cheese
Brownsville or Bent's Water Crackers*

Coffee

And the price? Incredibly for such a lengthy and individual bill of fare, *one dollar!* The 'Century's' one-dollar dinners, unsurprisingly, were a talking-point of travellers throughout the eastern US at the start of the 20th century.

Daniels' 'Century' did not go unchallenged in the New York–Chicago arena.

above: The observation saloon of the 'Twentieth Century Limited' in the early 1900s.   (Courtesy Arthur Dubin collection)

above left: The Pullman diner of the 'Twentieth Century Limited' in the first decade of this century. The interior was finished in Santiago mahogany.   (Courtesy Arthur Dubin collection)

By the opening of the 20th century New York Central–Pennsylvania rivalry was intense, for the rich passenger business between New York and Chicago especially. Pennsylvania had the shorter 908-mile route, but this was sharply graded west of Philadelphia and Central's Publicity played continually on the comparative tranquillity of travel by its longer but placidly graded 'Water Level Route.' In those days a major rail development was good for as much coverage by the media as Concorde's earthshrinking in the 1970s, so the banner headline type founts were busy when the Pennsylvania suddenly announced that on the very same day of the 'Century's' debut it would slash eight hours from its previous best New York–Chicago time and hurry a new 'Pennsylvania Special' between the two cities in exactly the same time, 20 hours.

The lightweight 'Special' lasted only 18 months in its first incarnation, too seriously hampered by freight congestion in the Pittsburgh area, but when the layout there had been enlarged the Pennsylvania attacked again in June 1905 – now with an 18 hour timing. Central promptly trimmed its 'Century' schedule to the same level. Throughout the Eastern US the public was enthralled as the two railroad giants battled it out, but within a year or two it was clear the Central had one weapon to which the Pennsylvania had ineffectual counter: the marketing expertise – enshrined above all in that 'Twentieth Century Limited' title – it had cultivated under Daniels. In November 1912 the 'Specials' were discarded and the crack Pennsylvania New York–Chicago service was reborn as the heavier and slower 'Broadway Limited' (the original title, derived from the Pennsylvania's six-track layout throughout from New York to Philadelphia, was the 'Broad Way Limited').

But Central, totting up the bill for safeguarding such a tight 'Century' schedule, had also had enough of the speed contest. By the end of the World War I both 'Century' and 'Broadway' were on 20-hour timings, which stayed that way until 1932. In the inter-war era with the emergence of heavier, more capacious and more solidly riding all-steel Pullmans, the two trains concentrated on building up their worldwide status as the flagships of American luxury travel, a title few grudged them right up to World War II. Both were all-Pullman and extra-fare.

left and below: Inside and outside a typical US 'limited' diner of the late 1920s, the twelve-wheeled *Martha Washington* of the Baltimore & Ohio. Note the Georgian-style leaded windows, the reproduction Hepplewhite chairs and (against the far wall) Sheraton sideboard. (Courtesy Author's collection)

above: The look of a US 'limited' in the 1920s. This is Baltimore & Ohio's Baltimore and Washington–Chicago 'Capitol Limited,' the first all-Pullman train to operate between Washington and Chicago. It was introduced in 1923. Headed by 4-6-0 No 5213, the train poses on Relay Viaduct in Maryland. (Courtesy Author's collection)

Highpoint of the 'Century's' career, probably, was the period immediately preceding the Great Depression of the 1930s. In the later 1920s the New York Central, overall the busiest mover of Pullman travellers in the country, was grossing in excess of ten million dollars a year from the 'Century' alone. Night after night the train had to be run in two or more sections, to the extent that the 'Century' pool of specially dedicated locomotives and Pullmans totalled no fewer than 24 and 122 respectively.

Peak day in 'Century' history was 7 January 1929, when the eastbound 'Century' ran in seven sections with a grand total of 822 fare-paying passengers. These days the $10 supplement they each paid for the privilege might sound pin-money: but it underlines their assessment of the train when one recalls that in 1929 the 'Century's' diner was offering roast ribs of beef with vegetables for just $1.10, Virginia ham, pineapple, spinach and baked potato for 95 cents, oysters for 75 cents, roast turkey with a fantasy of trimmings including fresh oyster and mushroom dressing and apples *glacé* for $1.35 and, say, apple pie *à la mode* to crown the meal for only 45 cents more.

Day in, day out the 'Century's' performance was a vital concern at Central headquarters right up to the president's office. Every morning the papers on the supremo's desk included a detailed report on the previous day's 'Century' loadings, gross revenue, timekeeping and – not least – a run-down on the cream of the political, commercial or showbiz world who had been aboard either way.

Rare was the night when the 'Century's' passenger list did not yield grist for the publicity department's mill under this last heading.

Much the same applied to Pennsylvania's 'Broadway Limited.' Both trains were kept refreshed with the latest in the coachbuilder's art, but the highpoints in their careers were the years of complete re-equipment from end to end. Golden year was 1938, in June of which both were reborn with magnificent new train-sets, each styled from the prow of its locomotive to its tail by a leading industrial designer of the period, Raymond Loewy for the Pennsylvania and Henry Dreyfuss for the New York Central. Both trains were simultaneously accelerated to a 16-hour schedule between New York and Chicago and both trains set a new

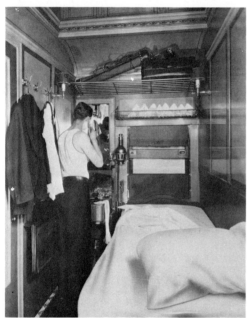

top: A characteristic Pullman sleeper 'section' of the early 1930s. The interior of this Canadian Pacific 1931-built car *Stockton* is finished in mahogany.   (Courtesy Author's collection)

above: A compartment of a Canadian National sleeper in the late 1920s. (Courtesy Author's collection)

right: The interior of *James Bay*, a lounge-car built for the Canadian National 'Confederation' in 1929. Its amenities included a hair-dressing salon and a small gymnasium.   (Courtesy Author's collection)

top center: A Canadian transcontinental in the late 1920s: Canadian National's Toronto–Vancouver 'Confederation' crosses Lytton Bridge in British Columbia.   (Courtesy Author's collection)

left: The 'Bay' series of lounge-cars which Canadian National acquired at the end of the 1920s had the latest trainboard diversion, a radio-gramophone alongside the writing desk.   (Courtesy Author's collection)

below (both): In summer passengers on CN's Montreal–Vancouver 'Continental Limited' in the 1920s could view the magnificent Rockies from an open observation car which was attached to the train between Jasper, Alberta and Kamloops, BC.   (Courtesy Author's collection)

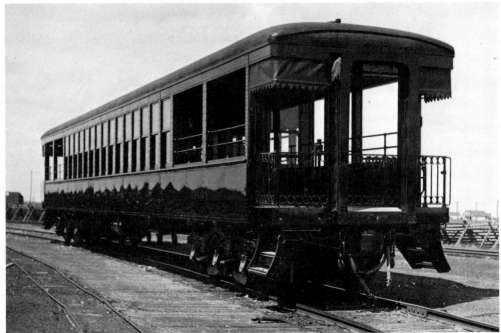

standard by eliminating the traditional Pullman upper-and-lower-berth section; all sleeping accommodation was in rooms of varying size and price range.

The 16-hour schedule was the crowning achievement with steam power, though the 'Broadway' had the benefit of electric traction from the Loewy-styled Class GG1 electrics, so beloved of Eastern American rail fans, between New York and Harrisburg. West of Harrisburg, however, the train was entrusted to the remarkable Pennsylvania K4 Pacifics, of which one, No 3768, had been dramatically streamlined by Loewy to help publicize the re-equipped 'Broadway.' The 1938 'Century' was steam-powered throughout, by ten new variants of Central's fabled Hudson 4–6–4s which Dreyfuss had semi-streamlined with imposing bullet noses.

After World War II in 1948 the trains were re-equipped yet again, with steam by now surrendering the 'Century' to diesel traction. The five cars of the original 1902 'Century' had cost no more than

$115,000, but in 1948 the capital investment in all the locomotives and cars needed to cover an each way, often multi-section, super-luxury long-haul train like the 'Century' or 'Broadway' was running out at more than $4 million. That sounds almost a discount store bargain compared with the $2.75 million price tag on each single new electric locomotive Amtrak was buying in the late 1970s for its revamped high-speed service over former Pennsylvania tracks in the US North-East Corridor, but it was a formidable sum three decades ago. In the false dawn of the US railroads' immediate post-war passenger boom it looked briefly likely to earn an adequate return, but within only two years air travel had bitten so deep into the premium trade and automobiles and buses had eroded so much of the ordinary rail travel business that the railroads had already abandoned practically half the 15,000 inter-city passenger trains a day they were running in the early 1930s. First of the two great New York–Chicago land-liners to be humbled

below: The 1932 'Twentieth Century Limited,' powered by one of New York Central's splendid 'Hudson' 4-6-4s on the shores of Lake Erie. (Courtesy Author's collection)

below right: The timings of the 'Twentieth Century' and 'Broadway Limited' frequently had the rivals racing each other out of Chicago's Englewood station; a Pennsylvania K4 Pacific heads the 'Broadway' on the left – an NYC 'Hudson' the tailing 'Century.' (Courtesy Arthur Dubin collection)

was the 'Century.' Unable any longer to command a satisfactory loading of extra-fare, exclusively Pullman clients, it was degraded from 27 April 1958 to the ordinary coach-and-sleeper format of the standard US long-haul train.

A ride on the 'Century' in its final, golden years was unforgettable. The first sign that it was the pearl of trains you were about to board at New York's Grand Central was the 260ft-long, 6ft-wide maroon carpet emblazoned with the train's title which, every afternoon from 1922 onwards except during the World War II years, was punctiliously rolled out the length of the departing 'Century's' platform.

Your Pullman berth would be in one of the train's eight to eleven sleeping cars, the number depending on whether the train was running an additional section that night. Cheapest accommodation was the roomette, the small single rooms ranged each side of a car's central corridor which were the latter-day refinement of the oldtime Pullman open-section

berth – and priced at an equivalent rate. By day it was a compact sitting-room. At bedtime a touch of a button lowered from the wall a comfortable bed, ready made up on one of the foam mattresses that were standardized in the 1948 'Century.' Next up the price scale were the double and single bedrooms, the latter more spacious than the roomettes because the bedroom cars were side-corridor (in a number of latter-day Pullmans, though not those of the 'Century,' the passenger/tare weight ratio of single-room vehicles was usefully increased without sacrifice of comfort by lowering the car floor between the bogies to make room for an interlocking 'duplex' arrangement of adjoining rooms at alternate levels). In the 'Century's' final all-Pullman manifestation, incidentally, every double room at whatever price had its own private full toilet facilities.

Penultimate luxury was a drawing-room, with the two sleeping berths against one wall (in which tiny windows were inset above the main window level for the benefit of the upper berth occu-

above: The enclosed ladies' lounge of the car *Elkhart Valley* in the 'Twentieth Century Limited' of the early 1930s; there was an adjoining buffet to serve lounge occupants. (Courtesy Author's collection)

right: June 1938 and the newly streamlined and re-equipped 'Broadway Limited,' with K4 Pacific No 3768 specially styled by Raymond Loewy, streams eastward out of Chicago on the train's maiden trip. (Courtesy Arthur Dubin collection)

below: The Loewy-styled main lounge in the 1938 'Broadway Limited.' The bar was in a small six-seater lounge and between that and the main lounge was an eight-seater card-room. (Courtesy Arthur Dubin collection)

pants) and the rest of the floor space was a roomy lounge area with individual chairs for the daylight sector of the journey. Top of the price-list was the so-called master room, which was effectively a suite, with two-berth bedroom and private shower bathroom and lavatory flanking a handsome lounge with four movable armchairs. In Pennsylvania's 'Broadway Limited' the master-room furniture even included a radio.

Awaiting your attention in your berth would be a brochure listing the wide range of on-train 'Century' services – valet, loan of electric shaver or dictaphone, complimentary newspaper (delivered with your freshly shined shoes next morning) and light refreshment at your whim throughout the trip. To summon any of this room service as in any quality hotel you had only to lift a dial phone by your bed; from end to end the 'Century' was threaded by an internal phone system in addition to the radio-telephone via which passengers could be connected to national and international networks outside.

Use of the dictaphone service in your own 'Century' room was completely free. A call on the train phone and the train secretary would soon be at your door to plug in the machine and advise you on its use. The dictaphone tape was also provided gratis. Your dictation finished, you could either mail it to your own secretary for attention or hand the reel to the train secretary who would have the letters transcribed at prevailing stenographic rates by railroad staff at New York Central's New York or Chicago offices on 'Twentieth Century Limited' headed

above: This was one of eight cars which Missouri Pacific rebuilt in 1933–34 as full-length lounges with a Spanish decor of red ceramic-tiled floor, fancy grilles, beamed ceilings and chandeliers. In the late 1930s one could be found in the 'City of Mexico,' a luxury train running between St Louis and Mexico City that was jointly operated by Missouri Pacific and the National Railways of Mexico. (Courtesy Author's collection)

right: Another much-loved family of late 1930s luxury streamliners was Southern Pacific's 'Daylight' series, introduced in 1937. Their strikingly red, orange and black-liveried 4-8-4s were claimed to be the largest and most powerful streamlined steam locomotives ever built. (Courtesy Author's collection)

left: A streamlined New York Central 'Hudson' noses out of La Salle Street station, Chicago on the 15 June 1938 maiden trip of the new streamlined all-room 'Twentieth Century Limited.' (Courtesy Arthur Dubin collection)

below: The lounge of the 1938 'Twentieth Century' was probably the summit of designer Dreyfuss' art. (Courtesy Arthur Dubin collection)

right, below and bottom: Union Pacific's diesel streamliners of the late 1930s featured some extremes of interior styling. These pictures show: (below) the replica of a Western barroom, with unfinished pine board walls and ceiling and period embellishments, in the *Frontier Shack* car of the 'City of Denver'; (right) the *Little Nugget* club car of the 1937 'City of Los Angeles' with its lace curtains, gas chandeliers, marble-topped tables, vivid colors, vaudeville portraits and mechanical warbling bird in a gilded cage by the bar; and (bottom) the sharply contrasting lounge-bar of the 1941 Hollywood car in the 'City of Los Angeles.' (Courtesy Union Pacific Railroad Museum collection)

paper, whence it would be posted to your addressee.

'Highball' or 'right away' for the 'Century' from Grand Central was 18.00 nightly. It was electric traction for the first $32\frac{3}{4}$ miles to Harmon because of ordinances prohibiting smoke or diesel fumes in the tunnels on the exit from New York, then diesels which worked unchanged the rest of the $925\frac{1}{4}$ mile journey to Chicago though their crew would be changed successively at Albany, Syracuse, Buffalo, Cleveland, Toledo and Elkhart.

As the 'Century' ended its superbly scenic run along the sinuous left bank of the Hudson and attacked the sharp climb up to its Albany stop it was time to make for the diner. Perambulating the train, women passengers especially would appreciate the air-operated vestibule doors, opening at a light touch of a hand-bar and closing automatically behind them, an improvement to which Europeans were not treated for another 15 years.

The 'Century' normally ran two diners marshalled the opposite way to each other, so that the two kitchens flanked the central dining area. Dreyfuss had been at pains to avoid the conventional, con-

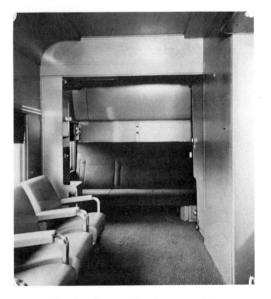

tinuous saloon layout of a railroad diner and each car's dining area was attractively partitioned into three separate areas. There were two eight-seater 'dinettes' with four-seater tables arranged in the orthodox fashion each side of the gangway, but the central 22-seater area was a seemingly casual but very ingenious mix of different-sized tables, some positioned longitudinally, others laterally, and of individual chairs and curved banquette sofas along the coach walls. Color schemes were a discreet gray and rust, with leather cloaking the walls of the main saloon to tone with its leather chairs and banquettes, rich walnut panelling in the dinettes and the whole softly lit by fluorescent panels in the ceiling (the whole train was fluorescently lit, incidentally). Entering the dining area and looking down through the semi-glazed inter-section partitions, you seemed to have come upon a whole series of small, intimate dining rooms.

Your place found at a table, the dinner-jacketed stewards would graciously present each lady of the party with an orchid, compliments of the New York Central (the men's turn would come next morning at breakfast, when they were offered *boutonnières*). If you were not a first-

timer on the 'Century,' the chances were that the steward would be addressing you by name. One famous 'Century' steward of the period claimed that he could put a name to 15,000 of his clientele and that on an average trip three-quarters of the diners would be known to him. Not only that, but the stewards kept their private *aide-mémoire* books of individuals' fads and fancies: for instance, that magnate Marshall Field would expect to find enough for two dry martinis in his cocktail shaker though his pre-prandial order was invariably one and that the late, great Bing Crosby liked to start his 'Century' day with hot wheatcakes at 06.00. As for the meal itself, as late as 1948 the 'Century's' five-course table d'hôte still cost no more than $1.75, and that for an enticing range of specialities such as clam bouillon, Peconic Bay Weakfish, apricot pie, orange pecan sticks and spiced melon rind.

Dinner over and cleared, the crisp white linen table-cloths would be removed, the tables covered with soft rose-colored cloths and the lighting would be dimmed. The easy beat of Artie Shaw, Tommy Dorsey, Benny Goodman or Glenn Miller, originating from a record-playing deck behind the scenes, would

top: Inside the observation lounge of the 1948 'Twentieth Century Limited.' (Courtesy Author's collection)

center: The diner of the 1948 'Twentieth Century Limited.' (Courtesy Author's collection)

above: A master bedroom in the 1948 'Twentieth Century Limited.' (Courtesy Arthur Dubin collection)

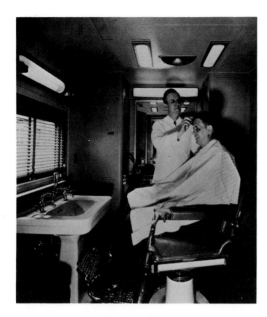

above: Barber's shop in the final version of the 'Twentieth Century Limited.' (Courtesy Arthur Dubin collection)

left: In its final years with its diesel locomotives a mix of the original two-tone and a later and simpler livery, New York Central's 'Twentieth Century Limited' threads the Hudson River Valley near the end of its run from Chicago to New York. (Courtesy Victor Hand)

thrum gently from concealed loudspeakers and the diner would be transmuted into a sophisticated nighterie.

The diner was not the only after-dinner night spot on the train, of course. You could move on to the 'Century' club car, another supreme example of Dreyfuss' art in downplaying the constricting corridor effect of a railroad car's shape on the senses. You entered the car through a circular foyer, inset in the walls of which were illuminated glass cases housing delicate, super-scale models of early New York Central steam locomotives. Beyond it the main lounge broke away completely from the traditional arrangement of lines of inward-facing armchairs along the side walls. Even more boldly than in the diner, Dreyfuss had conceived a layout of long serpentine settees and occasional chairs around staggered occasional tables that was strikingly intimate. Again the decor was subtly subdued, with natural cork finish on the walls and a light gray ceiling toning to perfection with the gray and rust pigskin leather of the seating. At the far end of the lounge, needless to say, was a well-stocked bar and beyond that a handsome octagonally-shaped barber's shop.

The far end of the club car was the crew quarters with its own shower and bunks for 18 staff. Staffing demands of a de luxe train like the 'Century' were formidable – and one of the primary reasons for the rapid accumulation of intolerable losses

by the great American long-haul Limiteds as soon as their premium trade started absconding to the airlines. Another outstanding cause of the Limiteds' bankruptcy was the prodigality of train catering which railroads regarded as essential promotion; even in the pre-World War II heyday of the Limited, the 'Pennsylvania' was reckoned to be losing upwards of a million dollars annually on its diners, while by the 1950s US railroads as a whole were spending on train catering a third more than they took in the till and squandering around $30 millions in the process.

Throughout its New York–Chicago run the 'Century' would have at least 40 staff on the train. Riding all the way would be the Pullman conductor, a Pullman porter in each sleeping car, the train secretary (who, with the railroad's travelling passenger department representative, had an office in the club car; this room, besides its equipment with typewriter and dictaphone, was also the radio-telephone booth), the barber, a ladies' maid and the numerous catering staff – two chief stewards, two chefs, six cooks, fourteen waiters and two barmen, one for the club car bar, the other for the bar in the rear-end observation lounge; the latter was designed and furnished similarly to the club car, but with the added interest of a speedometer inset in one partition. All these personnel were concerned exclusively with service to the passengers, and there would be no more than 140 paying customers in a typical first-section 'Century' with a complement of eight sleeping cars of various types. Superimposing the operating staff requirement on the purely service personnel one came up with a grand total of more than 60 people to cater for just 150 passengers on a 16-hour journey! The train itself was staffed operationally by a conductor, a baggageman and two brakesmen, who were relieved twice en route, at Buffalo and Toledo. As for locomotive crews, as we have already noted, they were changed no fewer than seven times en route, if one includes the Harmon change of traction shortly after departure from New York. Yet by 1948 the one-time $10 surcharge for the privilege of riding the 'Century' had been halved to $5!

It is an injustice to the many other great American luxury trains born in the first half of the 20th century to have spent so much space on the 'Twentieth Century Limited' alone, but broadly speaking most offered similar cossetting and comfort, the differences lying in style and decor, in the length of the diner's menu and the depth of its wine cellar, or in the nice touches of complimentary service – a 'hospitality hour' of free coffee and fruit juice in the lounge, maybe, or a free offering of the chef's own punch with the meal.

As early as 1923 the Chicago Milwaukee

& St Paul had gone one better than the increasingly familiar radio, or later radio-gram, in the lounge by putting on a film show in what it called a 'Movietorium.' Others followed suit, sometimes making film shows one of the diversions in a specially dedicated 'recreation car,' which would also be used for on-train bridge club sessions, or for dancing, sometimes to a live band. Towards the end of the pre-Amtrak luxury train era, the Baltimore & Ohio rivalled the airlines in the range of its on-train movie presentations, with roof-level screens showing different films in the diner and in one of the coaches.

Perhaps the most striking of all recreation cars were those built by the Pennsylvania in 1948 for its New York–St Louis 'Jeffersonian.' At one end of the car was a games and reading lounge, armchairs ranged along one wall, games tables and chairs against the other; adjoining that was an enclosed, well-equipped and nurse-supervised children's playroom; next came an attractive sunken buffet-lounge; and finally, at the far end of the vehicle, a compact newsreel theater!

Before we move on in Chapter 6 to pay fresh tribute to the American luxury train in its final flowering as the diesel streamliner and domeliner, however, one train demands some attention here simply for the renowned diversity of its on-train entertainment. That was the 'New York and Florida Special,' more crisply titled the 'Florida Special' in its later years. Its original *raison d'être* was the determination of Henry Flagler, one of the massively rich founders of the Standard Oil Company, to develop Florida as a winter haven which would lure wealthy Americans in the eastern US away from the Mediterranean coasts of Europe. His first move was to build the huge, flamboyant, Spanish-style Hotel Ponce de Leon at St Augustine. Since Flagler was also President of the Florida East Coast Railroad, the obvious concomitant to the hotel's opening in January 1888 was the inauguration on the same day of a luxury all-Pullman winter season-only train from New York, making the 1074-mile run over, successively, Pennsylvania, Richmond Fredericksburg & Potomac, Atlantic Coast Line and finally Florida East Coast tracks to Jacksonville in 30 hours.

George Pullman obliged with six-car train-sets that were decked out with the same panache as the pseudo-Moorish hotel. Even the staff seems to have been far more flashily arrayed than was usual at the time: to one pressman on the inaugural they 'resembled Prussian officers, so gaudy and gorgeous were their uniforms'. The diner menu of the 'Special' in its inaugural weeks is another that should be set out in full, especially as, yet again, the exclusive price was no more than a single dollar:

Mock turtle à l'Anglaise
Consommé Victoria

Salmon à la Chamborg
Parisienne potatoes

Boiled Beef Tongue
Boiled Chicken, Egg Sauce

Roast Beef with Browned Potatoes
Roast Leg of South Down Mutton,
Currant Jelly
Young Turkey, Cranberry Sauce

Fricandeau of Veal à la Richelieu
Salmi of Duck à la Jardinière
Banana Fritters, Port Wine Sauce

Roast Saddle of Antelope with
Currant Jelly

Lobster Mayonnaise   Lettuce Salad
Spanish Olives   Celery
Chow Chow   Pickled Onions
Gherkins

Boiled Potatoes   Mashed Potatoes
Baked Sweet Potatoes
Stewed Tomatoes   Squash
French Peas   Succotash

Mince Pie   Apple Pie
Coconut Pudding, Hard Sauce

Fruit   Ice Cream   Assorted Cake
Preserved Fruits   Marmalade   Figs
Dried Canton Ginger   Raisins
English, Graham and Oatmeal Wafers

Roquefort and Edam Cheese
Bent's Crackers
Café Noir
Table Water from Silurian Springs,
Waukesha

Even though the 'Special's' passengers had at first to transfer to a ferry at Jacksonville for the final stage of their journey to St Augustine on the other side of the St John's River, the train was an instantaneous commercial success. And so was the hotel, which sparked off the leisure development of Florida that became as hell-bent as a gold rush after World War I. The thrice-weekly 'Special' became daily in short order. Then, when Flagler finished his extraordinary sequence of bridges and viaducts south of Miami early in 1912, the 'Special' could hop from island to island as far as Key West.

It was the 'Florida Special' which in 1926 pioneered the recreation car. Three Pullman sleepers were gutted and refashioned with gay decor, including potted palms, for the role. Entertainment included bridge and horse-racing games, and at night the floor was cleared for dancing to a small band with an attractive hostess to direct the proceedings. World War II shelved the 'Special,' but it re-emerged

in 1949 as one of the new lightweight diesel-powered streamliners. Like the 'Century' of New York Central, it was all-Pullman and all-room, air-conditioned from nose to tail; every room, in whatever price range, had its own lavatory and washing facility, its own radio and recorded music apparatus, its own freshly circulating iced-water supply. To mark the 'Special's' diamond jubilee in January 1963 another brand-new train was applied to the service in the winter of 1962–3, commanding an extra fare even though it was no longer exclusively Pullman.

But in its final years the 'Florida Special' was a unique travel experience even on US rails, and all for a basic round-trip fare of $83.93 between New York and Miami (those were the days, by the way, of chronic airline hijacks to Cuba, which the 'Special's' operators turned to its commercial advantage with posters urging

'If you want to go to Miami without a stop-over in Havana, call us!') Champagne, compliments of the railroad, was served with sumptuous candle-lit dinners. Dinner over, you could watch TV. Alternatively, the recreation car might be staging a fashion show; otherwise it would be putting on bingo sessions or highly popular singalongs with a small group. And throughout the train pretty hostesses would be hovering to advise and pamper the passengers.

Those were the days when travel was a treasured end in itself, not just the-means-to-a-destination end it has almost universally become in the last quarter of the 20th century. Maybe, hopefully, dwindling energy resources will one day compel us all to put less of a premium on speed and re-awaken us to the travel pleasures we have sacrificed to squeeze more wage-earning hours out of a life-span.

top left: Atlantic Coast Lines's 'Florida Special' near Jacksonville, Florida in 1965. (Courtesy Atlantic Coast Line)

top and above: Hostesses conduct a bingo session and model swimwear to enliven the 'Florida Special's' journey south to Florida. (Courtesy Atlantic Coast Line)

left: A staggered table and seating layout was an attractive feature of diner *Moultrie*, a 1950 addition to 'Florida Special' equipment. (Courtesy Atlantic Coast Line)

CHAPTER 5
LUXURY IN EUROPE BETWEEN THE WARS

Milan station. Luxury excursion train headed
by an Italian state railway steam locomotive.
(Courtesy Italian State Railway)

left: The 'Flèche d'Or,' electrically hauled, awaits departure from Paris' Gare du Nord for Calais in 1963. By then the Pullman element of the train had been reduced to two cars. Crossing the bridge in the background is a Paris Metro train. (Courtesy Author's collection)

bottom: The Wagons-Lits diner of a European *train de luxe* in the 1930s. (Courtesy Author's collection)

below: A French Nord Railway 4-6-0 pulls away from the quayside with the Calais section of the 'Simplon-Orient Express' early in the 1920s. (Courtesy Author's collection)

The 'Simplon-Orient Express'

The first major development in European *trains de luxe* after World War I stemmed not from the railways but from the councils of the victorious Grand Alliance. The map of Europe had been redrawn at Versailles and new countries had been demarcated. To help cement the new shape of the continent the politicians were keen to have a new international train service between Western Europe and the Balkans which bypassed the traditional route through Germany and the old Austro-Hungarian empire. Counsel was taken of the Wagons-Lits company and in April 1919 the 'Simplon-Orient Express' was born.

It was the first step in the creation of a remarkable tracery of Wagons-Lits services between North and West Europe on the one hand and the Balkans and the Near East on the other. A first section of the 'Simplon-Orient' started from Calais and at Paris picked up the central part of the train, comprising sleepers to Istanbul, Athens and Bucharest. From Paris the make-up would be five sleeping cars, a restaurant car and a brake (which in later years would be one of the Wagons-Lits *fourgons* incorporating a small shower bath). After passage of Switzerland via the Simplon route the train made from Milan for Trieste, where the restaurant car crew was changed, then headed for Vinkovci, north-west of Belgrade, where two sleepers for Bucharest were put off.

The rest of the train continued to Belgrade, where in the later 1930s the 'Simplon-Orient' took on a still more cosmopolitan character. The Yugoslav capital became the rendezvous of a sequence of exotic trans-European *trains de luxe* – the 'Arlberg-Orient,' the 'Ostend–Vienna' and the resurrected 'Orient Express' as well as the 'Simplon-Orient' – and on different days of the week, from 1932 until the onset of World War II, the 'Simplon-Orient' would take on here additional sleepers from either Berlin,

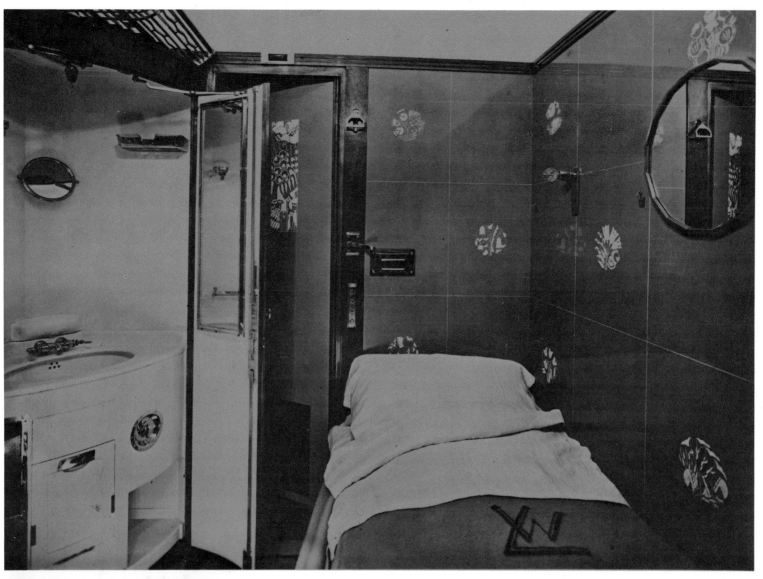

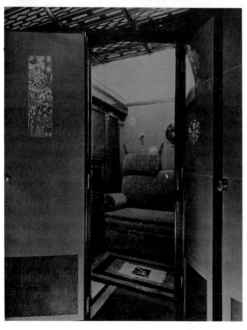

top and above: The single-berth compartment of a 'Blue Train' sleeper of the later 1930s, seen made up for both night and day use. (Courtesy Author's collection)

Ostend, Amsterdam, Vienna or Prague. Next strategic call for the 'Simplon-Orient' was at Nis, where the Athens sleepers were detached; there would be two from France plus, from 1932 onwards, one or more from one of the other originating points which, as just mentioned, were brought within the 'Simplon-Orient' at that date. The Athens cars, incidentally, fetched up eventually at the port of Piraeus for the benefit of passengers taking ship there, though you had to be patient through a long wait in the Greek capital while the sleeper crews were relieved and other bureaucratic business was leisurely conducted before the vehicles were hauled down to the harbor.

The rest of the train continued through Sofia to Istanbul. At first the restaurant car was removed at the Bulgarian border, but from 1933 it carried on the whole way to Istanbul, completing a 1899 mile journey from Paris that must have been the longest uninterrupted itinerary ever set a European diner in regular service.

Istanbul was by no means the limit of overland *train de luxe* travel from Western Europe in the inter-war period. In 1926, after Kemal Ataturk had transformed Ankara into Turkey's new capital,

Wagons-Lits secured a contract to extend its service in the Near East, and in 1930 inauguration of the 'Taurus Express' opened up the railway to the Middle East. 'Simplon-Orient' passengers were hustled in a special ferry across the Bosphorus (only an hour and a half was allowed for the transfer) from the Sirkeci terminus to Haydarpasa, there to board the new all-sleeper-and-restaurant-car *train de luxe*, which offered one section to the Iraki border at Tel Kotchek (the standard gauge railway to Baghdad was not completed until 1940) and another to Tripoli. You had to take a special bus from Tripoli southward to Haifa, but there you could take Wagons-Lits service on to the banks of the Suez canal. There was no rail bridge over the canal between the wars, so further recourse to a ferry was necessary before you could finish the journey from Kantara to Cairo in one of the Pullman trains the Egyptians had launched in the late 1920s. If you had started from London you would have taken almost exactly seven days for the trip.

In the age of Concorde a seven-day rail journey might smack of sheer masochism to some. It might even daunt one or two committed rail travellers who never came

below: Still officially known as the 'Calais–Mediterranean Express,' the more familiarly titled 'Train Bleu' hugs the Riviera coastline near Cannes soon after its post-World War II revival, headed by SNCF 'Mountain' No 241.A.120. (Courtesy G F Fenino)

upon the 'Simplon-Orient' until after World War II, after it had been vulgarized with ordinary coaches, or worse still in the final degraded years from the summer of 1962 as the 'Direct-Orient' to Belgrade, whence the Athens and Istanbul through coaches went forward respectively in the 'Athens Express' and the 'Marmara Express.' So impoverished had the service become by the mid-1970s that its extinction in the spring of 1977 was euthanasia.

For most of the inter-war era, however, competitive air service was non-existent and the only realistic alternative way from London to Cairo was by sea, a journey no less protracted. Consequently these trans-European *trains de luxe* did a substantial business in premium-rate international parcels traffic as well as high-ranking passengers from the Continent's nobility and its diplomatic and commercial milieus. The comfort and service on board the trains were exceptional for that age of travel, so much so that not infrequently royalty itself was well content to travel in a specially hired Wagons-Lits sleeper attached to a scheduled *train de luxe*. In Bulgaria the monarchy went one better. Both King Ferdinand and even more so his successor, Boris, were

steam engine fanatics; in the 1930s newspaper pictures of Boris unwinding from his royal burdens at the regulator of a Bulgarian locomotive – even, it is said, at the head of the 'Simplon-Orient' – were almost as commonplace as latter-day shots of British royalty being nuzzled by its horses. Mind you, in the heyday of the 'Simplon-Orient' the final course of the train's sections through the wilds of Serbia could harbor a variety of excitements. Once the train was hit by bandits in this area, but for voyeurs at least there was some compensation for that hazard in the probable spectacle of naked Serbian country girls innocently splashing about in the Varda – provided, that is, lechers were prepared to flout the Wagons-Lits conductors, who had strict instructions from their management to see that all blinds were drawn while the 'Simplon-Orient' traversed this bucolic Eden.

The 'Train Bleu'

A major *train de luxe* event of late 1922 was the delivery of the Wagons-Lits company's first all-steel sleeping cars, the first to be liveried in gold-lined dark blue instead of teak, and the flamboyant

launch of the 'Calais-Mediterranean.' That was the train's official title, but the new styling of the coaches tagged it with a name by which it was always famed worldwide even though this title was not officially recognized until as late as 1949. The 'Train Bleu' had been born.

Those first all-steel sleepers, incidentally, had been built in Britain by the Leeds Forge Company, a firm little-known as a coachbuilder which secured the order in face of fierce Continental competition, and not least in spite of acute problems of transporting the completed vehicles to France. The snag, of course, was the girth of cars built to the more ample Continental loading gauge. After exhaustive route surveys, the Midland and Great Central Railways conceded that it was just feasible to work them from the West Riding to Immingham for shipment, provided the cars were left part-finished in the matter of some exterior fittings. They were moved in groups on Sundays in the summer of 1922. Each convoy was reduced to walking pace anywhere there was risk of fouling clearances – through every station, on many curves and past many bridges; frequently no daylight was visible between vehicle and fixed structures, but they got through with slight physical contact at only one station platform.

Average cost of each car was £12,500, a phenomenal coach price for the period (British Rail's new Pullmans of 1960 were only £5000 more expensive). This in itself was testimony to the splendor of the finish, which extended to rich mahogany panelling in the lavatories as well as in the sleeping compartments. Each vehicle included both single and two-berth compartments (all first-class) and in some of the build each adjoining pair of two-berth rooms shared a separate and intervening dressing-room with washbasin; that arrangement of washing facilities vacated space in each compartment for a comfortable folding armchair so that by day couples could sit facing each other by the window.

A glittering company was invited to a sumptuous launch of the new service in December 1922. So prestigious was the affair, in fact, that the Crown Prince of Sweden and HRH the Duke of Connaught were moved to join ranks on the platform at Nice with the elite of Côte d'Azur officialdom and welcome the incoming trains. At first there were two separate services, the 'Calais–Mediterranean' and the 'Paris–Mediterranean,' but the 1930s slump saw them combined as one; thereafter Calais, which had previously originated a complete train of five sleepers, a diner (a roomily laid-out car with only 42 seats instead of the customary 56) and baggage cars, dispatched just two sleepers, one for San Remo and the other for Ventimiglia, which left the Channel port

right: The first of the newborn LNER's Pullman ventures, the London Kings Cross–Sheffield Pullman, heads north through the London suburbs behind Ivatt Atlantic No 4461. (Courtesy Author's collection)

at the rear of the 'Flèche d'Or' and then worked round the Ceinture from Paris Gare du Nord for attachment to the main train at the Gare de Lyon.

In later years a lounge-bar car handsomely and spaciously furnished in contemporary Pullman style enhanced the exclusivity of the 'Train Bleu.' Although dinner service was announced as commencing within half-an-hour of the train's 19.30 departure from Gare de Lyon, the bar was such an agreeable rendezvous, and the elegant patrons of the train so frequently on the same high society round, that it would be at least an hour-and-a-half before enough diners had filtered through to the flower-decked tables in the restaurant car to justify the *maître d'hôtel* signalling his staff into action. (Some 'Train Bleu' publicity of the 1920s, incidentally, depicted bowls of flowers in the sleeping compartments too, but I have a feeling this was a flight of the artist's fancy.) In steam days there was time to start dinner as late as ten o'clock and still dispatch a full menu of consommé, delicate sole fillets, entree, salad, cheese, *boule de neige* and fresh fruit in deliberate Gallic tempo before the restaurant was discarded at Dijon. Not so, of course, in today's electric age, when the train leaves later and is much faster all the way, especially between Paris and Lyons; – dinner service is under way while the train is still in the platform at Gare de Lyon. As I describe in a later chapter, the modern 'Train Bleu' is still a majestic all-sleeper train, often over-subscribed and retaining some of its old individuality in its restaurant car at least. But its exclusivity was first undermined by the insertion in its format of 'special'-rate P class cars with a duplex berth layout in 1956, then by the admission of tourist-class traffic in 1962 following emergence of the multi-purpose 'universal' sleeping-car design.

The 'Queen of Scots' and the 'Yorkshire Pullman'

The other major development on the European *trains de luxe* scene in the early years between the wars was the rapid spread of Pullman operation on both sides of the English Channel. In Britain the seed was sown by the American executive, Henry Thornton of the Long Island Railroad, whom the Great Eastern Railway imported as its General Manager in 1914, outraging the domestic railway world with a blunt assertion that it could find no Briton with all the right qualities for the job. Inexplicably for a man of undoubted commercial flair, Thornton believed supplementary-fare Pullmans would enrapture the short-distance travellers between London and East Anglia as much as they had the long-haul market in his own country. Unsurprisingly they did not, except on the boat trains to and from Harwich. But when the Great Eastern was absorbed by the LNER in the 1923 Grouping of British railways into the 'Big Four,' the new company was stuck with Thornton's Pullman contract, which still had years to run.

The LNER naturally switched the bulk of the Great Eastern Pullmans to the more likely premium-fare luxury markets on the Great Northern route between London Kings Cross and the industrial cities of Yorkshire and North-East England. After one or two false starts, notably a vain effort lasting only the summer of 1924 to interest Sheffield and Manchester in an all-Pullman train to and from Kings Cross, the LNER had, by the mid-1920s, settled upon two commercially rewarding services which, with minor variations of routing, were proud flag trains of the East Coast Main Line from London to the North for several decades (though interrupted, needless to say, by abandonment during World War II).

One was the 'Queen of Scots' as it was titled in 1928 after re-equipment with Britain's first rake of all-steel Pullmans. Between the wars the Yorkshire spa of Harrogate was very much in society vogue and the 'Queen' was routed that way instead of straight down the Anglo-Scottish main line from Doncaster to York and Darlington. That protracted the journey from London to Edinburgh or the Pullman's final terminus at Glasgow Queen Street. In the final pre-World War II years the 'Queen' took $7\frac{3}{4}$ hours over the Kings Cross–Edinburgh Waverley run, the 'Flying Scotsman' only 7 hours. Moreover by then the 'Scotsman,' as will be described shortly, had been refined into what was arguably Europe's most luxurious non-Pullman day train, yet one unburdened by any surcharge on the basic fare. Nevertheless the 'Queen' was the unhesitant choice of a substantial clientele for their Anglo-Scottish journeys right up to 1939.

A Pullman train had an exclusive club ambience equalled only in the diners of one or two morning and evening business trains. Meals were served at all seats from two or three kitchens spaced at intervals through the train. Even if you were a first-timer, therefore, the constant but discreet hovering of waiters at your elbow gave you a sense of cossetting not to be found in a non-Pullman express. The Pullman menu, too, was phrased with a flourish in keeping with the heavy polished tableware, the deep red-shaded brass table-lamps, the massive loose armchairs and the inlaid wood panelling of the walls which were Pullman hallmarks. The archetypal railway 'brown Windsor soup' would never defile a Pullman card. 'Real Tomato Soup with Golden Croutons' it would probably begin: then, not just roast beef but 'Roast Sirloin of Scotch Beef' plus – naturally – Yorkshire

left: The new all-steel 'Queen of Scots' Pullman train outshopped in 1928 en route from London Kings Cross to Edinburgh; headed by ex-Great Central 'Director' 4-4-0 No 5510 *Princess Mary*, it was photographed north of Grantham. (Courtesy Author's collection)

below left: The Southern Railway created the all-Pullman 'Bournemouth Belle' from London Waterloo to Bournemouth in 1931. For its first five years it was a Sundays-only service. The train is headed by 'King Arthur' class 4-6-0 No 780 *Sir Persant*. (Courtesy Author's collection)

The 'Sud Express'

Meanwhile Dalziel has been beavering away at the extension of the Pullman foothold on the European mainland. Desperate for vehicles, for his first post-World War I venture he appropriated all but one of an eleven-car order constructed in 1924–5 for British service and moved them to Milan, where they were adapted to Continental standards (eight of these exports returned to Britain in 1928 and survived to operate under the nationalized British Railways; one acquired further distinction when it was rebuilt as the post-World War II 'Golden Arrow's' bar car, the *Trianon Bar*). The Milan modifications included replacement of the kitchens' gas cookers with coal ranges, a characteristic of most Continental Pullmans until the end of their days. With these British cars the 'Milan–Nice Pullman' was inaugurated in the winter of 1925, then extended the following winter to become the 'Milan–Cannes Pullman.' This all-Pullman train was put on only during the winter Côte d'Azur season; attempts to find summer employment for crew and cars on a Milan–Venice run in 1926 and 1929 were a commercial disaster.

The first new Pullmans built specifically for mainland European operation after World War I were delivered to France in 1926 and applied to the 'Sud Express.' Unlike Wagon-Lits' pre-war saloons on the Continent, the new Pullmans were intended for day trains. Thus they were to a degree patterned on the British Pullman of the period, with most of their seating in armchairs around the tables of a spacious saloon, but some of it in the enclosed two- or four-seater coupés cherished by so many Pullman patrons as the equivalent of private drawing-rooms. At first the 'Sud Express' cars were even painted the same umber and cream as British Pullmans (though not indivi-

Pudding and a platter of fresh vegetables ennobled by descriptions like 'Crécy Carrots.' Fruit salad would be billed as appearing with 'Devon Double Cream'; and to end there would be no prosaic 'cheese and biscuits' but the 'English County Cheese Tray.'

This was not empty verbal filigree. Even after World War II and up to the acquisition of the Pullman Car Company by the British Transport Commission, some time after British Rail restaurant-car fare had been driven to the palate-dulling economics of too much present-day catering, the Pullman conductor was still effectively an old-style restaurant manager. The ordering of adequate and suitable raw materials for the kitchen remained his entire responsibility. Frozen foods were quite taboo, so was practically all pre-cooking and advance preparation of dishes in the company's kitchens on *terra firma*. Standards were so high

that even when, as quite frequently happened in the early 1950s, extra cars were added to the London–Newcastle 'Tees-Tyne Pullman' for a party off to launch a ship on Tyneside and their hosts ordered a five-course trainboard banquet of, say, trout, roast turkey and elaborate desserts, the whole meal would be prepared to their requirements in the cramped – and by then obsolescently equipped – kitchens on the train.

The LNER's other regular all-Pullman service stabilized as the 'West Riding Pullman' between Kings Cross and, chiefly, Leeds, but conveying also a section for Bradford and Halifax, down in the late afternoon from London and back in mid-morning (the Leeds section began its return journey at Harrogate). This train was renamed the 'Yorkshire Pullman' in 1935 to mark its acquisition of a further section for the East Yorkshire port and city of Hull.

The interior of a British first-class Pullman in the mid-1930s. *Violet*, seen here, was one of those built for the electric multiple-unit train-sets of the 1932 London–Brighton electrification. (Courtesy Author's collection)

dually named, as British first-class cars traditionally were until British Rail stamped the dull impress of standardization on its surviving cars in the winter of 1967–68), but in 1932 the external styling was changed to the dark blue below the waist-line and cream above which distinguished all European mainland Pullmans until their demise. Like the British cars, too, the Continental European Pullmans were originally designed to work in groups, or *'couplages,'* with a kitchen in one car capable of covering meal service in at least one adjoining car as well as in its own saloon. In later years, however, as Continental Pullman services gradually contracted to premium-fare sections of orthodox expresses, the Pullman kitchens

were abandoned and the Pullman passengers were attended from the kitchen of the train's Wagons-Lits restaurant car, next to which they would be marshalled.

Today's imposing overnight sleeper from Paris to Iberia, the 'Puerta de Sol' (see Chapter 8), disembarks its passengers in Madrid within 15 hours of leaving Paris, while the nowadays plebeian 'Sud Express,' pulling out from Paris Auster-litz, gets its couchette passengers to Lis-bon a little over 24 hours later. Both trains, as will be described shortly, have the benefit of modern electric traction and also of Franco-Spanish border apparatus which makes light of the gauge-break by smoothly exchanging the bogies beneath through-running vehicles and their re-

cumbent occupants. In the mid-1920s a whole day's rail journey would take you no further than the frontier. Just this side of it, though, was Biarritz, in those days as fancied by European high society as Monaco in the 1970s because of its patronage by King Edward VII; and Biarritz was probably a more appetizing commercial target for the 'Sud Express' of the 1920s than Iberia. Biarritz, anyway, was the destination of Dalziel's preview run of France's first all-Pullman train. As a mark of progress, it is worth recording that that inaugural run took more than $7\frac{1}{2}$ hours from Paris to Bordeaux, whereas today's 'Puerta del Sol' dismisses that sector of its journey in just over 4 hours!

In regular service the 'Sud Express'

was a lightweight assemblage of one first-class, one second-class and one part-kitchen Pullman, plus luggage vans at each end of the rake. Its Iberian passengers had luxury accommodation all the way, their comfort tempered only by the enforced change of trains at the frontier; there, in the late evening, they transferred to the Iberian-gauge 'Sud Express,' an exclusive sleeping-car and restaurant-car train, which conveyed portions both for Madrid and for Lisbon.

The 'Golden Arrow'

Within three weeks of the 'Sud Express' debut another French all-Pullman train was in business, the 'Flèche d'Or,' better known to much of the English-speaking

world as the 'Golden Arrow.' Those were the sadly far-off days when the global travel market harvested a fair proportion of its richest pickings in Britain, so Dalziel was naturally anxious to link the British Pullman network with his expanding European mainland services as effectively as possible. For a time he was thwarted on one ground or another by the management of France's Nord Railway, while on the other side of the Channel the Southern Railway – otherwise wholeheartedly furthering the enterprize – quirkily refused to adopt Dalziel's name for the service until it had been running for three years. Thus although the ten-car, all-first-class Pullman train which began to ply between Paris Gare du Nord and Calais Maritime on 11 September 1926 was titled 'Flèche d'Or' from the start and the Southern had been running a matching all-Pullman train between London Victoria and Dover since November 1924, the latter was not correspondingly christened 'Golden Arrow' until 1929, the year the Southern commissioned a new cross-Channel packet, the *Canterbury*, to complement the two *trains de luxe*. Chauvinism, it is said, was the reason for this British bloody-mindedness. The 'gold' in Dalziel's title was a proud allusion to the Wagons-Lits company's golden jubilee that inaugural year of 1926, and hence to have applied the name simultaneously to the British train might have implied fealty to some heathen enterprise across the water.

Anyone crossing the Channel in modern times on a filthy day in a ferry overcrowded with passengers and luggage, probably because mountainous seas have grounded the hovercraft, can faintly conceive what the passage to France was like before the creation of the 'Golden Arrow.' Boats were much smaller and chronically unpunctual, port facilities were cruder, the struggle to board or disembark purgatorial, the Customs on both sides of the Channel argumentatively meticulous and a prime aggravation of delays to boats and trains.

The 'Arrow's' first-class Pullman passengers were cocooned from practically everything but *mal-de-mer*. By registering their heavy luggage before departure from Paris or London, they could be relieved of it for the whole journey, like any latterday air traveller. The registered baggage was bulked into small, sealed containers which were massed on flatcars at the head of the Pullman trains on both sides of the Channel and transhipped to and from the packet-boat holds by quayside cranes; Customs examination was conducted after reclamation at the destination terminal. No need, either, to worry about scrabbling for a comfortable seat on the boat. The 'Arrow' was despatched from Victoria at 10.45, ahead of the ordinary boat train, to allow its passengers leisurely first choice of accommodation on board. On the other side, the French Customs graciously agreed to

forgo the quayside interrogation for which they were so notorious and deal with 'Arrow' passengers en route.

Not the least remarkable aspect of the service was the marketing acumen, years ahead of its time, shown by Dalziel in his concern to imprint a common identity on the British and French elements of his train service. A critical issue in the prolonged negotiation with the Nord Railway had been Dalziel's determination to equip the 'Flèche d'Or' with British-built Pullmans, a point he eventually won. His aim was to have the French cars finished internally in precisely the same style of upholstery, panelling and lighting as British Pullmans, as well as in the same external scheme of umber and cream (changed to dark blue and cream in 1932, when the 'Flèche d'Or,' its traffic eroded like that of many other *trains de luxe* by the economic depression, took in second-class Pullmans). Not only that, but every last item of tableware for the French cars was supplied from the Pullman Company's London depot. So successful was Dalziel's corporate image-building that some first-time 'Arrow' passengers, it has been alleged, were incredulous at finding they had to change transport modes at the Channel ports: surely the French and British Pullmans were one and the same, and crossed the water by train-ferry? A service of that kind was some years away, but the Pullman Company did the best to take the worry out of

passenger transhipment wherever it could. In particular, it operated its own road bus service between London's Kings Cross and Victoria termini to smooth transfer between the LNER Pullmans and the Southern Pullman boat train services, and to encourage Europe-bound travellers from the North of England to go Pullman the whole way.

The 'Edelweiss' and the 'Rheingold'

New Pullman trains were tumbling on to European mainland tracks in 1927. First to appear, in May, was a precursor of one of today's TEEs, the 'Etoile du Nord' or 'North Star,' operating from Paris two pairs of cars, each a first and a second-class, one of which terminated at Brussels while the other continued to Amsterdam.

With British Pullman service of Harrogate a conspicuous commercial success, Dalziel was optimistic of comparable profit from a summer train to the French spa, Vichy. But the 'Paris–Vichy Pullman,' to which a 'London–Vichy Pullman' section originating from Boulogne was attached in the French capital, did not prosper as an all-Pullman train; after 1930 it was

reduced to a Pullman section in an ordinary train and never revived after its World War II cessation. Within a day of the Vichy train's debut a 'Calais–Brussels Pullman' was launched and two years later timed to link up with 'Golden Arrow' travel in England; on this train Franco-Belgian frontier formalities were also organized on the move. The Brussels

top left: Southern Railway 4-6-0 No 850 *Lord Nelson* climbs the bank out of London's Victoria station at the head of the Dover-bound 'Golden Arrow.' Note the six-wheelers conveying the registered passengers' baggage containers behind the engine's tender. The leading Pullman is still in all-umber livery. (Courtesy Author's collection)

top right: A high-stepping Nord Pacific speeds for the English Channel coast with the Calais portions of three *trains de luxe:* up front, the Wagons-Lits sleepers from San Remo of the 'Train Bleu' and from Istanbul off the 'Simplon Orient Express,' and at the rear, the 'Flèche d'Or' Pullmans. (Courtesy G F Fenino)

extreme left: The 'Sud Express' of 1933, comprised of three Pullmans and two *fourgons*, leaves Orleans Les Aubrais behind Paris–Orleans Railway Pacific No 3563. (Courtesy G F Fenino)

left: Inside a first-class Pullman of the 'Sud Express' in the 1930s. (Courtesy Author's collection)

train saw the inter-war years out. but a summer 'Milan–Ancona Pullman' introduced in July 1927 failed to survive its third season. Other all-Pullman train developments of 1927. which also saw the addition of Pullmans to a number of ordinary French expresses. among them Boulogne–Paris boat trains connecting with Pullman-equipped Southern Railway services from London to Folkestone. included a weekend 'Deauville Pullman Express' between Paris and Deauville. and the 'Gotthard Pullman.' This last. Switzerland's first Pullman venture. gathered in two two-car *couplages*. one from Basle and the other from Zurich. at Arth-Goldau for onwards operation as one train to Milan. Subsequent modification of its timetable to allow attachment at Basle of a third *couplage* coming from Paris Gare de l'Est failed to generate satisfying business. however, and the Swiss had the 'Gotthard Pullman' expunged from the timetables at the end of the 1931 summer.

If the Swiss themselves were indifferent to the blandishments of daytime *trains de luxe*. their more well-heeled English visitors certainly were not. The 'Edelweiss Pullman' and the 'Rheingold,' both created in 1928 to forge a luxury link with Switzerland via the North Sea passage from England. were two of the most consistently successful of all the inter-war international premium-fare trains. The 'Rheingold,' of course. was not a Pullman and brings Mitropa into this narrative for the first time.

Mitropa. a contraction of the German concern's full title of Mitteleuropaische Schlafwagen-und-Speisewagen AG. was a political creation. After the outbreak of World War I the German Government in 1915 ordered the sequestration of all Wagons-Lits assets in the Reich and barred the circulation of Wagons-Lits vehicles in their territory. Until then Wagons-Lits had been sharing sleeping car operations in the Reich with the

Prussian State Railway and had also, through a German subsidiary, deployed some refreshment cars on German services. Brusquely laying claim to Wagons-Lits equipment as enemy material. the Germans in 1916 then passed all the vehicles it had grabbed to the new Mitropa company. formation of which they had instigated with the railways and banks of several of their Allies as co-partners and shareholders. After the war the Wagons-Lits company intrigued unsuccessfully to put Mitropa out of business. but in 1925 it had to concede Mitropa not only a monopoly of internal German sleeping and refreshment car services. but also the right to project German vehicles into Holland. Austria. Switzerland and Scandinavia. In return. Wagons-Lits won transit rights through Germany for their own cars on international itineraries between Germany's neighbors. Within a year Mitropa. which had been building its own new vehicles since the early 1920s. had become to all intents and purposes a subsidiary of the post-war national German railway system. the Reichsbahn.

The Mitropa story might as well be brought up to date at this juncture. After World War II its headquarters was left stranded in the Russian-controlled sector of Berlin and that put paid to Mitropa's role in Western Europe. A new company. the Deutsche Schlafwagen-und-Speisewagen Gesellschaft. or DSG. was established in 1949 to undertake all sleeping and refreshment car service on the post-war West German railway network (the Deutsche Bundesbahn or German Federal Railway). of which the DSG was made and today remains a wholly-owned subsidiary. The remains of a war-battered Mitropa fleet with which DSG began life have long since been superseded. Today's DSG equipment. which gets appropriate tribute in Chapter 8. is all of its own build and unsurpassed in Europe for quality.

But to revert to 1928. Mitropa had already scented English tourist blood with a luxury train it had improvised between Hook of Holland and Berlin with refurbished coaches from the vanquished Kaiser's imperial train. If they needed any persuasion to build on that foundation. it came loud and clear from the worldwide publicity attending the 'Golden Arrow' inauguration and that train's immediate trawl of traffic.

The obvious course for Mitropa to exploit was the route from Holland to the Swiss Alps. with its spectacular passage of the Rhine gorge between Cologne and Mainz. An order for new Pullman-style cars of supreme comfort was laid with German builders in the spring of 1927 and that autumn the Germans announced that the new vehicles would be run in a premium-fare train from Hook of Holland. whence departure would be just before breakfast after arrival of the night boat from Harwich. to Lucerne. German mythology. familiar to any Englishman who had ever come within earshot of Wagner. offered an apt title for the new train: the 'Rheingold.'

Only four weeks after the 'Rheingold's' debut on 15 May 1928 the Wagons-Lits company threw its hat into the same ring with the 'Edelweiss.' an all-Pullman train also from Amsterdam to Lucerne. but drawing in English traffic from the other nocturnal service from London's Liverpool Street terminus via Harwich. the night boat from that Essex port to Antwerp. Needless to say. the 'Edelweiss' routing did not touch Germany. but from Antwerp ran via Brussels. Luxembourg and Strasburg to Switzerland. Eventually both trains settled on Basle as their Swiss focus. each projecting on to Lucerne and Zurich portions which the Swiss Federal Railway coupled as one very colorful train with its contrasted blue-and-cream Pullman and purple-and-white Mitropa 'Rheingold' liveries. Eventually, in the

top extreme left: Lord Dalziel of Wooler, the Wagons-Lits and Pullman Chairman, at the doorway of a European mainland Pullman. (Courtesy Author's collection)

top left: An ex-Nord Railway Atlantic makes speed near Orry-la-Ville with the all-Pullman Amsterdam–Paris 'Oiseau Bleu' in 1933. (Courtesy G F Fenino)

top: Former Bavarian State Railways class S3/6 Pacific No 18.527 threads the Rhine valley at Oberwesel with the Switzerland-bound 'Rheingold' in the early 1930s. (Courtesy Archiv Bellingrodt)

above: A Swiss Federal electric locomotive hauls the combined 'Rheingold' and 'Edelweiss' from Basle to Lucerne. (Courtesy Swiss Federal Railways)

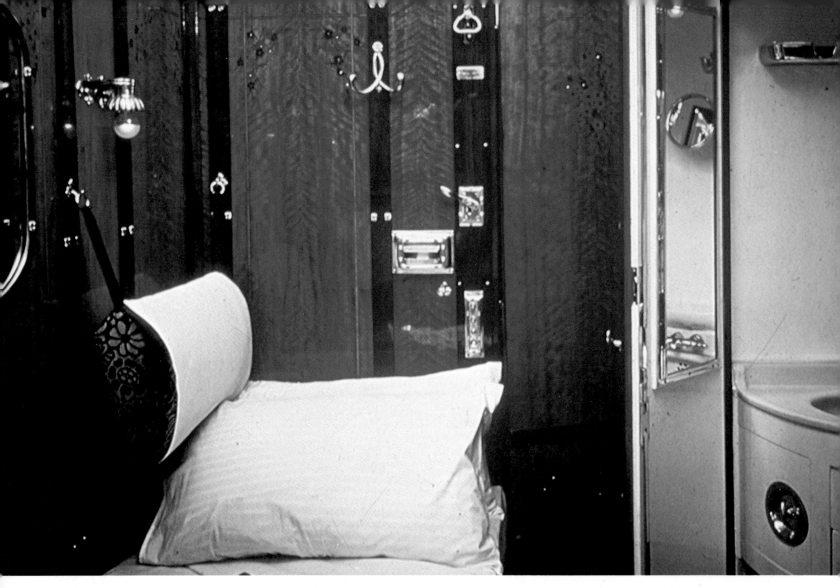

spring of 1938, the Germans broke out of this common mold by extending a section of the 'Rheingold' from Basle over the Gotthard main line to Milan.

Englishmen heading for the Alps between the wars were confronted with a difficult choice between 'Edelweiss' and 'Rheingold.' There was little in it as regards overall journey time to Switzerland. From London's Liverpool Street both connecting boat trains, the 'Hook Continental' and the 'Antwerp Continental,' featured Pullmans and Pullman-catered dinner service. Cabin comfort on the Hook of Holland and Antwerp night boats from Harwich was of the same standard. There was an option of first- or second-class Pullman accommodation on both 'Edelweiss' and 'Rheingold' and neither train significantly outshone the other, for the layout of the 'Rheingold' cars was patently modelled on that of the Pullmans, even down to the table lamps and a mixture of coupés and an open saloon arrangement of tables each with two heavy free-standing armchairs in the first-class cars. However, if other Europeans had by now grown accustomed to the extravagant roominess of a first-class Pullman layout, the Germans had not. In the early 1970s one German journalist who rode on the inaugural 'Rheingold' could still vividly recall his awe when he first boarded one of its first-class cars and

top: The Mulhouse Museum in France also houses a fully restored Type Lx10 Wagons-Lits sleeper of 1929. This is one of its single first-class compartments made up for the night. (Courtesy Cie Internationale des Wagons-Lits et du Tourisme)

above: The short-lived narrow-gauge 'Golden Mountain Pullman' on the Montreux–Oberland–Bernois Railway of Switzerland in 1931 crossing the viaduct at Gstaad. (Courtesy Author's collection)

top: The original 1928 Mitropa cars of the 'Rheingold' which have been restored to their original livery in Cologne are mobilized for a special Hook of Holland–Lucerne run in May 1978 to mark the train's jubilee. Seen at Hook of Holland the train is headed by Netherlands Railways' electric locomotive No 1139. (Courtesy Charles Long)

above: Inside a narrow-gauge 'Golden Mountain Pullman' car. (Courtesy Author's collection)

diffidently relaxed in an armchair: only crowned heads, he murmured to himself, had previously travelled in such state. One minor consideration might have swayed some Britons to pick the 'Rheingold'; its staff could usually be relied upon to speak reasonable English, whereas French was the accepted business language throughout the Wagons-Lits empire and their conductors' command of English tended at best to be fractured.

The 'Golden Mountain Pullman'

Rivalry between Mitropa and Wagons-Lits in the heart of Switzerland led to the quaintest of all inter-war Pullman enterprises. Hungry for new commercial territory, and taking the crafty line that its agreement with Wagons-Lits not to run operational restaurant cars in Switzerland implied a veto only on standard-gauge cars, Mitropa dumbfounded the enemy camp at the start of the 1930s by persuading the narrow-gauge Rhaetian Railways to accept specially-built Mitropa diners. That deal eventually generated the most extraordinary rail catering service in Europe. Following extensions of the narrow-gauge network in the rugged terrain between the Swiss Valais and Engadine, where the little railways are vital all-year-round lifelines, and the fitting of one of the Mitropa diners to work on the rack system, full-scale restaurant-

car service was bestowed upon the narrow-gauge Zermatt–St Moritz 'Glacier Express' over the western sector of its journey, despite the route's stretches of 1 in 9 gradient on its grind up to the line's 6670ft summit at the Oberalp Pass.

Wagons-Lits rather desperately retaliated by contracting with the meter-gauge Montreux–Oberland–Bernois system to run the world's only narrow-gauge all-Pullman train from Montreux through the mountains via Gstaad to Zweisimmen (a Spanish railway also ran narrow-gauge Pullmans between Bilbao and San Sebastian, but singly, as an adjunct to orthodox trains). The MOB Pullmans were patterned as closely as possible on the standard-gauge model, even down to their characteristic leaded oval lavatory windows, but their bay windows were a novelty. Titled the 'Golden Mountain Pullman,' the MOB train was launched for the 1931 summer in conjunction with a connecting standard-gauge Pullman ser-

vice on the Bern–Loetschberg–Simplon branch from Interlaken to Zweisimmen and the insertion of Pullmans in a Paris–Interlaken service. A few American tourists were tempted to fork out the Pullman surcharge, but most visitors were unimpressed and at the end of the 'Golden Mountains's' first summer the MOB demanded that Wagons-Lits take its baubles elsewhere. The Pullmans were subsequently sold off to the Rhaetian, which relegated them to the status of ordinary stock and ran them as such well into the post-World War II era. Some still survive.

Pullmans in Egypt and Rumania

To catalog the numerous fresh standard-gauge Pullman services which were added to the European mainland time-tables before World War II would be tedious, but one or two deserve extended mention. The existence of Pullman services in Egypt has already been noted, *en passant*, in discussion of the 'Simplon-

Orient Express.' The Wagons-Lits company had been operative there since the late 19th century, and given the substantial Anglo-French military and naval presence in the country and the Suez Canal Zone in the 1920s it was natural for Dalziel to add Pullmans to the enterprise. Operation of single cars was crowned in November 1929 by the inception of a three days weekly all-Pullman day train, the 'Sunshine Express,' between Cairo and Luxor during the winter. It complemented the overnight 'Star of Egypt' on the same route, which was another exclusively Wagons-Lits equipage of sleepers and restaurant cars (garbed, incidentally, in a striking all-white livery).

Except that the Pullman staff were preponderantly Maltese or Turco-Greek and the armchair upholstery was leather, the Egyptian Pullmans both inside and out were almost carbon copies of the European standard of the period, though any illusion that you were forging out of

London or Paris rather than Cairo was quickly demolished by the imperfections of Egyptian track and the ham-fisted techniques of Egyptian enginemen. Nevertheless, an excursion up the Nile one way by steamer and the other by the Pullman was an eagerly anticipated fixture in many an Anglo-American tourist's Egyptian itinerary of the 1930s. The 'Sunshine Express' was not resumed after World War II, but some Egyptian Pullman workings were revived for a short time until 1950 and Wagons-Lits still deployed sleeping-cars in the country until the early 1960s.

Another forgotten arena of Pullman operation between the wars was Rumania. The culmination of Pullman activity in that country was the inception in May 1933 of the last of the two dozen all-Pullman trains created before 1939 and one of the most rewarding commercially. Bearing the ponderous title of the 'King Carol the First Pullman Express,' this was in essence a high-grade commuter ex-

press, steaming up from Black Sea resorts to Bucharest in the early morning and back in the evening – and steaming to some purpose, since it was timed from end to end of the main part of its journey, the 146 miles from Bucharest to Constanza, at close on 50mph including two intermediate stops, a very creditable performance for the times. In summer business was so brisk that the usual rake of four Pullmans had to be supplemented by three ordinary Wagons-Lits diners masquerading as Pullmans.

The 'Côte d'Azur Pullman'

Lord Dalziel added two more achievements to a formidable record shortly before his death in 1927. One was the foundation of the International Sleeping Car Share Trust whereby a controlling interest was established in the Wagons-Lits company. The other was the French PLM Railway's acquiescence to one of the most splendid of all Europe's inter-war

trains de luxe, the 'Côte d'Azur Pullman,' which took the tracks in the summer of 1929.

The new cars built for the 'Côte d'Azur' marked the zenith of the European Pullman era. It was not just that first-class seating in a 'couplage' had been trimmed from the customary 56 to 48 in each pair of kitchen and parlor cars to enhance the already spacious Pullman ambience, or that the satin-covered armchairs had adjustable lever-operated backs to mollify some French patrons who shared my disenchantment with Dalziel's cherished Pullman chair design. The cars were things of peculiar beauty thanks to the company's commissioning of Prou and Lalique, two protagonists of the *Art Nouveau* movement, to execute their interior decor. It was the 'Côte d'Azur' cars which sustained the vestigial mainland European Pullman services on French *rapides* like the 'Mistral' and the 'Train Bleu' and on some Italian *rapidi*

after World War II, until the last Pullman facilities were deleted from the Milan–Rome route and France's Paris–Irun 'Sud Express' in the spring of 1971. Some, however, including one converted into a bar car for the post-war 'Train Bleu,' still survive, reverently refurbished and in operation under the management of private entreprenuers on the latter-day land-cruise trains described in detail in Chapter 12.

Even though the Pullman train's load was usually just two couplages flanked at each end by a *fourgon*, totting up to no more than 300 tons (which, neverthe-less, was a generous train-weight for a maximum payload of only 96 passengers), it took over 14 hours from Paris to Nice in those days. That was by no means slug-gish for the period, but in sharp contrast to the 9hours 5minutes booking for the same distance of the Pullman's electri-cally-hauled 1970s successor, the 'Mis-tral.' You pulled sedately out of Paris Gare de Lyon at 8.50 and were not into Nice until 23.00, Monte Carlo just over half-an-hour later and Ventimiglia on the stroke of midnight. The felicities of Pull-man cuisine, of course, could be guaran-teed to engross you for much of the jour-ney – and inflate your substantial bill for the trip: Pullman supplement on top of the ordinary first-class fare was £1.60 from Paris to Monaco, a pretty sizeable impost set against the mere 25p the LNER sur-charged passengers on its handsome high-speed 'Silver Jubilee' across the Channel from 1935, not to mention the 17½p which was the price of *table d'hôte* lunch on the same train!

Should gourmandism pall on the 'Côte d'Azur Pullman,' the Wagons-Lits com-pany at first offered other diversions. One car in each of four 'couplages' was fitted up with a record-player, or electrophone as it was termed then, and loudspeakers, and floor space was cleared for dancing. Bright young things were ecstatic, but older patrons seem to have reacted rather as they might to the intrusion of a whelk-stall on Nice's Promenade des Anglais, and within two months the Wagons-Lits company had deferentially silenced the electrophones. Instead, the more decorous extra of a smoking saloon was added to the train the following year.

The 'Night Ferry'

By the mid-1930s the Pullman concept was in sharpening contention with the de-veloping luxury of front-rank trains in ordinary service, in Britain especially. The return across the Channel to review them is the moment to record that from October 1936 that tiresome stretch of water could at last be crossed without intermediate change of transportation mode. After the Southern Railway had built a train ferry dock at Dover, the Wagons-Lits company built a series of Continental-style sleeping-cars contour-ed to the British loading gauge for through overnight service between London Vic-toria and Paris Gare du Nord via Dover, train ferry across the Channel, and the French ferry dock at Dunkerque. You left Victoria at 22.00, dined in a Southern restaurant car which was attached to the sleepers as far as Dover, retired to your berth, hopefully slept untroubled through

the shunting of the cars on to the ferry, their shackling to the deck, the ill-temper of the Channel, and unshackling and un-loading at Dunkerque, then woke, dress-ed and repaired to a French buffet car for coffee and *croissants* (a 'meat breakfast,' as the Continentals term it, was available if you were incorrigibly British) before arrival in the Gare du Nord at 09.00.

The 'Night Ferry,' as it was eventually titled, deserved to rank with the luxury trains of the inter-war period. It survives today, little altered, but only blunted senses and an access of charity could acknowledge it as a luxury service in the contemporary travel environment. The trouble is basically that the train has changed so little. Partly through optimism of a Channel Tunnel, no one on either side of the Channel has been willing to invest in new equipment. With the addition of six sleepers inexplicably built by Wagons-Lits in 1941 under German domination, the cars are the same as those which launched the service, innocent of up-to-date ventilation and noisy in gait, especi-ally over the multiple-unit train-ham-mered tracks of Britain's Southern Region. Up to the mid-1960s the 'Night Ferry' still commanded very good business, especi-ally after the 1957 addition of a London–Brussels section (though the 1967–8 experiment of a London–Basle through-sleeper was a fiasco), but only a hard core of Europe-trotting railwaymen, bureau-crats and pathological aerophobes sus-tains it nowadays. With the cars coming up to heavy overhaul date the French washed their hands of them in the mid-1970s and British Rail now staffs the train

throughout. To the great inconvenience of travel-weary passengers its restaurant cars have been eliminated on both sides of the Channel and with them the full English breakfast on the run up from Dover, always a model of the meal that is British Rail catering's *tour de force*. At the time of writing the bleak outlook for the 'Night Ferry' is no better than re-equipment with British Rail's post-war, non-air-conditioned Mk I sleepers when the latter are at long last superseded by modern, air-conditioned vehicles using BR's Mk III body-shell, which is due to be introduced in the second half of 1981, although this may well be delayed.

'Scot,' 'Scotsman' and Streamliners

To revert to the evolution of luxurious standards in ordinary British expresses of the inter-war period, the stimulus was the same as that which had sparked off the major advances at the previous turn of the century, the recrudescence of intense rivalry for long-haul Anglo-Scottish traffic. The LMS was first off the mark in 1927, building for its London–Glasgow 'Royal Scot' and other front-rank trains a range of first-class compartment coaches with the opulence of two-a-side seating, plus some part-luggage brake firsts with individual leather armchair or settee seating. Oddly the latter were not too

above, extreme left: The Paris–Menton 'Côte d'Azur Pullman' near Combs-la-Ville in 1934, fronted by a PLM Class 231G Pacific.   (Courtesy G F Fenino)

above, center: Interior of a first-class 'Côte d'Azur Pullman' car.   (Courtesy Author's collection)

above: London–Paris 'Night Ferry' sleepers are propelled on board a train ferry at Dover.   (Courtesy British Rail)

left: An artist's impression of one of the first-class lounges introduced to the LMS 'Royal Scot' in 1927.   (Courtesy Author's collection)

popular, probably because their windows were too shallow and from the depths of his armchair an occupant could see little below the lineside telephone wires.

The following year the LNER thoroughly eclipsed the LMS with two magnificent new trains complete for the world-famous 'Flying Scotsman.' Centerpiece of each set were the restaurant cars. A distinguished contemporary interior designer, Sir Charles Allom, had been deputed by the LNER to create an ambience which would set a new trend in interior rail vehicle design. For the diners he had conceived a perfectly integrated Louis XIV style, with loose individual armchairs, concealed lighting behind elegant translucent pelmets (vestibule wardrobes obviated luggage racks) and hand-painted decor; one car was delicately finished in soft blue and stone, the other of each pair in a pastel red and stone. The following year the 'Scotsman' was further enhanced by the addition of vehicles embodying a unisex hair-dressing saloon and a ladies' retiring room, staffed by a woman attendant throughout the London–Edinburgh run; in 1932 a cocktail bar was also built into these cars. And in 1930 the train's first-class accommodation was re-styled to match the restaurant cars, with deep two-a-side seating. The hair-dressing saloon-ladies' retiring room-cocktail bar vehicles were withdrawn from the 'Scotsman' in 1938, but only because the express was that year equipped with even more splendorous train-sets, pressure-ventilated and double-glazed throughout. These included the most elegant buffet-lounges ever seen in Britain except for Pullman's. The bar area, which occupied the car's entire body except for a ladies' retiring room at one end, was walled off from the side-corridor by a glass-panelled screen and its handsome tables and chairs were as Chippendale to a do-it-

above: Gresley Pacific No 4475 *Flying Fox* steams out of Edinburgh Waverley with the LNER's London-bound 'Flying Scotsman' in July 1936. (Courtesy Author's collection)

above right: The LNER experiments with radio for its passengers' entertainment in the 1930s. (Courtesy Author's collection)

right: A first-class compartment in the 1938 'Flying Scotsman.' (Courtesy Author's collection)

top left and above: The buffet lounge and the Louis XIV-style first-class diner of the 1938 'Flying Scotsman.' (Courtesy Author's collection)

right: The front cover of a brochure advertising the glories of London and North Eastern Railway's luxury service 'The Coronation' which covered the 392 miles between London and Edinburgh in six hours.

left: LMS 'Princess Royal' class Pacific No 6209 *Princess Beatrice* takes water from Bushey troughs as she storms through the northwest London suburbs with the Euston–Glasgow 'Royal Scot' in the late 1930s. (Courtesy Author's collection)

The "CORONATION"
THE FIRST STREAMLINE TRAIN
KING'S CROSS FOR SCOTLAND

DOMINION OF CANADA

LONDON & NORTH EASTERN RAILWAY

yourself home furnishing kit compared with today's execrable plastic-topped buffet fixtures. Little but tradition and the pampering of continuous waiter service at your seat could persuade you that it was worth the extra money to head north by Pullman rather than the 'Scotsman' in the late 1930s.

The LNER was also a pioneer in its efforts to adapt *terra firma* entertainments to British train travel. Between 1930 and 1935 it fitted out a London–Leeds and two London–Edinburgh train-sets with headphone sockets so that passengers could, like today's jet travellers, tune in to radio programs or recorded music dispensed from apparatus in the guard's quarters. And from 1935 to 1939 a Kings Cross–Leeds and a Leeds–Edinburgh service were provided with cinema coaches, converted from full

luggage brakes, which unfolded an hour-long program of newsreels, cartoons and travelogs for an admission charge of five pence.

Before this chapter culminates in the LNER's supreme World War II achievement note must be taken of the Great Western's 1931-built 'Super Saloons.' Those were the days when Plymouth port did a lucrative business with trans-atlantic liners to vie with Southampton. Between Southampton and London the Southern Railway greeted liner passengers with Pullman boat trains. So, across the Channel, did the Etat Railway of France at Le Havre. So, in 1929, the GWR was persuaded to sprinkle a Pullman or two in its Plymouth–London boat trains. At the same time it agreed to try an all-Pullman train between London and what Britons fondly imagine to be their

own Riviera, Torbay on the Devon coast. But, inconveniently timed, the 'Torquay Pullman' was a commercial disaster. It reappeared in the summer of 1930, but palely, linked with ordinary coaches for Kingsbridge, and thereafter was killed off. Though it rid itself of Pullmans proper, however, the GWR accepted that incoming Americans now expected something of the sort on the Plymouth boat trains. It therefore built its own version – some say it had had the Pullmans slyly measured in every parameter while they were on GWR premises – and the outcome was the very Pullman-like 'Super Saloons,' all named after members of the British royal family. They were staple GWR Plymouth boat-train equipment until the Devon port's transatlantic traffic had dwindled to such an extent that, in 1962, it suited British Rail to opt out of railing what was left to London in special trains.

The LNER's final luxury accomplishment, of course, was its high-speed steam streamliners. This is not the place to dwell on the 1935 London–Newcastle 'Silver Jubilee' and its revolutionary pace, for in terms of our subject its interior was basically of the same pattern as the 1938 'Flying Scotsman' equipment. The innovation in internal design came with the two-tone blue train-sets of the 1937 London–Edinburgh 'Coronation' and London–Leeds and Bradford 'West Riding Limited' (in sharp contrast to the stock of the rival LMS 'Coronation Scot' which within was strictly conventional). The LNER train-sets were open throughout, but with each first-class bay and every pair of third-class bays enclosed by partitions to preserve some privacy but still allow meal-service at every seat in the train from a pair of kitchens. Seating at each table in the third-class area was two-and-one, but only one-and-one, in swivelling armchairs, in the first-class cars. The tail of the 'Coronation,' moreover, was brought up in summer by a beaver-tailed observation car with heavy loose armchairs which were available for a charge of 5p an hour.

Sadly these superb trains died with World War II. Some of the vehicles were destroyed by German air action and the residue eked out such post-war life as they were vouchsafed as single units dispersed among run-of-the-mill East Coast Route expresses. At least the two beaver-tail observation cars from the 'Coronation' have been preserved to this day in private ownership.

top left: LNER's gleaming two-tone blue 'Coronation' streamliner prepares for its 16.00 departure from London Kings Cross for Edinburgh in 1937, headed by Gresley class A4 Pacific No 4491 *Commonwealth of Australia*. (Courtesy C C B Herbert)

above: A first-class saloon of the LNER 'Coronation' showing how each four-seater bay with semi-rotating armchairs was partly enclosed. (Courtesy Author's collection)

left: Armchair seating in the beaver-tail observation saloon at the rear of the LNER 'Coronation.' (Courtesy Author's collection)

right and below: Inside and outside *Princess Royal*, one of GWR's Pullman-like saloons built for transatlantic traffic between Plymouth and London. (Courtesy British Rail)

CHAPTER 6
THE DOMELINERS OF NORTH AMERICA

The 'California Zephyr' on the Rio Grande
sector of its run near State Bridge,
Colorado.   (Courtesy Victor Hand)

On 26 May 1934 a sleekly streamlined three-car train winged across the USA from Denver to Chicago non-stop at an average of 77.6mph for the entire 1015.4 miles and changed the face of the American long-haul train. The 'Pioneer Zephyr,' fruit of General Motors Electromotive Division advance in diesel engine design, coachbuilder Budd's expertise in light-weight bodywork technology and the enterprise of the Chicago, Burlington & Quincy Railroad in harnessing both sciences, had dramatically demonstrated the ability of diesel traction to transform express train speed. And to transform it economically: the fuel bill for that whole journey at 1934 prices was $16! A few months later on 22 October 1934 Union Pacific strengthened the evidence by running the second of their early diesel streamliners, the six-car Pullman sleeper-equipped M-10001, the breadth of the country from Los Angeles to New York in five minutes under 57 hours, a shattering $14\frac{1}{2}$ hours faster than the standing coast-to-coast record posted by a steam special run for magnate E H Harriman in 1906.

Those early flyers were self-contained train-sets in which the emphasis, at that stage of the diesel engine design art, was on light train weight. Hence the scope for luxury accommodation was restricted, though the Burlington's twelve-car 'Denver Zephyrs' of 1936 were starting to acquire the expected trappings of a transcontinental, with a cocktail as well as an observation lounge and several sleeping accommodation options. Key to the golden age of the American luxury train, in which a full range of hotel-like amenities internally was combined with world-beating end-to-end speed for most of the 1940s and 1950s, was Electromotive's 1938 perfection of its famous 567 series of diesel engines which spawned the world's first successful mass production diesel locomotives. By the early 1950s these machines had been the prime factor in lifting daily mileage scheduled at 60mph or better to over 150,000, five times the total on the timecards of 1936.

The Burlington was the pace-setter with a concept that added a last new dimension to the US luxury train. The idea itself was unoriginal. If you like, it was traceable to the ingenious and unknown freight train conductor of the 1860s who improvised a skylight in his roof for a better lookout and inspired the standard rooftop cupola of American cabooses. As early as 1890 Canadian Pacific modified some observation cars with a pair of rooftop cupolas for operation through the Rockies, but left the idea dormant when the rebuilt vehicles were withdrawn through age in 1913. It was not resurrected until 1944, when a General Motors executive riding the cab of a freight diesel on the Rio Grande's spectacular

passage of the Rockies was bowled over by what he could see from that privileged vantage point. Some people, he mused, would shell out $500 for his fireman's seat coast-to-coast in preference to the comfortable but limited view within the train. That night in his hotel he sketched out an idea for a glass-roofed coach. His company was impressed, proved it practical and ordered construction of a demonstration dome-car train, the 'Train of Tomorrow,' which was eventually built in partnership with Pullman-Standard, sent on a nationwide exhibition tour of the US from 1947 to 1950, and finished up on Union Pacific's Portland–Seattle service from 1950 to 1958.

But meanwhile Burlington's president had glimpsed GM's first outline drawings, grasped the idea's potential and had his own workshops convert an existing streamliner car into the country's first Vista-Dome, with a raised lounge beneath an elevated glass-covered cowl which gave the occupants uninterrupted all-round and overhead viewing. The prototype car, *Silver Dome*, carried its first paying customers in July 1945 and captivated them immediately. Before the year was out Burlington had ordered from Budd new 'Zephyr' train-sets each incorporating five Vista-Dome cars. That General Motors man who revived the dome concept has not gone unhonored,

incidentally. Near the trackside at Gresley, Colorado, just where the awesome scenery so inspired him, the railroad has set up a stone cairn surmounted by a scale-model Vista-Dome car.

Most celebrated and beloved of the Vista-Dome 'Zephyrs' was the 'California Zephyr.' The Burlington, the Denver & Rio Grande Western and Western Pacific Railroads had added a new transcontinental route to the US network in 1934 following Rio Grande's completion of the Dotsero cut-off. It was longer than the rivals, but its magnificent scenery in the Colorado Rockies and the Feather River Canyon of the Sierra Nevada had attracted very satisfying business to the steam-hauled, largely orthodox-equipped 'Exposition Flyer' which the three railroads had combined to run from Chicago to San Francisco, 2532 miles, since 1939. In 1945 the three companies decided to capitalize on that experience by investing $15 millions in a new transcontinental train concept. With some 300 miles further to run from Chicago to San Francisco than the competition there was no point in going for speed as a prime selling point. Travel amid such scenic splendor would be sold as a pleasurable end in itself. Care would be taken to schedule the new Vista-Dome trains through most picturesque sectors in daylight, never mind what that sacrificed in transit time.

above: A dome car of General Motors 1947 'Train of Tomorrow.' (Courtesy Author's collection)

above right: On the upper floor of a dome car in the GM 'Train of Tomorrow.' (Courtesy Author's collection)

right: Band-leader Phil Harris and his film-star wife Alice Faye lend their services to GM publicity in this view of the 1947 'Train of Tomorrow's' dome restaurant. (Courtesy Author's collection)

The 1947 'Train of Tomorrow' had three dining rooms, one in and one below a dome, and the main space (seen here) at normal floor level. (Courtesy Author's collection)

And the whole exercise would be shaped as a land-cruise rather than focussed on the destination objectives.

That philosophy was patent in the lavish provision of non revenue-earning space in the eleven-car format of the Budd-built 'California Zephyr.' Fare-paying capacity was 245: of these 138 were in the ground floor coach-class areas of the dome cars, which offered very relaxing reclining seats with individual leg-rests; the remainder were in sleeping accommodation that ranged from sections through roomettes and compartments to 7ft-wide double bed-rooms and (in the elegant Vista-Dome buffet-lounge-sleeper-observation car at the tail) a drawing-room suite with private shower. But elsewhere in the train were no fewer than 224 seats for optional use free of charge: 120 in the dome lounges alone, plus those in the diner, in two buffet lounges and in the observation lounge.

In other words, there was room, as near as makes little matter, for everyone on the train to stretch their legs and try another seat for a while whenever they felt like it, maybe in the domes or maybe in one of the buffets for a between-meals coffee and snack. Hostesses, the 'Zepyh-rettes,' were aboard in addition to the usual train staff to cosset passengers, and a public address system throughout the train added a background of soft music to the panorama beyond the windows. There was no need to worry about a place for dinner: you reserved in advance for a choice of three successive sittings, and after a leisurely cocktail in the bar you would take a flower-decked table for the Italian cuisine which was a 'CZ' speciality – antipasto, minestrone, pasta, then maybe a veal *scalloppine à la Parmesan* with salad and toasted garlic rolls, cheese and finally a Marsala-fortified nut sundae, with which came a six-ounce bottle of California wine compliments of the house. The postlude to dinner and relaxing prelude to bed was, for most travellers, a last spell in one of the now-darkened domes. Thank goodness no other rail-road, so far as I know, aped the Baltimore & Ohio's philistine fitting of searchlights to some of its domes in a misguided concern to make the scenery more compelling viewing after dark. (A time to seek out a 'CZ' dome seat for an eerie experience was at Denver or Portola, California where the loaded train was put through

top: A ground-floor lounge of the 'Train of Tomorrow.' (Courtesy Author's collection)

above: Rooms in the 'Train of Tomorrow' were arranged longitudinally in the car body. The foreground room is made up for day use. Through the communicating door, the conductor is making up the lower bed in the adjoining room. (Courtesy Author's collection)

left: 'California Zephyrs' meet on the Denver & Rio Grande Western in Glenwood Canyon, where a GM executive dreamed up the vista-dome concept which the trains now display. (Courtesy Denver & Rio Grande Western Railroad)

above: A dome diner of the Union Pacific. The 85-foot-long, 15-foot-10-inch-high car had an 18-seater restaurant on the ground floor, an 18-seater restaurant in the dome and intimate 10-seater restaurant in the Gold Room under the dome. (Courtesy Union Pacific Railroad)

below: The Baltimore & Ohio ran the only dome cars in the eastern US, where tight clearances otherwise inhibited the use of these oversized vehicles. One was featured in the coach-Slumbercoach 'Columbian' between Washington and Chicago, seen here on Relay Viaduct in 1949. (Courtesy Baltimore & Ohio Railroad)

above: Santa Fe's 'Super Chief' rounds the
last bend of the double horseshoe curve
near Ribera, New Mexico on its daily 39.5-
hour trek between Chicago and Los
Angeles.   (Courtesy Santa Fe Railway)

right and far right: Relaxing in the 'Pleasure
Dome' lounge of the 'Super Chief'
introduced in 1951.   (Courtesy Santa Fe
Railway)

car-washing plants during its journeys.)

Until about the mid-1960s the 'California Zephyr' consistently did capacity business – in fact it was frequently sold out a month or more ahead of each trip. But from then on takings nosedived until in 1969 the operation, which demanded six complete train-sets for daily execution because of the journey's time-span, was losing almost $2 million dollars annually. It was ended as a Chicago–San Francisco service in March 1970, though the impending birth of the Federally-sponsored and subsidised Amtrak organization led to retention of a replica of the original between Chicago and Oakland for a while.

One of the many advanced ideas embodied in General Electric's 1947 'Train of Tomorrow' was the use of a dome for a 'roof garden' restaurant. Arguably the most attractive cars to take up this scheme subsequently were the dome diners built in 1955 for Union Pacific's 'City of Los Angeles' and 'City of Portland' streamliners from Chicago to the West Coast. Each housed three separate dining rooms, an 18-seater on the upper floor under the dome, an intimate 10 seater, the 'Gold Room' at a recessed lower level beneath the dome, and an 18-seater main dining room at normal floor level at the far end of the car to the kitchen. The main restaurant was fetchingly laid out with free-standing circular tables, two-seaters on one side of the center aisle and four-seaters on the other. These cars were not as doted on by their staff as they were by their passengers, however: coping with three separate rooms, even with the aid of a dumb waiter to the 'roof garden,' was much more difficult in a railroad car-body's confines than in a snack bar on the ground.

Domes were an outstanding feature, too, of the train that had only to contend with New York Central's 'Twentieth Century Limited' for the title of America's most prestigious train worldwide, Sante Fe's Chicago–Los Angeles 'Super Chief.' (It also conveyed Los Angeles sleepers from New York off both 'Twentieth Century' and 'Broadway Limiteds,' and from Washington off Baltimore & Ohio's 'Capitol Limited.') Re-launched in 1937 as the USA's first diesel all-Pullman streamliner, the 'Super-Chief' had stunned them with the extravagant finish of its Budd cars, more prodigal in their interior use of tropical woods than any in public operation before or since. After World War II it was again renewed with equally imposing cars but in the idiom of the 1950s. As noted earlier in the book the all-private-room, all-Pullman 'Super Chief' was one of the few US trains to command a supplementary fare in its own right – $15 in the 1950s, not a sum to put down idly in those days, but a worthwhile investment in the 'Super Chief's' special ambience.

For instance, every apartment in the train, from roomettes to the suites into which several neighboring bedrooms could be converted by withdrawing partitions between them, had its own push-button radio and enclosed toilet facilities. Cuisine in the diner was justifiably acclaimed some of the finest on American rails and champagne of the finest quality was included in the $6.50 tab for the train's widely reputed Champagne Dinner. Catering was the responsibility of Harvey House, the company which sprang from the enterprise of a London-born mail clerk, Frederick Henry Harvey – better known as Fred Harvey – who earned an imperishable niche in American railroad history not only by founding a string of eating houses along the Santa Fe line in the latter half of the 19th century, but also by helping a Missouri postmaster to put the latter's idea of a travelling rail postal sorting office to practical proof in 1862. This last was the direct genesis of the American railroads' once highly lucrative Railway Post Office traffic.

Marshalled next to a brand-new diner in the 'Super Chief' of the early 1950s was one of the Rolls-Royces of dome cars. At the end of the vehicle adjoining the diner, at normal floor level, an exquisite private dining room with seating for ten, the Turquoise Room, was offset from the car's side passageway. Turquoise, naturally, was the dominant and rich color scheme, but the room's appellation was justified above all by the wall-mounted silver medallion inlaid with genuine turquoise which Santa Fe had specially made by the Zuni Indians of New Mexico to top off the decor. From the corridor alongside the

Turquoise Room you either stepped up into what Santa Fe dubbed the 'Pleasure Dome,' the upper level observation saloon which was palatially laid out with individual rotating armchairs, or down into a modernistically-styled cocktail lounge below the dome. At the further end of the vehicle, back on normal level, was the main lounge, with a segregated writing desk alcove and a table specifically designed for card-players as well as a generous provision of armchairs and settees. In its 1950s heyday the 'Super-Chief' carried a barber's shop and showerbath facilities, and offered a trainboard valet service. Passengers were kept briefed on the outside world throughout their transcontinental run by news bulletins and stock reports. The train even had its own special headed stationery for passengers' use.

Some of these luxury trappings, sadly, were trimmed in the years of nibbling economy which preceded the American long-haul passenger train's near-extinction and then resurrection, Lazarus-like, in the clothes of Amtrak. So jealous was Santa Fe of the 'Super-Chief's' memory, nevertheless, that in the spring of 1974 it brusquely exercised a right on which it had insisted when it reluctantly agreed to Amtrak's perpetuation of Santa Fe's crack train titles: that permission would be rescinded if it seemed that, under Amtrak, the services concerned had been degraded to the point of tarnishing Santa Fe by association. In the Santa Fe view that was happening: diner and lounge accommodation had been so savagely curtailed that there was chronic overcrowding in just those parts of the train which, asserted Santa Fe's Presi-

above: Dining in the 'Turquoise Room' of the Santa Fe 'Super Chief.' The silver medallion was made by the Navajo Indians. (Courtesy Santa Fe Railway)

far right: The scene in a 1939 'Hiawatha' diner. (Courtesy The Milwaukee Road)

below: The steam-age prime of the Milwaukee 'Hiawathas.' A class F7 4-6-4 gathers speed out of Milwaukee in August 1941. (Courtesy R H Kindig)

dent, 'determine the entire character and comfort of a long-distance train trip.'

The next logical step in dome-car technique was to extend the upper-storey panoramic lounge the full length of the car. By the early 1950s more than one carbuilder was toying with the concept, but the pioneers in actual hardware were Pullman-Standard. In early 1953 the world's first full-length dome cars took up service on the Milwaukee Road's 'Morning Hiawatha' and 'Afternoon Hiawatha' between Chicago and the Twin Cities, St Paul and Minneapolis. The Chicago-Twin Cities route was one of the most sharply-contested of all intercity corridors in the heyday of the US streamliner. On the Milwaukee Road the competition had bred in the later 1930s the apotheosis of the steam streamliner in the 'Hiawathas.' At first they were hauled by high-stepping Atlantics, but as swiftly expanding traffic demanded new, heavier train-sets the Milwaukee in 1938 evolved its superb Class F7 streamlined 4-6-4s for 'Hiawatha' duty. The 'F7s'' feats of speed and load haulage are legendary. So tight were 'Hiawatha' timings that these engines were one of the elite classes in steam history which were forced to run consistently at 100mph or even more daily to keep schedule. But by the 1950s, when the rival Burlington 'Zephyrs' were required to average up to 87.9mph over sections of their Chicago–Twin Cities route, even the Milwaukee 'F7s' had succumbed to the invincible diesels.

There were no less than 625 square feet

of glass in the curved roof of a Milwaukee 'Super Dome.' That predicated air-conditioning plant of decidedly abnormal capacity, controlled by roof-mounted solar-heat-measurement devices. The whole concept, in fact, was an abnormal constructional achievement, given that a car turning the scales at a massive 224,000lb had to be assembled unconventionally, because the extension of a low-level floor the entire body length ruled out orthodox center-sill underframing. Upstairs the dome had standard two-and-one seating for 68. The lower floor was given over to a capacious cafe-lounge.

These first full-length domes were not totally satisfying, however. One complaint was that the dome seats were set too low and the bulkheads at the fore and aft ends of the glass canopy too high for good all-round viewing. Another was that the cars were boisterous riders by recognized 'Hiawatha' standards. When one of the 'Hiawatha' services, the 'Olympian Hiawatha,' was abandoned in 1964 six of these 'Super Domes' were sold to Canadian National.

Most singular of all dome cars, probably, were the so-called 'three-quarter-length domes' which Southern Pacific improvised from existing vehicles for its 'Daylight' streamliners and Overland Route services, the latter operated jointly with Union Pacific. Apart from a small crew dormitory at one end, a split-level bar-lounge took up the whole of the car body: that is to say, there was no two-level

By 1968 Santa Fe's 'Super Chief' and 'El Capitan' were running as one train. A pair of Santa Fe's FP45 diesels leads the train on its climb to Raton Pass, New Mexico. (Courtesy Victor Hand)

above: The Tip-Top-Tap lounge bar of the 1939 'Hiawatha'; passengers would be kept advised of the next stop by illumination of the appropriate name under the clock. (Courtesy The Milwaukee Road)

right: A 'Super-Dome' stands out from the consist of the 'Afternoon Hiawatha,' diesel-hauled in the early 1950s and photographed between Winona, Minnesota and Las Cross, Wisconsin. (Courtesy The Milwaukee Road)

center right: The 'Skytop' observation lounge at the rear of the 'Olympian Hiawatha.' Six of these cars were later bought from the Milwaukee line by Canadian National. (Courtesy The Milwaukee Road)

far right: Nearest the camera, one of Great Northern's full-length 'Great Domes' graces the 'Empire Builder' as it threads the Montana Rockies. (Courtesy Burlington Northern)

passenger space division, but most of the lounge was at a raised floor-level under glass,' which also extended over the saloon area at normal car-floor level to achieve an extraordinary effect of vaulted spaciousness at that end.

Few would dissent from an acclaim of the Great Northern's and Santa Fe's full-length domes, both Budd-built, as the supreme examples of the concept. The Great Northern's 'Great Domes' were acquired in 1955 for its far-famed Chicago–Portland and Seattle transcontinental, the 'Empire Builder,' which had been the first long-haul service in the US to be totally re-equipped after World War II. Those five 1947 train-sets, which set the 'Big G' and Burlington Lines, its junior partner in the enterprise, back a Pullman-Standard bill of some $7 millions, were stunning enough: but four years later the 'Empire Builder' was again re-equipped from end to end, this time for $12 millions. (The 1947 train-sets were then handed down to the railroad's 'Western Star.') The addition of 22 new domes, among them the six 'Great Domes,' in 1955 added another $6 millions to the 'Empire Builder's' post-war capital account.

The record of the post-war 'Empire Builder' is studded with distinctions. It was the first train, for instance, to embody duplex roomette accomodation, the first to offer iced water on tap in its sleepers, the first to equip its bedrooms with wardrobes on the aisle side of the room. If its exterior shading of dark green and brilliant orange set off by yellow and silver edging was pleasing, still more so was the theme of Northwest Indian culture carried through the stylish interior and supported by Winold Reiss murals and reproductions of paintings by the

Western artist Charlie Russell. A star vehicle of each 1951 train-set was the Ranch Car, a coffee shop which was distinctive in service as well as decor. Open throughout the daylight hours of the journey, it offered the traveller on a budget continuous over-the-counter service of excellent and adequate meals – soup, pork chop and vegetables, dessert and coffee, maybe – as an alternative to the formal dining car, with its specially commissioned and executed silverware, napery, glassware and chinaware, the last a particular delight with its embellishment of Glacier Park scenes and flora in natural color. One should add the catering was always one of the 'Empire Builder's' many brilliant facets: between the wars, for instance, this was one of the trains in which a delicate service of English-style afternoon tea and cakes in the lounge was a treasured ritual. The setting for that 1920s and 1930s tea service, though, was very different from the ambience of a 'Ranch Car,' which was laid out as a Western log cabin, with oak-faced walls, pseudo-cedar-log pillars, leather chairs dressed to look as though they were partly cattlehide-covered and dominated by a 'G Bar N' device which the railroad had actually registered with the Montana Livestock Association.

In pre-Amtrak days the 'Empire Builder' was also unique in its inclusion of two types of dome car, orthodox short center-dome cars for coach-class passengers and a 'Great Dome' adjoining the diner for the exclusive use of Pullman clients (until the later 1960s, that is, when dwindling business drove the 'Big G' to curtail the train's amenities and the lower-floor lounge of the 'Great Dome' was opened up to coach passengers). The

dome-floor sofas, considerably angled a little towards the windows for comfortable viewing, had room for 74. Below was an enticing 35-seater lounge bar, with magazines on display and writing tables laid with 'Empire Builder'-headed stationery; an electrically-powered dumb waiter made it simple to hoist drinks and snacks from the bar to passengers relaxing in the air-conditioned solarium above.

In its mid-1950s prime the 'Empire Builder' ran to 15 cars grossing over 1100 long tons to convey only 323 passengers, assuming an absolutely full payload. And to look after them the 'Empire Builder' deployed on each trip a conductor, two coach porters, two stewards, five chefs, six waiters, a lounge car attendant, a Pullman conductor, six sleeping car porters, a uniformed railroad passenger department representative (whose role was broadly that of courier: his voice would be one of the most frequently heard on the train's public address, drawing attention to points of interest en route as well as disseminating operational information) and a brakesman, plus locomotive crews. Such prodigality on top of the enormous capital cost of a streamliner like the 'Empire Builder,' of course, was a millstone about the neck of every great American luxury train as soon as air and land competition dimmed the early post-World War II false dawn of improved business and load factors began their remorseless slump to catastrophe levels.

The 'Chair-Lounge-Dome' cars, as they were officially termed, of the Santa Fe were structurally similar to Great Northern's 'Great Domes,' but differed in internal arrangement. All had a similar

Union Pacific's 'City of Portland' eastbound in the Columbia River Gorge near Wyeth, Oregon. (Courtesy Union Pacific Railroad Colorphoto)

layout under the dome, where most of the space was given over to angled two-seater sofas, but one end was occupied by a refreshment lounge with most of its seating at inward-facing bench settees fronted by small tables. On the lower floor one batch of cars had a lounge bar, a compact writing room and train nurse's quarters, the remainder, a small cocktail lounge and a crew dormitory.

One cannot talk of Santa Fe and two-storey cars without a mention of the complete train-sets of this type of equipment which Budd built for the railroad's 'El Capitan' in 1956 and in the mid-1960s for the 'San Francisco Chief,' though some

might quibble that as an all-coach Chicago –Los Angeles service, even though tagged with a supplementary fare, 'El Capitan' does not strictly make the grade as a luxury train. The design objective of these Santa Fe 'Hi-Level' cars, in face of already palpable economic pressures on the traditional American rail trans-continental, was to increase payload/ tare train weight ratio without sacrifice of comfort and amenities. The solution was to build every vehicle with two storeys from end to end to a ceiling height 15½ft above rail, concentrate all the principal passenger accommodation upstairs and use the ground floor for all the functional

top: The domes of the 'City of Portland' in another Columbia River Gorge scene near the Hood River. (Courtesy Union Pacific Railroad Colorphoto)

above: The main lower-floor restaurant of a Union Pacific dome diner. (Courtesy Union Pacific Railroad Colorphoto)

right: The upper deck of a 'Great Dome' in Great Northern's transcontinental 'Empire Builder.' (Courtesy Burlington Northern)

center right: The remarkable 'Ranch Car' coffee-shop lounge of the 'Empire Builder' was decked out in the style of a Western log cabin. The 'G bar N' brand above the bar was registered with the Montana Livestock Association. (Courtesy Burlington Northern)

far right: This was the buffet-lounge on the lower floor of the 'Empire Builder's' 'Great Dome.' (Courtesy Burlington Northern)

bottom right: The diner of Great Northern's 'Empire Builder.' (Courtesy Burlington Northern)

necessities – baggage space, crew quarters, restrooms, lavatories, kitchens and auxiliary electrical plant. The result was a train-set able to accommodate over 40% more passengers than a 'Super Chief' consisting of near-identical unladen weight.

The 'Hi-Level' configuration has been taken a stage further by Amtrak. One of the many crosses this body has had to shoulder (as Amtrak sees it, naturally) since the Nixon administration gave it reluctant midwifery in 1971 has been lack of funds to renew its long-haul equipment. The long-distance services which it was handed in its Federally-determined route structure are still protected almost entirely by the domes, diners, lounges and sleepers of the pre-Amtrak streamliners, jewels of the coachbuilder's craft in their day, but two decades or even more later not only dated stylistically but often down-at-heel, not least in mechanical and electrical condition. At last, in the mid-1970s, Amtrak was granted the cash to work out a replacement design for its Chicago–West Coast services with the builders, Pullman-Standard.

The outcome was clearly derived from the 'Hi-Level' idea, but took advantage of subsequent technological development. Higher above rail by $7\frac{1}{2}$ in than the Santa Fe cars, the 'Superliners,' as Amtrak has dubbed them, exploit the maximum floor space on both levels for passenger accommodation. Whereas previous cars carried their own auxiliary plant, the modern vehicles take supply for their electrical equipment from generators in the locomotive, saving weight and making more room for payload. The 'Superliners' are built for 120mph maximum speed and mounted on air-cushion suspension bogies of German design. They are being produced in several versions: mixed class sleepers, with bedrooms on the upper floor and economy berths below (recalling that in 1957 Budd abortively sketched for the 'Super Chief' a 'Hi-Level' sleeper, which would have had highly desirable full car-width bedrooms upstairs); all-economy cars; standard day cars; and 'Sightseer' lounges with a bar-lounge on the ground floor and a partly glass-roofed saloon with individual armchairs above. Sadly the 'Superliners' have been dogged first by protracted labor disputes at their manufacturing plant, then by technical snags of the sort designers half-expect from a vehicle packing a great deal of innovation as yet unproven in a combined structure. At the time of writing the first has yet to be seen on the road.

Some of Santa Fe's full-length domes have been finishing their career in the world's most colorful automobile-and-passenger package services, those which the private Auto-Train Corporation was at last authorized to run from Lorton, near Washington DC, to Sanford, Florida, in December 1971 after six years of patiently lobbying Federal agencies for permission. It was the then passenger manager of British Rail's Eastern Region who, in the mid-1950s, grasped that there was rail revenue to be extracted from the upsurge of private motoring, given the road congestion it was aggravating. What better than to get to your destination area with your feet up, well fed and slept, and with your automobile cool and fresh, having done the long haul on rail wheels, loaded in a rail vehicle at the back of the train, not on its own? With automobile-carrying vehicles improvised out of parcels vans and attached to sleepers and a diner, British Rail put the idea to the proof between London and Perth. It was an immediate success. Since then British Rail has evolved a network of what it calls Motorail services between several of the country's conurbations and its tourist areas or the car-ferry ports for mainland Europe, and the idea has been copied throughout Continental Europe. None of the European trains, though, offer the diversions of the American Auto-Train, with its TV-fitted double bedrooms (plus room service), its trainboard movie shows, the 'Night Club under the Stars' in the full-length dome where professional entertainers have the backing of an electronic organ and the bar is in business until the small hours, the all-night snack service in other lounges, the free self-service coffee bars throughout the train, the help-yourself-as-much-as-you-want buffet meal service (pre-cooked on the ground and put aboard in plug-in hot cabinets or refrigerated containers, but no way impaired by that), the hostesses, and reclining leg-rest armchairs with which the domes have been re-equipped.

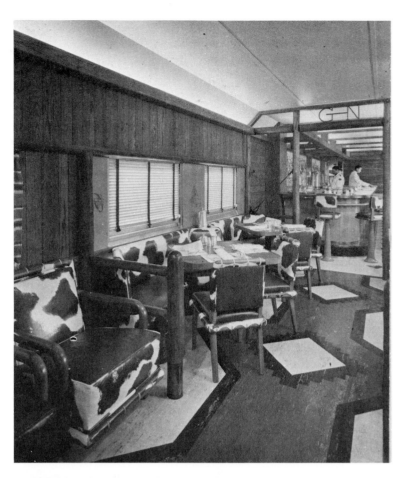

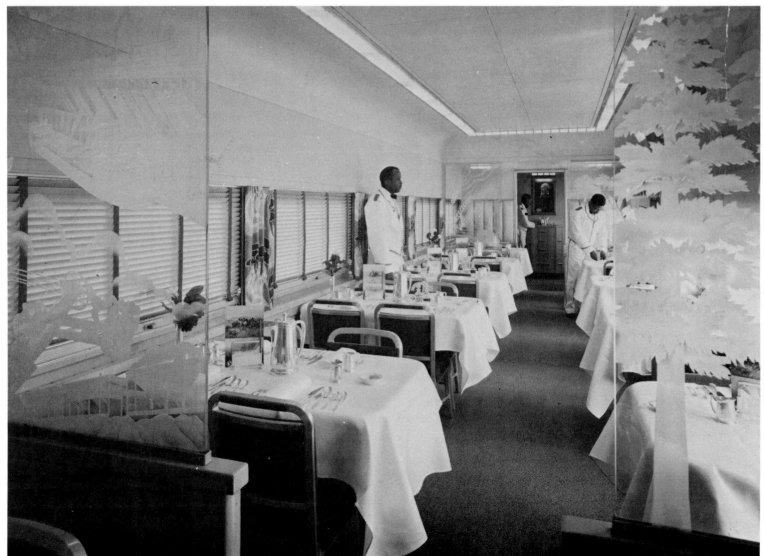

Auto-Train has commanded a satisfying demand on its original Lorton-Sanford route, but a 1974 attempt to launch a similar operation from Louisville, Kentucky to Florida was a commercial catastrophe; the railhead was too far from the Mid-Western cities of Ohio, Michigan and Illinois which were the prime marketing target, but the state of tracks further north debarred Auto-Train from setting up base any closer to them. The financial effect of that fiasco was compounded in 1976 by two very costly derailments of the Lorton-Sanford train. As a result of this and other harassments, especially a rise in railroad material costs outpacing the national inflation rate (which has, for example, swollen the cost of each new Amtrak 'Superliner' coach to around £500,000), Auto-Train confronts a worrying re-equipment problem. Sooner or later renewal of the second-hand passenger cars on its existing service will be unavoidable, never mind what would be needed for the start of others. There has been talk of a joint operation with Amtrak, but in the late 1970s that looked remote in view of the moves in Washington to curtail Amtrak's operation so as to contain its losses. A more likely prospect is operation from the US-Mexican border at Nuevo Laredo to the outskirts of Mexico City, for which outline agreement was reached between Auto-Train and a group of Mexican investors in 1974. Mexican National Railways gave the concept its formal blessing in August 1978.

If ever rail routes cried out for domes they were, of course, the transcontinental lines of the Canadians – especially perhaps Canadian Pacific, with its climb to the 5339ft-high Continental Divide amid the 11,000ft peaks of the Rockies and then, after negotiation of the spectacular Kicking Horse Pass and the boiling gorge of Kicking Horse Canyon, the ascent into the Selkirk Mountains. In the prime of CP's transcontinental train service in 1929, on the eve of the Great Depression, the railroad sent no fewer than five crack trains daily each across the country via this route: the all-sleeper Montreal and Toronto–Vancouver 'Trans-Canada'; the 'Toronto–Vancouver 'Dominion'; the Montreal–Vancouver 'Imperial'; and from Chicago to Vancouver the 'Soo-Pacific' and the all-sleeper 'Mountaineer.'

As already remarked, CP pioneered the first primitive dome cars in North America for fuller enjoyment of its mountain grandeur as early as the 1890s. Before it took up the conventional North American observation-lounge car concept with railed and gated verandah in 1909 it also deployed a unique fully open car, quite uncovered above the waistline, in the mountain territory. The view from its slatted wooden seats was superb, but even so it must have taken a little stoicism to put up with their discomfort and a chill

mountain breeze for any length of time. Small wonder, perhaps, that steaming hot 'English Plum Pudding and Brandy Sauce' figured on the CP diner menus of the period as a follow-up to the sirloin steak.

Immediately after World War II it was CP of the two Canadian systems which was optimistic of the rail passenger business, CN which was at best lukewarm. By the early 1960s that balance was to be completely reversed. It was CP, however, which in 1953 laid down a huge sum with Budd for 173 new stainless steel cars, including domes, to refurbish the 'Dominion' and establish an entirely new train, the 'Canadian,' these two to provide a paired transcontinental service each way daily between Montreal and Toronto in the east, and Vancouver in the west. The 'Canadian' was the faster train, taking about half a day less than the 'Dominion,' which was assigned a considerable amount of secondary mail and passenger business on the way. At first both trains carried the same range of modern equipment all year round, but as business fell away in the 1960s the 'Dominion' was reduced in format outside the main vacation seasons and eventually excised from the timetables in 1965.

The new equipment excited more interest than anything railborne in Canada for years. In part this was generated by the promise of a 16-hour cut in the previous best Montreal–Vancouver time westbound, though eastbound the new 'Canadian' managed an acceleration of only $10\frac{1}{2}$ hours. But the new vehicles were also sent on barnstorming coast-to-coast tours of Canada and of parts of the northern US before they were put into service, backed by an intensive media campaign. One fruit of the latter was dedication of the whole April 1955 issue of *Vogue* to an account of the 'Canadian,' its attractions as the mode for a vacation trip across Canada and what the *Vogue* reader should wear, day and night, on the trip. Much was made of the fact that CP would be offering the longest dome journeys in the world.

The trains certainly justified the attention. They featured two types of dome car. Marshalled near the front of the consist was a dome-buffet-lounge, similar in layout to the design applied to Burlington's 'American Royal Zephyr,' with normal floor-level cafe for the service of economy meals at one end, a bar-lounge and kitchen beneath the 24-seater dome, and then a a coach-class section accommodating 26 at the further end of the vehicle. At the rear of the train was the second dome, an observation-lounge-sleeper, embodying three double bedrooms, a drawing room, then the two-level section with the dome above and a bar-lounge below, and a relaxing observation lounge at the tail end. Every bedroom in the 'Canadian' was wired for

above: The two-storey 'Hi-Level' train-set of Santa Fe's Los Angeles–Chicago 'El Capitan' gets a mechanical wash-and-brush-up at an intermediate stop. (Courtesy Author's collection)

below and bottom: In 1956 the Seaboard Coast Line created for its 'Silver Meteor' three 'Sun Lounge' cars, with five double bedrooms at one end of the vehicle and at the other, an elegant lounge with a partly glazed roof. (Courtesy Seaboard Air Line Railroad Company)

above right: The full-length upper floor dining room of Santa Fe's 'El Capitan'; electric lifts communicated with the kitchen below. (Courtesy Santa Fe Railway)

right and bottom right: Upper and lower floors of the 'Skytop Lounge' in Santa Fe's 'El Capitan' train, formed entirely of 'Hi-Level' equipment; the lower lounge has the main cocktail bar. (Courtesy Santa Fe Railway)

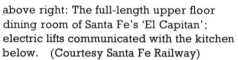

left: The fully open observation car which Canadian Pacific deployed in its mountain territory early this century in Alberta. (Courtesy Author's collection)

right: Dome cars in Canadian Pacific's 'Canadian' near Lake Louise, Alberta. (Courtesy Canadian Pacific)

below: Amtrak takes over the domes: this is the latter-day 'North Coast Hiawatha' climbing the Gallatin range of the Rockies from Livingston, Montana. (Courtesy Amtrak)

center left: The lower-level lounge of one of Southern Pacific's unique dome cars which carried the raised glass roof over an area at normal floor level (as seen in this Amtrak-age photograph). (Courtesy Amtrak)

left: An artist's impression of how Amtrak plans to lay out the upper-level lounge in one of its new Superliner cars. (Courtesy Amtrak)

three-channel sound, with an option of two taped music programs and the third band forming the train's public address system.

For nearly a decade after World War II the Federally-owned Canadian National was not in the market for new passenger equipment. For one thing its resources were under too much pressure to cope with the freight demands of booming industry, for another it was denied the pricing latitude to keep pace with general inflation. Thus when it was finally in a position to re-order in 1953 CN filed the biggest requisition ever assembled by a North American railroad within one year – in all 389 cars valued at over $60 millions. They were high-quality but not fancy. They did not check the recession which eroded CN passenger business in the later 1950s in common with that of every other North American railroad.

Uncommonly – uniquely, in fact – CN vigorously counterattacked. The traffic was there for the taking, CN management concluded. What was lacking was marketing acumen, customer relations and

effective packaging on the railroad side. Timetables were restructured, staff retrained, a new tri-seasonal fare scheme – the celebrated Red, White and Blue – was devised, trainboard amenities and entertainments were diversified, and a great deal of passenger equipment was refurbished. In addition CN went shopping south of the 49th Parallel for any luxury streamliner cars that passenger service-weary US railroads might be happy to clear from their property. Top of the shopping basket pile on the buying party's return was a complete streamliner train-set, the Reading Railroad's 'Crusader' (which served as the Montreal–Quebec 'Champlain' from 1964 to 1967), and six ex-Hiawatha 'Super Domes' and 'Skytop Lounge' observation cars from the Milwaukee. CN renamed the 'Super Domes' its 'Sceneramic Cars,' refashioned their upper decks as very appealing club lounges with a mix of easy chairs, settees and tables as well as conventional coach seating, and applied them to principal services over the Rockies sector of CN's transcontinental route between Winni-

peg and Vancouver, such as the 'Super Continental' and the 'Panorama.'

A decade later CN was glumly conceding defeat. Its bold enterprise had boosted passenger journeys, certainly, but nowhere near enough to overtake the rapidly escalating costs of maintaining the reinvigorated service. As in the US, the Federal Government had ultimately to take over the country's intercity rail passenger services and vest the administration and marketing of a rationalized route system in a new Government-financed agency, VIA Rail. Under VIA Rail there would still be a transcontinental rail service – but over the central sector of the cross-country route one only. Separate trains would originate from Montreal and Toronto, but from the autumn of 1978 they would merge at Sudbury and operate as a combined train over the CP route thence to Winnipeg, there dividing to follow the CN and CP tracks to Vancouver as separate trains once more. It was a miserable castration of two of the world's most scenically-rich luxury train services.

CHAPTER 7
THE BIRTH OF TRANS–EUROP EXPRESS

Trans-Europ Express, or TEE. was the brainchild of the Netherlands Railways' able President in the early 1950s. F Q den Hollander. Long before the 1958 creation of the European Economic Community (EEC) or the European Common Market, developments such as the 1952 formation of the European Coal and Steel Community were plainly signposting rapid growth of commercial links between the mainland European countries. That would generate an equivalent growth of international business travel. And the greater part if not all of it would be snapped up by the reawakening airlines unless the continent's railways collaborated to establish a new concept of international service which dismissed frontiers almost as contemptuously as an airplane.

The urgent need, den Hollander foresaw, was for a network of de luxe trains between Western Europe's main commercial centers that brought a large number of them within the compass of a day's out-and-home journey of each other, yet allowed sufficient time at destination in the middle of the day for transaction of business. The traditional international expresses did not meet the need. Heavy with second-class cars and baggage or mail as well as quality accommodation, they were too slow. Many of them made intermediate calls that were irrele-

vant to business market demand, and some of those calls were horribly protracted by the transfer of through coaches between trains. And then, of course, there were the dreary waits at frontier stations while the border authorities conducted their rituals and the crews and locomotives of one system gave leisurely place to those of another.

I have always imagined that den Hollander drew his inspiration from the prewar German Reichsbahn, which from 1933 onwards developed nationally what was essentially a luxury business executives' service with high-speed two- and three-car diesel multiple-units. These were Europe's first regular 100mph trains, first-class only and with a high standard of interior appointments for the times. Right from the start the service's pioneer, the 'Fliegende Hamburger,' was timed from Berlin to Hamburg at a start-to-stop average of 77.5mph. The operation was steadily expanded and by 1939 when war brought down the curtain on the enterprise a tracery of these trains interwove almost all the Reich's chief centers of commerce and industry with each other and with the focal point of the scheme, Berlin. By then the fastest, the 'Fliegende Kölner,' was daily covering the 158 miles from Berlin to Hannover at an average of 83mph and the 109¾

A Swiss four-voltage electric TEE train-set on the Gotthard main line and an interior

view of its diner. (Courtesy Swiss Federal Railways)

right: One of the German Reichsbahn's pre-1939 first-class only, high-speed diesel train-sets leaves Berlin. These trains may well have been the inspiration for the first post-war 'Trans-Europ Express.' (Courtesy Deutsche Bundesbahn)

far right top: French Railways' first contribution to the TEE pool was a two-car diesel train-set, classified RGP; this unit has just arrived in Paris Gare du Nord on the 'Parsifal' service from Dortmund, West Germany in 1958. (Courtesy Yves Broncard)

below right: Breakfast is served in one of the early French TEE diesel train-sets. (Courtesy Author's collection)

miles thence to Hamm at 82mph in the course of a 719-mile round trip between Cologne and Berlin. These trains brought major cities like Munich, Nuremburg, Stuttgart, Frankfurt, Cologne and Bremen within a comfortable day's business journey of the German capital.

Den Hollander wanted a supra-national approach to his concept. He envisaged a standard European luxury train-set of superlative comfort to be run as far as operationally practicable to a standard level of speed on each itinerary and he urged that the whole scheme be managed by an independent international body which was associated with, but administratively and financially divorced from, the participating railways. But like their political masters railroad managements were very reluctant to yield sovereignty and the eventual TEE scheme was a decidedly imperfect realization of den Hollander's vision.

The seven national railway systems which embraced the TEE idea in principle –France, Western Germany, Luxemburg, the Netherlands, Switzerland and Italy – were agreed on some fundamentals. They acknowledged that the TEEs would command a supplementary fare, exclusively first-class market which would not prejudice the loadings of the orthodox international services, and quite quickly they settled on an initial ten international routes which would link as many as 73 important centers of commerce and industry. They agreed on broad design and operating characteristics: the trains must be capable of at least 140kph maximum speed (87mph), seat no more than three-a-side, have restaurants and be equipped for execution of Customs and immigration formalities on the move, to

eliminate those tedious frontier stops. Standards of passenger seating, lighting, heating and air-conditioning were meticulously specified – even a common TEE red-and-cream livery, to the finicky extent that every builder eventually involved in constructing TEE train-sets was bidden to employ a precise shade of cream paint of which samples were supplied from a Swiss manufacturer.

A standard train-set to wear the livery, however, was not agreed. It had begun to look chimerical when the seven participating countries' transport ministers turned down one of den Hollander's key propositions, that the project be handed over to a separate management body which would be financially autonomous, once it had been appropriately capitalized by the various railways involved. That, wrote den Hollander sadly in 1960, 'was a draconian blow to the idea, above all from the viewpoint of technical standardization, and a unified commercial and operating approach.' No less disappointed was the then President of the German Federal Railway (DB), who had wistful hopes that the seven governments would confer some sort of extra-territorial status on the TEEs, so that they would get concessionary treatment at frontier posts. (In much later Common Market years, before the worrying upsurge of European terrorism in the later 1970s, it did become progressively more perfunctory on some services in my experience.)

In the event TEE management was left to a loose grouping of the seven railways devoid of statutory power. Each one in turn would act as manager for a four-year term and a small TEE Commission would look after administrative detail. But each system would pocket all the TEE revenue

it originated and, within the broad specifications previously agreed, design and be responsible for its own contribution to the TEE train fleet. In no way was it obliged to take account of other railways' opinion.

No one, therefore, could block the immediate French decision to adapt as their first TEE equipment contribution the RGP diesel multiple-unit they had applied to their domestic inter-city services in 1954, which straightaway torpedoed any lingering hope of progress to standardization; besides which, it blurred the distinction between TEEs and standard inter-city services. After that each railway naturally went its own way. There was not even a consensus on open-saloon or compartment format, or whether meals should be served at seats or in separate restaurant cars.

Several other sensible proposals that would have usefully distinguished TEE service were discarded for reasons that would have been superable by more imaginative collaboration. One railway, for instance, wanted to cocoon the passenger from bother with incidentals as soon as he had booked his ticket (at least, in a trailer for today's computer seat reservation systems which neighboring railways in mainland Europe are progressively integrating with each other, the participants agreed to establish an international TEE teleprinter organization that would enable a passenger easily to pre-book a seat anywhere in the TEE network). It was suggested that the TEE ticket be priced to include main meals. That was negated because the various train catering organizations – Wagons-Lits over most of the network, the DSG in West Germany and the Swiss company –

since compact multi-voltage traction equipment capable of working with Western Europe's four different current supply systems – 1500V dc in the Netherlands and parts of France, 3000V dc in Belgium and Italy, 15,000V ac in Germany, Austria and Switzerland and 25,000V ac in most of France's post-war electrification – had yet to be perfected. So for the slender benefits of easier turnrounds, the TEE operators at first paid a substantial bill for extra traction costs through use of diesel power over electrified routes: for inflexibility because of the snags of breaking up a fixed-formation train-set to maintain or replace individual vehicles (besides which, the traction was unusable for any other assignment); and for markedly inferior comfort since at that time no one had mastered the technique of designing a multiple-unit to ride as sweetly as the best of locomotive-hauled vehicles.

It has always been believed that a good deal of the considerable pre-1939 image of the German diesel flyers as the ultimate in European rail travel survived the war to color early TEE thought. Ironically the fallacy that a flashily streamlined multiple-unit had special sex appeal in the travel market even though the top speeds in mind would not be high enough to give it significant aerodynamic point (which is, of course, a critical reason for the streamlining of train-sets like British Rail's 'Inter-City 125' units) gripped British Rail just as it was being discarded in post-war Germany. On these illusory commercial grounds the then British Transport Commission unwisely built Britain's first fully air-conditioned train-sets, the 'Blue Pullmans,' as diesel multiple-units which blunted the impact of their undoubted interior luxury by deplorable riding.

The German Federal's first TEE train-sets were, in fact, the last diesel multiple-units the system built for long-distance operation. They were unquestionably the cream of the early TEE equipment. They offered a choice of compartment or open saloon seating and found room for an attractive bar as well as a separate restaurant. Among the first rail vehicles in Europe to be disk-braked, these were easily the smoothest-riding of the first TEE trains, helped by the Germans' dedication to rapid installation of continuously welded rail from the mid-1950s onwards. I remember riding in the cab of the German equipped 'Helvetia' soon after the TEE scheme's inception in 1957. We were on the then single-track stretch between Hannover and Celle – single-track because the pre-war Reichsbahn had never conceived this line as the key north-south trunk route it had become in the post-war partition of Germany – and rolling happily at near the permitted maximum of 87.5mph. The turnout for resumption of double track loomed up and I tensed

protested that it would be administratively too much of a chore to harmonize their prices. Also rejected was a scheme to man each station in the network with special TEE staff who would relieve passengers of their luggage as soon as they entered the station and usher them to their booked seat. On the trains a corps of TEE conductors, like the Wagons-Lits and DSG men on international sleeping-car trains, would take over passengers' tickets and passports and relieve them of the nuisance of frequent checks by ticket inspectors and frontier staff; but that too was ruled out of court.

More excusable, though not totally uncontroversial, was general acceptance that the initial TEE train-sets should be diesel multiple-units. The double-ended train format was deemed essential because several of the TEE routes involved reversal at terminal stations, such as Frankfurt, Munich and Stuttgart in West Germany, but in later years, when the TEE fleet became predominantly locomotive-hauled, the operators were nowhere taxed to re-engine TEEs smartly during terminal turnrounds. Once the multiple-unit choice had been made, there was no alternative to diesel traction,

A unique TEE – Spain's 'Catalan-Talgo' from Barcelona to Geneva employs the patent Talgo steered single-axle suspension and embodies devices that enable the wheel-gauge to be changed at the Franco–Spanish border. The views show the train's exterior, its diner and a typical first-class saloon.   (Courtesy RENFE)

more than a little as the driver made no move to slow for it. The lurch as we took the points, however, was trifling and probably almost imperceptible in the train. There was nothing remarkable in the comfort of the other first-generation TEEs to linger over, least of all in the Italians' ungainly two-car sets of extreme vehicle length, which were not even fully air-conditioned.

The shorter-distance TEEs, like the 'Paris–Ruhr,' were naturally pathed for round-trip-in-a-day business with very

early – almost indecently so – morning departures and late night returns. But some TEEs were on lengthy itineraries that added up to useful service to different markets over successive sectors of their route. No businessmen, for example, would have given a second thought to use of the 'Helvetia' throughout its day-long run from Zurich to Hamburg, but it afforded a viable out-and-home day service between Zurich and Frankfurt, and useful afternoon luxury travel each way between Frankfurt and Hamburg.

Outstanding omissions from the first batch of TEE services were any direct links between industrial northern Italy and Paris or Zurich. A cogent reason was the hard grind of the steeply graded, sinuous Gotthard and Simplon routes through the Alps, which would have exacted diesel power plant of extravagantly high output to attain even the fairly modest TEE speed standards of the scheme's early years. But by 1958 the Swiss were convinced that multi-voltage traction technology had progressed suf-ficiently for a confident order of new TEE train-sets able to operate with equal facility on Western Europe's four main electric traction current supply systems. So, in the summer of 1961, the first straight electric TEEs took up 'Gottardo' and 'Ticino' service between Milan, Zurich and Basle, and – more interestingly – one of the fastest TEE workings up to that date as the 'Cisalpin' between Milan and Paris.

The new Swiss multi-voltage TEE train-sets were still double-ended multiple-units, though that format was justified only by the obligation to reverse at Zurich on the Milan–Basle run.

These Swiss units lifted the TEE concept into a more distinctive grade of speed and comfort. Each set's twelve-wheeled power car was practically a full-blown 3400hp locomotive, although the compactness of the electrical gear left room within the bodywork for a kitchen and pantry, train staff quarters, customs staff compartment and baggage room. Such power was essential to satisfy a commercial specification seeking unprecedentedly high sustained speed over the transalpine Gotthard route. The power plant was required to keep the six-car, 257-ton train-set moving at a steady 55mph – the limit enforced by incessant sharp curvature – up the long 1 in 40 grind to the 3786ft summit at the Gotthard Tunnel in order to lop as much as 23 minutes southbound and 37 minutes northbound off the previous fastest schedule between Zurich and Milan.

The Swiss train-set's speed potential on easier track profiles was demonstrated on the Paris–Milan 'Cisalpin' service. Agreement by the three railways involved – French, Swiss and Italian – to early afternoon departure each way enabled the French to route the new TEE between Paris and Dijon at 4–5 minutes' headway from their crack Paris–Riviera 'Mistral' (of which more in Chapter 8), a grouping which minimized disruption of the existing, heavily-loaded Paris–Dijon–Lyons main-line timetable by the insertion of the new train. As a result – and to the chagrin of some French railway aficionados – the Swiss interloper was allowed to share the contemporary glory of the 'Mistral's' European pace-setting timetable average speed of 81.9mph going south and of 79.2mph coming north over the 195.2 miles between Dijon and Paris. This sprinting at the northern end of its

route boosted the 'Cisalpin's' overall average speed on the 511-mile Milan–Paris course to a very creditable level for those days of 63.7mph, despite five intermediate stops and necessarily restrained running over the Simplon route through Switzerland and even more so over the winding, largely single-track stretch threading the Jura mountains between Vallorbe and Dole.

One is tempted to dredge the travel-writer's thesaurus of easy superlatives every time a transalpine journey comes up for discussion. On the 'Cisalpin's' route it starts with the rich blue beauty of Lake Maggiore, then the steady advance of the mountain backcloth to crowd the railway into its 12¼-mile Simplon Tunnel; on the Swiss side of the tunnel the train emerges into the beetling-browed Rhône Valley, with its castle-crowned centerpiece of Sion and glimpses of higher peaks up the steep valleys cascading water into the Rhône; then comes the broadening into Lake Geneva, past the turreted castle of Chillon nestling in the lakeside trees near Montreux, with the ice-and-rock layer cake of the gaunt Dents du Midi dominating the panorama across the water.

On a cloudless summer's day every rail ride through the Alps is a little less awesome and exhilarating than one's

first, but it was a blissfully new experience altogether to absorb the color and the grandeur from a semi-reclining armchair in the fully and very effectively air-conditioned 'Cisalpin.' Both sound and climatic insulation had been substantially improved throughout the train-set compared with previous air-conditioning applications by a new style of totally-enclosed inter-car vestibule connection which the Swiss vehicle manufacturers, SIG, had evolved. Also seen for the first time in these Swiss TEE train-sets was the comfort of electrically-powered venetian blinds enclosed within the panes of the double-glazed windows, individually and effortlessly adjustable by push-buttons at the side of each passenger seat. Seating was entirely in open saloons, maybe not specially remarkable by 1970s standards, but significantly more relaxing and attractive than the premium-fare norm of the late 1950s. Another refinement was separate lavatories for each sex, with the bonus of an outer powder room in the ladies' accommodation.

Most striking internally of the set's cars was the restaurant car, finished in brilliantly contrasted red and yellow. The designers had given it an airier ambience by use of rather light-weight, freely movable chairs, which was misguided given the train operators' determination

left: A Swiss four-voltage electric TEE train-set skirts Lake Geneva and passes the Château de Chillon near Montreux. (Courtesy Swiss Federal Railway)

bottom left: The Italians' first contribution to the TEE network was also a two-car diesel train-set; here a pair forming the Milan–Marseilles 'Ligure' passes Menton on the French Riviera in 1965. (Courtesy Yves Broncard)

below: At the start of the TEE scheme the Swiss Federal and Netherlands Railways jointly provided these diesel train-sets, Dutch-built, of which the six-axle power car was virtually a locomotive. One is leaving Paris on the 'Arbalète' service to Zurich, which these units covered until 1969. (Courtesy Yves Broncard)

bottom: One of the first German TEE diesel train-sets, here seen after supersession by new locomotive-hauled equipment and covering one of the German Federal's 'Inter-City' services, the Hannover–Frankfurt/Main 'Mercator.' (Courtesy Yves Broncard)

above: Spain's TEE, the 'Catalan-Talgo,' runs between Barcelona and Geneva. (In this photo the train had been diverted and is seen leaving Lyons behind French Railways 1.5kV DC electric locomotive No BB9329.) (Courtesy Yves Broncard)

right: Lunch in a Swiss Federal electric TEE train-set. (Courtesy Swiss National Tourist Office)

to squeeze the last allowable mile an hour out of the speed limits over the curvature between Zurich and Arth-Goldau or on the Gotthard slopes of the sets' 'Gottardo' and 'Ticino' TEE itineraries. The Swiss TEEs rode as sweetly on curved track as they did on the straight in terms of rail-induced oscillation, but the smoothest suspensions and running gear are not proof against centrifugal force if they attack bends at speeds for which the track is not ideally superelevated (to mitigate wear and tear on both track and vehicles the degree of cant through a curve has to be a compromise between the optima for the fastest and slowest trains using the route). I still cherish a memory of lunch on an international press demonstration run of one of these Swiss TEE sets between Zurich and Milan, before the start of public service. One of Britain's best-known savants in food and drink, a very dapper little gentleman, was caught off-balance by one of the sharper curves in the middle of an extravagantly pantomimic evaluation of the wine that had just been set before us. You could only admire the vestigial elegance he somehow – but characteristically – managed to retain as he was smoothly decanted by his heeling chair and slid gracefully across the center gangway clear under a table on the other side of the car. Not surprisingly, as we shall find in a subsequent chapter, the Swiss Federal is one of the few world railway systems which seems to have decided that the irrestistible commercial

demand for speed as well as comfort will sooner or later have to be met by expensive resort to automatic body-tilting mechanisms. They exaggerate a vehicle's lean into a curve, thus allowing it to take a bend at higher speed than the superelevation normally prescribes without detriment to passenger comfort.

The 'Cisalpin's' considerable contraction of journey times between Milan, several major Swiss towns or cities and Paris, coupled with its enhanced supplementary-fare comfort, quickly attracted excellent business – so much so that in 1965 the Swiss had to add a coach to each train-set. Two years later they went further and built an extra train-set so that at peak traffic periods the 'Cisalpin' could be run as a twin-unit formation.

By the early 1970s, however, railway management opinion throughout Western Europe was hardening against the fixed-formation, multiple-unit format for medium- to long-haul inter-city services, chiefly because of its operational inflexibility. In the case of the 'Cisalpin,' for instance, once the basic single-unit formation had been fully booked for a specific working the operators had two stark options: turn away any further business or add a complete six-car set, with the chance that 297 extra tons of train weight and an additional 3400hp of traction might be burning up energy for only half a load or even less.

By that time, too, TEE clients were showing signs of preference for the meal service at seats which French Railways

had introduced in their second-generation TEE coaching stock to be described in the next chapter. Increasingly cost-conscious railway managements also preferred that arrangement for the obvious reason that it saved the extra train tonnage incurred in laying out two seats for every passenger likely to dine en route. Finally, there was the perennial issue, where design of European long-haul coaches are concerned, of compartment versus saloon arrangement. The exclusively open-plan layout of the Swiss sets had its critics. They rounded off the case for re-equipment of the prestigious and well-patronized 'Cisalpin' from the summer of 1974 with the latest French locomotive-hauled TEE cars; at the same time the 'Cisalpin' was extended beyond Milan to Venice for the duration of the summer service each year. Although French Railways had by the 1970s perfected and put into service on the Paris–Brussels–Amsterdam TEEs some powerful four-voltage locomotives with 150mph capability, the CC40100s, these were technically unsuited to the mountaineering sector of the 'Cisalpin's' route. So the three railways involved decided to forego through operation with unchanged traction (which anyway would have saved a trivial number of minutes set against the overall time of the Milan–Paris journey)

and run the train with their own loco-motives up to the limits of their own borders.

The original Swiss train-sets were not put out to grass, by the way. The 'Ticino' TEE is no more, but the Basle–Milan 'Gottardo' survives, down to Italy in the morning and back at night; nowadays it is extended to Genoa in the summer. The other Swiss sets these days cover the two pairs of TEEs between Brussels, Luxembourg, Strasbourg and Basle or Zurich, the 'Edelweiss' and the 'Iris.'

By the start of the 1970s den Hollander's original TEE concept was still more clouded. With the French and German Federal Railways in particular disinclined to equip the flagships of their internal premium fare-commanding services any less opulently than international trains, it looked highly probable that before long some TEEs' distinctions might be confined to the size of the TEE supplementary fare and the international character of their routes. Conceivably standards of both speed and luxury on some front-rank domestic services of the TEE scheme's member systems might even creep ahead of those on the TEE network. The only logical course was to admit the various railways' internal services of acceptable comfort and speed standard to TEE status.

As a result 'Europ-Express' has become an apter brand name for the network than '*Trans*-Europ Express.' Of course, the changed policy has saved the railways the very considerable cost of designing different varieties of high-grade coaching stock for domestic and international premium services, which is eminently sensible in the economically stringent last quarter of the 20th century. But in Western Germany especially, where the internal supplementary-fare Inter-City and TEE services use not merely identical types of vehicle but the same red-and-cream, originally TEE livery, distinction between the two networks has in fact diminished to the scale of supplementary fare, the 'IC' and 'TEE' logos by which the respective networks are promoted and described in official notices, and – of very recent years – the German Federal's decision to infuse second-class accommodation into the 'IC' trains, whereas the TEEs remain exclusively first-class. Not that in the process the pursuit of admirable comfort has been relaxed: what has happened, as we shall see in the succeeding chapter, is that the German Federal has lifted the standards of a mounting number of its purely domestic trains to TEE level.

But in general, promotion of more and more trains to TEE status has defaced den Hollander's vision of a standard inter-national luxury train service beyond recognition. Especially incongruous in the present-day TEE network is the Barcelona–Geneva 'Catalan-Talgo,' with which RENFE, the Spanish national system, infiltrated the scheme in June 1969 by some subfusc barter of contracts to re-equip Spanish railways for a chance to win a bridgehead outside Spain for the locally-patented Talgo system. This book is not the place for a detailed description of the Talgo method: I can only interpolate briefly for any reader unfamiliar with it that it was an ingenious invention devised to overcome the speed-limiting characteristics of many principal RENFE routes by use of extremely lightweight, short (only 11 meters/43ft long) and low-slung coach bodies, each carried on a single pair of independent, cleverly guided half-axles at one end and at the other carried on the shoulders, as it were, of the adjoining vehicle. Since RENFE's 5ft 6in gauge is at variance with the standard 4ft 8½in in Western Europe outside the Iberian peninsula, for the 'Catalan–Talgon' service (and for the non-TEE 'Barcelona–Talgo' through sleeper which operates between Paris Austerlitz and Barcelona) the Spaniards had to come up with more dexterity to fulfill their international ambitions: an apparatus at the Franco–Spanish border station of Port-Bou to vary the gauge of the Talgo's wheels, which is done as the train is moved steadily through the special installation at around 6mph.

There is no doubt that Talgo is by far the most successful and durable of several early post-World War II essays in ultra-lightweight coach construction allied to novel running gear, all aimed at curbing running costs. The 'Catalan–Talgo,' one must also stress, is comfortably furnished and sports a small bar as well as a Wagons-Lits-staffed kitchen which serves alternatively a separate restaurant or meals at seats in two of the train's cars. But in the nature of things no single-axle running gear will ever come up to the ride quality of a full-length car mounted on the latest in bogie technology from any of at least four Western European railway design schools.

The special case of the Talgos apart, latter-day TEE development has throughout Western Europe been a by-product of the general drive to enhance the competitive appeal of inter-city rail travel. To bring the story of Europe's luxury trains up to date, therefore, the next chapter surveys the cream of today's services and equipment country by country rather than confining the rest of the narrative to TEEs. Without den Hollander's vision of the 1950s, one wonders whether today's Western European travellers would have come into a heritage of such comfort quality on so many of the continent's inter-city services.

CHAPTER 8
MODERN LUXURY TRAINS OF EUROPE

A present-day TEE of the Italian State Railways heads south down the coastline south of Genoa behind a class E444 electric locomotive. (Courtesy Fototeca Centrale FS)

Italy's 'Settebello'

There was nothing very luxurious about Italian express trains before World War II, except for the few that featured Pullmans. Up to the mid-1930s, in fact, there was nothing much of anything to recommend Italian long-distance rail travel. Speeds were as humdrum as the appointments of the coaches and punctuality could be execrable. A commonplace of popular history has it that Mussolini at least made the Italian trains run to time, but more importantly in his drive for supremacy in the land, sea and air lanes he had them speeded up more dramatically than those of any other European country in the last half of the pre-war decade. Climax of that process was a world-record-breaking demonstration run in July 1939 when the 195.8 miles of quite severely graded and curved main line from Florence through the Apennine Mountains to Milan were eaten up at a start-to-stop average speed of no less than 102mph by an electric multiple-unit train-set.

Gloomily surveying their battered system after the war, the Italian State Railways realized it would be years before they could reconstruct it to standards which would allow even an approach to the inter-city speeds on the everyday horizon in 1939. What could be done to stop internal air services and especially the emergent north-south *Autostrada de Sol* from skimming the cream of the railways' inter-city business? This was a particularly critical concern to the Italian State, in whose gross revenues passenger traffic figured to a much greater extent than it did with any other of Western Europe's railways at the time. Their answer was to put on rails the continent's first post-war essay in supplementary-fare, luxury day train design in

1953. The Italian State originally proposed to build an initial series of eight electric multiple-units of this ETR300 type, then had second thoughts and built only two in 1953, adding a third in 1959.

The first two ETR300s were launched on a thrice-weekly service in each direction all the way from Milan to Naples, but in 1954 the itinerary was cut back to Rome. Four years later both the Milan–Rome service and its striking light gray and bright green-hued train-sets were officially titled 'Settebello,' or 'Lucky Seven' in colloquial Italian; the name comes from a popular Italian card game and matches the seven-car format of each exclusively first-class ETR300.

A quarter-century after their premiere, the ETR300s are still arguably the most sumptuously furnished day trains in all Western Europe, though in quality of ride they now yield several points to vehicles embodying subsequent pro-

gress in running gear technology. The Italians gave them a unique timetable designation of 'electric trains de luxe' – and appropriately piled a really massive supplementary fare on top of the basic first-class price for a 'Settebello' journey.

The 'Settebello's' highly original nose-end design rivets your eye before you have crossed the airy concourse of Rome Termini station and reached the train's platform. At each end of the ETR300 unit the driving cab has been set back from the front of the vehicle and raised into a squat dome protruding from the roof. Cockpit is a much more apt term than cab for this cupola: its height above the ground, its necessarily rather stunted height and the neat grouping of the controls and displays in front of the two motormen's seats give it very much an aerospace ambience. Removal of the driving nerve-center from its usual position clears the considerable space vacated in the main coach body for a passenger observation saloon. Each saloon has a four-seater settee at the rear and individual rotating chairs for eight more passengers ranged round the uninterrupted 'U' of the window curving right round the nose.

It is an unforgettable experience, particularly, to have one of those individual seats in the front-end saloon when the 'Settebello' is on its passage of the Apennines between Florence and Bologna. It is preferable to get a seat in front rather than the settee at the back, because a sunblind is draped over the tops of the observation windows, which are anyway rather shallow, so that one does not see much but the ballast from a standing position. Curves are fairly frequent on the mountain sector of the route, but on the straighter sections the 'Settebello' is allowed up to 140kph (87.5mph). The ETR300's combination of air and re-

above: Inside the Italian 'Settebello's' nose; there is one of these observation lounges at each end of the set. (Courtesy Fototeca Centrale FS)

left: An Italian State Railways Type ETR300 electric train-set on 'Settebello' service. The driving cab protrudes above the roof; in the nose is an observation saloon. (Courtesy Fototeca Centrale FS)

far left: An Italian State Railways Type ETR 300 electric train-set on the Rome–Milan 'Settebello' service. (Courtesy Italian State Railways)

left, below and bottom: Inside the elegant Rome–Milan 'Settebello': a compartment, the diner and the bar. (Courtesy Italian State Railways)

generative electric braking is very efficient. Consequently the driver always seems to leave braking from top speed for the next curve looming up ahead well beyond what the averagely neurotic passenger thinks must be the last safe moment. Of course, the braking is always professionally timed, but over the years many a nervous front-seat automobile passenger must have scuffed the observation saloon skirting, subconsciously stabbing his feet at non-existent brake pedals as each fresh curve comes into sight.

The two outer two-car units of an ETR-300 set, every axle of which is powered for a total of just over 3000hp, house most of the passenger space. This is arranged entirely and uniquely in delightful lounges, each about 13ft from lateral wall to wall and each seating ten, three on each settee against the compartment walls and four on free-standing armchairs. Besides the latter there are neat occasional tables in the central floor space and above each settee is a locker for hand luggage, the door of which is etched with attractive Roman scenes. Both wall and door on the corridor side are glazed from top to bottom, which enhances the impression of spaciousness, though the occupants can curtain off the whole of the corridor wall from inside their compartment. Unobtrusive fluorescent lighting sets off a restful color scheme of blue and gray ideally, and the whole is most effectively air-conditioned and soundproofed.

Originally the first vehicle of an ETR-300's non-powered central three-car unit was devoid of passenger seats, but three more ten-seater loungers were inserted in this vehicle of the 1959 unit and subsequently the two earlier units were rebuilt to match. The original provision of only 160 seats in a seven-car train

grossing 364 tons was naturally a compelling reason for such a crippling supplementary fare, which in the early 'Settebello' years all but doubled the normal first-class rate for the Rome–Milan journey. Space for the additional lounges was secured by cutting out the bookstall and souvenir shop incorporated in the first two ETR300s and by reducing the volume of a large baggage room. One is bidden to deposit all bulky luggage here, which keeps the train's vestibules and lounges admirably clear of obstacles, but reclaiming belongings back after arrival can be a test of temperament if one has a tight connection to make. The opening minutes of a Harrods sale had nothing on one crush I remember around the 'Settebello's' baggage-room door at Milan as a crowd of anxious Italians were brandishing their cloakroom tickets under the train attendant's nose. Apart from the baggage room, the rest of the bodyspace in the center triplet's leading car is occupied by the radio/telephone office, from which passengers can be connected to the national telephone network and from which the train's public address is operated for music, radio programs or multi-lingual announcements.

The center car of the triplet is mostly taken up by a gleaming all-electric kitchen, but also accommodates a train office base of the train's two attractive hostesses, and staff quarters. Beyond it is a restaurant-bar car with decor of the old-style elegance. There is no tawdry plastic in the diner, but a nice, understated blending of polished wood finishes, graceful murals, deep tan and green coverings to the seats, the tables and the floor and evidence of the acclaimed Italian style of the 1950s in every design detail.

Catering on Italian State trains is still exclusively by the Wagons-Lits company. On a premium-fare train like the 'Settebello' the *table d'hôte* lunch menu will take the characteristic Italian shape of an *antipasto*, or *hors d'oeuvres*, then pasta – ravioli or canelloni, maybe – an entrée, usually chicken or veal well garnished with vegetables, an ice-cream confection or cheese and fresh fruit. If you do not feel like a full meal then you can make up a card of, say, soup, a dish of cold meat, fresh fruit and coffee from the pleasing bar at the far end of the dining car, but in my experience that tends to work out proportionately more expensive than the set meal.

Be warned – with only three ETR300 units available and a timetable which at the time of writing has the 'Settebello' on a breakfast-time departure from both Milan and Rome, so that two sets are needed for each day's working, there is a risk of booking a 'Settebello' trip and finding different equipment in use. If you are lucky, the substitute will be one of the four-coach variants of the same spectacular front-end design, but without the full range of facilities, which the Italian State had built in 1960. However the deputy may be some of the much more prosaic but still comfortable Ale601 series multiple-units; even, if your star is right out of the ascendant, a unit or two of the pre-war ETR220 class.

The 'Settebello' has 125mph capability, but at present it is limited to 100mph and that only across the flat Po Valley plains north of Bologna, and also on the stretches so far completed of the new *Direttissima* line, engineered for speeds up to 150mph, which the Italians are very expensively and rather laboriously building to bypass the traditional rail route

between Rome and Florence. The new railway bores through the successive ranges of hills and leaps over valleys on long viaducts to achieve the straightest possible alignment, whereas the original railway was economically bent round natural obstacles wherever possible, with the result that the first 90miles or so out of Rome are chronically curved and demand a continuous speed limit of 110kmph (68mph). The *Direttissima's* once-planned timescale has been hopelessly compromised by a combination of environmental argument, particularly over the new line's penetration of Florence, and Governmental pressure on the purse-strings. The greater part of the bypass is now predicted to be complete by 1983, but as yet no one is prepared to pin a firm date on the opening of the controversial stage from Rovezzano into Florence.

The topographical contrast between the northern and southern halves of the 'Settebello's' route was always patent in its schedules. From Bologna to Milan it could be timed at a start-to-stop average of up to 83mph at one stage of its career, but from Rome to Florence the booked average was below 65mph. Even partial opening of the Rome–Florence *Direttissima* has already cut 20 minutes from the 'Settebello's' previous best schedule overall and northbound the train is at the time of writing on its best-ever booking of 5 hours 25 minutes for the 391 miles end-to-end, inclusive of Florence reversal and Bologna stop.

Despite the age and the unique character of its equipment, the 'Settebello' was admitted to the TEE network in the summer of 1974, presumably in the belief that the still undimmed splendor of its interior appointments made up for the

shortcomings in its ride quality by comparison with latter-day locomotive-hauled TEE vehicles. Yet another inconsistency of the TEE structure is that it shares the selfsame Milan–Rome route with two other daily TEEs, the 'Ambrosiano' and the 'Vesuvio' (a Milan–Naples through train), which are locomotive-hauled and formed of vehicles nearly 20 years younger.

To win TEE status for any of its purely internal services the Italian State had to improve upon the dismal two-car diesel train-sets which were its inaugural contribution to the network. Neighboring railways despised them: Swiss railwaymen, who took them in on the Milan–Geneva 'Lemano' service, branded them *'les camions'* (the lorries), while the German Federal eventually refused to accept them at Munich on the 'Mediolanum' TEE link from Milan and insisted on substituting one of its own diesel train-sets. For the 1970s, therefore, the Italian State had Fiat build a new range of locomotive-hauled coaches, of both compartment and saloon layout, which now serve both TEEs and non-TEE, first-class-only *rapidi* of the Italian State; coaches in TEE use are liveried in the scheme's red-and-cream, the others in dark blue and light-gray with broad horizontal red lining, to match the recently-introduced high-performance Type E444 electric locomotives by which they are usually hauled on front-rank services.

The first sets of the new vehicles were ready to supersede the vilified Italian diesel twin-units on the international TEE services for which the Italians were responsible in the summer of 1972. The following summer they put the stamp of approval on the first of Italy's domestic TEEs, the Milan–Bari 'Adriatico.'

Today's Italian TEE rides as smoothly and silently as any in the international network, and the air-conditioned comfort of its accommodation is exemplary if not specially remarkable, apart from the facility of a full-length wardrobe let into a lateral wall of each compartment (though you can only get at it by asking any occupant of the center space to move so that you can swing forward the hinged back of his seat). Another unusual feature of certain Italian TEEs, specifically the Milan–Naples 'Vesuvio' and the Milan–Rome 'Ambrosiano,' is the extent of meal service provision. Each train includes two full restaurant cars (on the 'Vesuvio' one goes no further south than Rome, and consequently is marshalled separately from its twin). These combine to offer 94 seats for the full *table d'hôte* meal services, but if you do not fancy full board then lighter tray meals can be served at any of the 96 seats in each train's open saloons.

The Italian TEEs traverse some of the network's choicer scenic routes and the Fiat coaches are an unrivalled vantagepoint, especially when a blazing Mediterranean sun is baking the ground outside the car's cool saloon. You might go particularly for the spectacular sweep of the Italian Riviera by the 'Cycnus' as it hugs the rocky coastline on its way from Milan and Genoa to the French border at Vintimiglia, but my pick will always be the Milan–Munich 'Mediolanum,' back with Italian equipment since the availability of the Fiat locomotive-hauled coaching stock. Once the northbound train has cleared the Po Valley, then the long, steep-walled gorge of the Eisack above Bolzano, now so hideously disfigured by the never-ending stilts of the Brenner *autostrade*, the steady ascent to the snowline or in winter above it at the Brenner pass, followed by the sharp winding descent through lush, mountain-girt valleys into the Austrian Tyrol at Innsbruck is one of the really sublime experiences of European railroading.

West Germany's TEE and Inter-City Trains

Vying with Italy's 'Settebello' for a rosette as Europe's most luxurious train in the early 1960s – and taking the honor for the superior quality of its riding if nothing else – was the 'Rheingold' of the German Federal Railway (Deutsche Bundesbahn, or DB). The 'Rheingold' had been revived in the spring of 1951, but at the start of its post-war reincarnation only its title and route reflected any of the pre-war service's aura. Roughly a third of the pre-war Mitropa 'Rheingold' cars had been destroyed, but even if all had survived the German Federal would probably not have dusted them off, preferring at that stage to cast the train in its standard 'F'-train mold of the period.

above: The German Federal 'Rheingold' in the early 1960s. (Courtesy Author's collection)

top left: The latest Italian locomotive-hauled TEE equipment forms the Milan–Avignon 'Ligure,' hauled by French Railways dual-voltage electric No BB-22258. (Courtesy Author's collection)

left: A first-class saloon of present-day Italian TEE equipment. (Courtesy Italian State Railways)

As a result the early post-war 'Rheingold' was not only formed of standard DB coaching stock but adulterated with second- and third-class accommodation. It was still steam-operated the whole way to the Swiss border, too, but throughout the 1950s the Dutch and the Germans were stringing up catenary so rapidly that by the early 1960s only the short stretch from the Dutch–German border at Emmerich to the fringe of the DB's Ruhr network at Oberhausen was unelectrified. The stage was ready for a new concept of DB inter-city express, and the DB selected the 'Rheingold' to model it.

The new 'Rheingold' of 1962, once more first class only, was possibly the most opulent public service train Europe has ever seen. Its ordinary seating coaches set the style for so much subsequent inter-city vehicle construction on the mainland of Europe that today's seasoned TEE travellers complacently take them as the norm of premium-fare travel. Two decades ago the 'Rheingold's spaciousness, comfort and wealth of

detail and refinement caught the breath when one boarded the re-equipped train for the first time.

Like the Italians in the 'Settebello,' the German designers had given the compartment coaches an added sense of width by glazing the inner walls of the corridor practically from ceiling to floor, then recessing every detail in the corridor itself to preserve an absolutely clear line from vestibule to vestibule. The semi-reclining seats in the compartments, each with its own movable footrest, were comfortable enough, but it was the alternative saloon vehicles that were the really dramatic break with previous post-war European coach styling, the 'Settebello' of course excepted.

I still rate this German open saloon design the most relaxing in all Europe for a long day journey. Ergonomically its roomy armchair seats are supremely comfortable in any position, and there is a really generous choice of tilting attitudes by use of a simple control in one of the armrests; tilting, moreover, brings your feet neatly up to the level of a footrest at the base of the seat in front. Every seat or pair of seats is reversible, so that you can sit in seclusion or face-to-face as you will – in theory, that is: locating the foot pedal beneath the seat and lunging at it is a job which usually defeats most passengers unless and until they can button-hole one of the train's staff for assistance.

left: Train secretarial service in a German 'Inter-City' express. (Courtesy Deutsche Bundesbahn)

top, far left: A German Federal class 103 electric locomotive heads the 'Rheingold' up the Rhine Valley. (Courtesy Deutsche Bundesbahn)

center, far left: The 'Rheingold's' lounge bar. (Courtesy DSG)

above: Reclining armchairs of the German Federal TEE and 'Inter-City' equipment. (Courtesy Deutsche Bundesbahn)

bottom, far left: Lunch in a German TEE diner. (Courtesy DSG)

below: One of three German Federal class ET403 high-speed first-class-only electric train-sets. (Courtesy Deutsche Bundesbahn)

One of the former 'Rheingold' dome cars, now owned by the West German tourist agency Apfel Reisen, repainted in their vivid colors along with other vehicles the company owns and operated as land-cruise trains. One is seen here in the Rhine Gorge near Oberwesel. (Courtesy Brian Stephenson)

The present-day 'Rheingold,' headed by a DB class 103 electric, heads south through the Rhine Valley near Oberwesel. (Courtesy Brian Stephenson)

The 'Rheingold' was the first train in Europe to be fitted with the now commonplace air-operated automatic vestibule doors. Unwisely, the Germans did not at first think it necessary to brief passengers that the doors functioned at the touch of a finger, then closed themselves after a ten-second interval. The apparatus must have been pretty resilient to put up with all the baffled manhandling I saw the doors get from untutored Customs or Immigration men and passengers until the railway belatedly pasted informative notices throughout the train.

Centerpiece of the 'Rheingold' was a pair of vehicles with no European design precedent. Seen from the platform, a pronounced, part-windowed bulge in the roof at one end of the restaurant car clearly indicated originality within – a kitchen on two levels. Above was the kitchen itself, below the scullery, and beyond them, at normal car-floor level, a serving area that doubled as a counter for the restaurant car staff and a buffet for snack service, and which was connected to each 'business' room by electric lifts which lowered cooked dishes from the kitchen or dispatched dirty crockery to the scullery. Each working area was interconnected by a two-way internal telephone system. But the concept was too extravagant of staff and heavy on upkeep costs. The eventual stock of five such cars has since been retired.

The highpoint of the 'Rheingold's' journey, of course, is the train's passage of the sinuous, romantic Felsenrhein – the deep valley through which the broad Rhine river forces a passage from Mainz first through the Taunus mountains and then, after the confluence with the Moselle at Koblenz, between the Eifel and Westerwald uplands. For miles on end the sweep of the vine-spread valley walls, the countless Gothic castles perched on the hillcrests, at the water's edge or in mid-river, the towns huddling at the river edge and the incessant commerce of main roads and railways on both banks, plus the jam of huge barges and pleasure craft of all sizes and vintages on the river itself, compel most passengers to drop their books and papers. To maximize this scenic selling-point of a 'Rheingold' journey (mind you, one should not underrate the appeal of the southernmost sector of the train's routing in Germany, where it skirts the densely wooded eastern slopes of the Black Forest), the German Federal contrived to adapt the American Vista-dome to the European loading gauge.

Approaching the 'Rheingold's' dome car from the adjoining diner, you stepped first into an urbane lounge-bar, with bar-stool seats, a settee and some tables for two. In the early years of the refashioned 'Rheingold,' moreover, it was respected as a lounge-bar, attended throughout the journey by a hostess of the German restaurant car company, DSG. It was not allowed to deteriorate into the nondescript sort of buffet-bar, drearily familiar on British Rail, where serious drinkers have to contest elbow room with matrons deep in Maxpax tea and fruit cake, or scrabble among a clutter of empty ale cans and crumb-strewn plates for a place to rest their glass. But as time went on, unfortunately, the German Federal's bars were relegated to little more than service as reserve dining space.

At the far end of the 'Rheingold's' bar, steps climbed away to the raised central saloon, its floor 6ft 8in above the track and its completely glazed roof 14ft 8½in from rail level. There was no supplementary charge for occupation of its 22 armchair seats – which was not altogether a blessing, as only conscience inhibited anyone who had grabbed a seat in the dome at the start of one of the train's highly scenic sectors from hogging it to the bitter end. Up in the dome one really tested the impeccable efficiency of the 'Rheingold's' air-conditioning and tinted window-glazing. Even on a baking, cloudless summer's afternoon the only discomfort I ever sensed came visually from the endless flicker of electric traction current wire supports above and around the dome's windows. The dome was the place, too, to take the full measure of the Germans' significant early-1960s lead in European ride quality, thanks to a combination of vehicle size and length (26.4m – but subsequent series of kitchen-diners in the same family of coaching stock have been even longer, at 27.5m), a rapid spread of continuously-welded rail and very effective running gear design in the so-called Minden–Deutz bogie. 'Gliding' is a cliché-word for a glib description of good vehicle riding, but in the remarkable silence of the dome at speed and at that height above the track it was not so inapt a term in the 'Rheingold' of the 1960s. Unhappily, ride quality on the German Federal these days, though still in the very top bracket of European experience, is not what it was a decade ago.

Back on normal floor level at the other end of the dome car one came upon a telephone kiosk and a train secretary's office. The 'Rheingold' was the first German Federal train to acquire these facilities after World War II and since then they have become a hallmark of premium-fare expresses in West Germany to a much greater extent than on any other Western European rail system. Some, like British Rail, have never believed demand would justify the expense of providing such services while others, like French Railways, have discarded them. But the German Federal, though from time to time it has subjected the facilities to critical economic analysis, now believes them to be such a sales asset in the executive travel market that, like train catering, they should not be appraised on a self-accounting basis. Thus today both secretary and telephone are available on well over half the DB-equipped TEEs and the country's internal supplementary-fare Inter-City services in daily operation. In 1978, moreover, the train telephone system was re-equipped with self-dialling instruments just like those on terra firma; passengers no longer have to put all their outgoing calls through the train secretary.

The German Federal fortified the impact of the new 'Rheingold' by making it simultaneously one of Europe's fastest trains. In its first post-war years it had started intact from Hook of Holland, to stress the revived luxury link with Britain via the Essex port of Harwich, and made for Germany via Rotterdam Central and Venlo. From 27 May 1962, however, the main train was transferred to its historic starting point at Amsterdam and a portion from Hook of Holland was picked up at Utrecht. This protracted the train's mileage, but that was offset by re-gearing some of the German Federal's Class 110 electric locomotives for 100mph, by exploiting this maximum wherever the track geometry permitted and by timing the 'Rheingold' up to the hilt of the route's potential in the Ruhr and in southern Germany, where there is comparative freedom from severe curvature. In the southern sector the 'Rheingold' was assigned Germany's first post-war timing at over 80mph for the 83.1 miles from Freiburg to Karlsruhe. That was screwed up to an 84mph average, stripping the French 'Mistral' temporarily of its European long-haul speed crown, in the summer of 1963 when the companion 'Rheinpfeil' ('Rhine Arrow') from Dortmund to Munich was re-equipped with similar vehicles. The two trains were organized to conduct a complex exchange of through coaches at Duisburg, and the German Federal was anxious to recoup the overall journey time these maneuvers exacted.

Both 'Rheingold' and 'Rheinpfeil' were admitted to the TEE network in the summer of 1965 (since then, in the redevelopment of German Federal first-class-only services under the Inter-City brandname, the 'Rheinpfeil' has surrendered TEE status). That was inevitable. Until it happened there was the ludicrous anomaly of greatly inferior TEE trains elsewhere in West Germany carrying the much higher scale of TEE supplementary charges, while the two new luxury trains were subject only to the modest German Federal 'F' train surcharge of the period. So 'Rheingold' and 'Rheinpfeil' changed their initial blue-and-cream livery for TEE red-and-cream. Nowadays blue and cream is the standard livery for all German Federal passenger locomotives and long-haul passenger vehicles not assign-

ed to regular TEE or Inter-City work.

The 'Rheingold' and 'Rheinpfeil' were the first multi-portion TEE trains, the former comprising sections for Munich, Chur, Geneva and Milan, the latter sections for the same destinations except Chur. That posed a problem: did the various portions rank as TEEs over stages of their journey made as part of an ordinary train? It was decided they did not. Beyond Basle, therefore, you can still ride the Chur through coaches without payment of TEE supplement, though nowadays the other sections make their entire journeys as part of a TEE or a supplement-bearing German Inter-City train.

Unsurprisingly, with multi-voltage electric locomotive traction now very much a practical possibility, the German Federal made the 'Rheingold' design the basis of its second generation of TEE coaching stock. Next to be re-equipped with the new-type vehicles, in that same summer of 1965, were the Hamburg–Zurich 'Helvetia' and the Hamburg–Munich 'Blauer Enzian.' Neither were embellished with dome cars, however, and in the mid-1970s the five 'Rheingold' and 'Rheinpfeil' dome cars and two-level kitchen cars were dismissed from TEE service.

Although the domes had been carefully shaped to shave within the loading gauges even of the Swiss and Italian tracks on the 'Rheingold' itinerary, they were never

worked beyond Basle in regular service. Even in Germany their spectacular dimensions were liable to crease operators' brows should an emergency demand the 'Rheingold's' diversion from its normal route. With economy an ever more nagging concern to every rail management, too, the German Federal was always conscious that each heavy, expensive car had only 12 revenue-earning seats in two abnormally roomy compartments at one end. The discarded domes have been bought by one of the big West German travel agencies which runs its own charter cruise trains the length and breadth of Europe; the new owners, Apfelgold, have had the dome height trimmed so that the cars, repainted in the agency's own orange and green livery, are a comfortable fit over all the routes to the French and Italian resorts to which they operate their trains.

At the start of the 1970s the German Federal decided to create an internal network of two-hourly interval, first-class only trains between the country's major commercial centers, all individually named, which would be precisely comparable to the international TEEs in standards of speed and comfort – even in scale of supplementary charges, which was set at an identical level. British Rail's brand name of 'Inter-City,' ('IC' for logo purposes), was borrowed for the new scheme launched in the autumn of 1971.

At the start the only distinction between TEE and IC trains was that some of the latter were furnished with the original German TEE train-sets, the bulbous-nosed diesel-hydraulic multiple-units. Gradually that difference was erased as the IC trains were fully equipped with red and cream 'Rheingold' pattern vehicles, similarly offering options of compartment or that superb open saloon seating. Customary power for trains of both networks was also the same: the sleek, extremely powerful 8750hp six-wheeled electric locomotives of Class 103 which the German Federal introduced in 1965.

The 103s were designed for 125mph, since the German Federal was anxious to lift the speed ceiling to this figure over every part of the IC network that was amenable to it as soon as possible. The 103s were to display their top speed potential with a train of 'Rheingold' stock between Munich and Augsburg in the summer of their debut, as a sideshow of an international transport exhibition that was staged in Munich that year. The following spring the 'Blauer Enzian' TEE was allowed up to 125mph over this specially signalled stretch and over another between Hanover and Celle. But a year or so later the German Federal abruptly pulled the limit back to 100mph. The wear and tear on track and vehicles of consistent 125mph running, they felt, was excessive.

In the belief that a spread of traction gear weight over all the axles of a light-weight electric multiple-unit would mitigate this nuisance, the German Federal in 1973 unveiled a trio of four-car articulated train-sets, classified ET403, furnished to the same standards as the locomotive-hauled TEE and IC coaches if a mite less roomily, because the ET403 car bodies were slightly tapered upwards from the floor to allow for automatic body-tilting (a subject to be discussed in the next section of this chapter). The ET403s went into regular IC operation between Munich and North Germany, but at a maximum of 100mph.

Within a few years the German Federal had learned afresh that the fixed multiple-unit format was commercially too inflexible. No more ET403s, they decided, would be built. At the same time the Germans somehow overcame their misgivings over 125mph with the Class 103 locomotives, equipped more stretches of their trunk routes with the means to actuate automatically the continuous locomotive cab signalling display and computerized speed control essential for 100mph-plus, and in the summer of 1978 sprinkled their TEE and IC schedules with 74 instances of 125mph running spread over four sectors: Munich–Augsburg, Augsburg–Donauwörth, Hannover–Uelzen and Hamburg–Bremen. Germany's TEE and IC trains, therefore, are now among Europe's fastest trains as well as challenging all comers for comfort.

One area in which they are quite unsurpassed is in the range of DSG's catering on the move. The diner of a TEE or IC train puts on a *table d'hôte* lunch or dinner at the usual times, and in the context of contemporary West German living costs the set meal is very good value. There is a choice of two menus. The more expensive one, priced at DM21.50 inclusive of all service and taxes at the time of writing, might offer a soup, then an omelette with asparagus or ham tubes filled with asparagus on toast; as the main dish a veal steak with mushrooms, buttered rice and side-salad or a pork steak with grilled tomato, French fries and side-salad, and finally a dessert of patisserie, an ice cream confection or fresh fruit. The cheaper card costing DM17.50 omits the second course and offers a slightly less sophisticated entrée. Portions are always liberal and to top off the meal the car carries a reasonable selection of high-quality German wines. These, too, are not expensive by local restaurant standards, running at DM4–5.40 for a quarter-liter of Moselle to DM7.00 for a quarter-liter of Franken.

Should you board a German Federal TEE or IC too late for the start of the *table d'hôte* service, you will not miss out. No other organization in Western Europe offers such a comprehensive à la carte menu as the DSG and has it fully available

top left: The first style of French locomotive-hauled TEE equipment forms the Paris–Amsterdam 'Ile de France,' photographed behind a French Railways four-voltage Type CC40101 electric locomotive near Compiègne. (Courtesy Yves Broncard)

top: Europe's fastest TEE, the 'Etendard' which, in common with the 'Aquitaine,' covers the 360 miles between Paris and Bordeaux non-stop in 3 hours 50 minutes. Here, hauled by a French Railways 8000 hp CC6500 electric locomotive and formed of 'Grand Confort' equipment it is making speed near Dax in the Landes area of southwestern France. (Courtesy Yves Broncard)

above: The diner of the 'Etendard' TEE. (Courtesy Maurice Mertens)

left: French Railways' 'Aquitaine' TEE,
Europe's fastest long-distance train (paired
with the 'Etendard'), leaves Bordeaux for
Paris behind electric locomotive No CC6524.
The train is formed of French 'Grand
Confort' stock.   (Courtesy Yves Broncard)

above: Inside French Railways' 'Mistral':
(top) the bar, (left) the shop – in the same
car as the bar, and (above) an open saloon.
(Courtesy Author's collection, French
Railways and Cie Internationale des
Wagons-Lits et du Tourisme respectively)

for the greater part of a train's itinerary. There is the choice not only of a score of cold dishes, from a plate of liver sausage, bread and butter at DM5.30 up to two chicken drumsticks, bread and butter or cuts from a roast joint and salad at around DM10, but a selection of half-a-dozen or so egg dishes and of up to ten entrées, from grilled sausages to pork schnitzel, potatoes and salad or veal escalope, French fries and salad at between DM12.50 and DM15. Boarding the 'Rheingold' just too late for the main dinner service in the period I was writing this chapter, I found a place in the diner before the last of the coffee-drinkers had retired to their coaches and quickly got very agreeable service of an excellent steak, salad, French fries and a beer for a total of about DM22 from one of the DSG's hard-worked hostesses.

As you might expect, contemplating the scale of provisioning and staffing this unrivalled service entails, the DSG's train catering balance sheet is the most lopsided in Western Europe. Revenue fails to cover even the costs of trainboard staff and materials, but the DSG is a wholly-owned subsidiary of the German Federal, which counts such providence a vital element of its overall TEE and IC marketing package. Nevertheless of late the financially beleaguered German Federal has been forced into a harder-nosed attitude and is gradually confining full diner service of the kind I have described to its supplementary-fare TEE and IC trains. Over the rest of its network catering will now be from the self-service cafeteria cars which the railway and DSG have not too euphoniously brand-named 'Quick-Pick.' Incidentally, although the 'Quick-Pick' cars cannot generically qualify for much attention in this book, I must add that, in their own category, they reflect the sort of service offered in DSG diners. As well as a long list of cold snacks, they serve up nearly a dozen different hot and cold main dishes, including roast veal or pork, goulash and chicken stew, none of them priced at more than DM10.50. The full-color, gatefold 'Quick-Pick' menu itself, which appetizingly pictures all these dishes in direct-color photography, shames those of most steakhouse chains on terra firma.

Launched as an internal carbon-copy of the TEEs, and timed primarily for business market convenience, the German IC trains have not been proof against the fierce competition of the airlines and more particularly of the superb road network into the continuous expansion of which the West Germans have plowed – and still are plowing – such immense capital. In the mid-1970s second-class accommodation was filtered into a few IC trains as an experiment, to increase load factors. The results persuaded the German Federal to embark on a comprehensive redraft of the whole service. By 1980 every West German trunk route will have an hourly premium-fare train each way, adding a profusion of new train-names to the timetable. Every IC train will include second- as well as first-class accommodation. (At the time of writing the German Federal is building a new range of air-conditioned second-class coaches to match the hitherto exclusively first-class IC vehicles.) The objective is 80mph average end-to-end transits over most of the IC network, with 125mph top speed wherever feasible. The TEEs will be shoehorned into this hourly pattern, but the new concept has probably numbered the days of some of them. From year to year fewer of them have an unchanged passenger complement for long stretches of their itinerary: and the further a train runs the more prone it becomes to delay especially when it is crossing frontiers. That nuisance is a growing aggravation within the framework of an intensified, accelerated domestic express service.

The High-speed TEEs of France

Most lucrative of the first clutch of TEE services, unquestionably, was that between Paris and Brussels. At only 195 miles distance from each other the two capital cities were near-ideally related for a commercial killing by a good rail service, and when Brussels was adopted as the administrative capital of the European Economic Community a healthy traffic in international bureaucrats was added to an always substantial business executive flow to and from Paris.

Consequently demand for Paris–Brussels TEE space quite soon saturated the capacity of the first-generation Dutch–Swiss diesel train-sets that pioneered the service. As the 1960s wore on, in fact, business was overflowing the trains on some of the workings. With electrification complete throughout the route by 1963 – though at three different voltages: 25,000V AC in the French sector, 3000V DC in Belgium and 1500V DC in the Netherlands – the case for re-equipment was complete. The Belgians could now be persuaded to invest in TEE equipment. They picked up roughly 40 percent of the bill for a fleet of new air-conditioned, locomotive-hauled coaches to French Railways' designs which transformed the service from the summer of 1964.

One's first experience of this new French TEE material was as memorable as that in the new 'Rheingold' a year or two earlier. The styling was the work of the industrial designer who has been responsible for most of French Railways' visual panache since the last war, Paul Arzens. As can be seen from color photos in this book, he had been even bolder than the Germans and the Italians in his deployment of glazing to achieve a spacious effect. The master touch in this

The 'Trans-Euro-Nacht' brandname on a German sleeper.   (Courtesy DSG)

respect was the wide, fully-glazed double door leading from each open saloon to the car's end vestibules. Seen from one's lunch table the far end of the car looked as much like the ante-room of a first-class hotel restaurant as made no matter.

Both French and Belgians turned out new multi-voltage electric locomotive designs to power the refurbished TEEs. The Belgian 3560hp Class 150 four-axle machines were fairly conventional in technology as well as looks, the latter apart from a bright peacock blue overall hue. The French six-axle 4540hp CC40101 type, on the other hand, not only riveted the eye immediately with its strikingly raked, vertical 'Z'-form cab and nicely red-trimmed metal body finish, matching the style of the coaches, but turned out to be the first European locomotives arranged for a maximum speed as high as 150mph. As I have already remarked, however, regular operation in public service at over 100mph demands more sophisticated safety aids than a driver's reliance on intermittent lineside signalling and these the Franco–Belgian route does not yet have, so the full speed potential of the CC40101s has yet to be realized in revenue-earning operation. In 1974, when the TEE service between the two capitals had been augmented, the Belgians bought themselves a batch of locomotives (Belgian Class 180) vir-

tually identical to the CC40101. The CC40101's jagged cab front subsequently became a standard feature of French main-line electric locomotive shaping, the motivation being that inward-sloping cab windows protect the driver from sun glare and distracting reflections. One more stylistic innovation of these Franco–Belgian TEEs deserves mention (it aroused some critical comment at the time): they were the first TEE vehicles to depart from the hitherto standard red-and-cream livery.

Since its inception the Paris–Brussels TEE service has been twice strengthened and it now runs to six trains each way daily, the most intensive on any route in the TEE network. They are on near identical departure times from each capital: approximately 6.45, 7.30, 11.45, 17.30, 18.45 and 20.45. Two of the trains, the 'Ile de France' and the 'Etoile du Nord,' include a section which is through to and from Amsterdam; the remainder, the 'Brabant,' 'Oiseau Bleu,' 'Memling' and 'Rubens,' ply exclusively between Paris Gare du Nord and Brussels. All but one, which makes a couple of additional stops en route through Belgium, link the French and Belgian capitals in under 2½ hours, the fastest, the 6.44 'Memling' out of Paris, taking only 2 hours 21 minutes for an end-to-end average speed of just on 83mph – and that is a city center-to-center

transit time invincible to air competition.

In the late 1960s French Railways patterned an order for more new TEE vehicles on the highly successful Paris–Brussels–Amsterdam design. Among the trains to be endowed with the new stock, from the spring of 1969, was the post-war successor to the 'Cote d'Azur Pullman,' the midday flag train each way between Paris and the Riviera which in the first two post World War II decades had earned worldwide repute to challenge long-venerated European names like the 'Flying Scotsman' or 'Train Bleu.' Named 'Mistral' in 1950 and created a TEE in 1965, this express was not only one of the first in Europe to boast full air-conditioning throughout but also was one of the final few on the mainland continent to include a Pullman in its formation. (The Pullmans employed were specially fitted out to accept air-conditioning.) It was the luxury train on which French Railways lavished all the accelerative benefits obtainable from their first post-war main-line electrification of the main line from Paris to Dijon and Lyons. As early as 1959 the 'Mistral' had become Europe's first post-war express to be timed at an average of 80mph or more, when it was booked to eat up the 195.3 miles from Paris Gare de Lyon to Dijon in only 146 minutes – and that despite the fact that it was one of the heaviest trains on the route.

Its performance today remains pretty impressive. From Nice to Paris is 676.2 miles, but despite speed limitation over a good deal of the initial 137 miles to Marseilles, where the line hugs the beautiful Riviera coastline much of the time, and nine intermediate stops, of which the Marseilles halt involves a reversal, the 'Mistral' covers the whole journey northbound in a minute over nine hours. That represents an overall average of almost exactly 75mph, stops included.

Even if you're taking the 'Mistral' the whole way from Nice to Paris the nine-hour journey is remarkably unexacting. Much of the credit for this is attributable to the partnership of excellently manicured track throughout this vital artery of French Railways and the air suspension and extremely effective sound insulation of the air-conditioned 'Mistral' coaches, which in my recent European travel experience achieve the quietest and silkiest ride of any trains on the present-day Continental mainland (France's own *Grand Confort* vehicles possibly excepted: these we shall review shortly). The armchair seating is faultlessly shaped and substantially adjustable as to angle, and is available in compartment or open saloon, some of the latter accommodation supplementing the restaurant cars for meal service at seats. Tinted windows nicely temper the sun's glare, but should you want relief, the touch of a button by your seat lowers electrically-powered

venetian blinds between the double panes.

It is almost as effortless to walk the train as to move between rooms in your own house. Vestibule doors open automatically as you approach, actuated by electrical contact pads in the floor ahead of them, then slide smoothly closed behind you. Even the external doors to and from the platform are power-operated and open at a clasp of their handgrips, but not unless the train is at a stand or crawling to it at less than about 3mph; a safety override takes care of that. This French TEE stock was Europe's first to embody what has now been made mandatory in long-haul European coaching stock by the International Union of Railways, or UIC: a facility whereby the conductor can close and seal every door in the train from a central control before departure, as on any Métro.

There is not quite as much diversion on a 'Mistral' journey nowadays as there was in the first half of the 1970s. Among the range of vehicle types created for the service was a car roughly two-thirds occupied by a buffet-bar, the other third by a small fancy goods, confectionery and book-magazine shop, a train secretary's office and a unisex hairdressing salon, this last decked out in a very exotic shade of Pompeian red; it was the first time hairdressing had been added to a European train's facilities since the LNER's 'Flying Scotsman' of the 1930s. But it was also, almost certainly, the last of its kind. For a luxury service aimed at the higher strata both of the Riviera's hedonists and the business world concentrated more densely along the Paris–Lyons–Marseilles axis than anywhere else in France, both salon and secretary looked commercially justifiable. Not so, however. The cars still run in the 'Mistral' and the bar and the shop are fully operative, the latter staffed by the train's hostesses; but in the mid-1970s French Railways discarded both train secretary and barber and their premises nowadays are just extra train-staff offices.

The 'Mistral' is the heaviest train in the TEE network – and reportedly the most profitable because of its consistently good loading – between Paris and Marseilles. Over that sector the usual formation is 14 or 15 cars with space for over 500 first-class passengers and grossing over 700 tonnes in train weight. Five or six of these cars, however, go no further than Marseilles, where detachment and attachment consumes little extra time because the train has to reverse there. Each section includes its own kitchen-diner, with a roomy two-and-one seating layout in the saloon.

The diners are no longer conspicuous by their dark blue Wagons-Lits external livery, of course. Nor, for that matter, are the catering cars of any French Railways'

The diner of the French Railways' 'Mistral.'
(Courtesy Cie Internationale des Wagons-
Lits et du Tourisme)

expresses. That betokens the company's
changed role, so far as its railway operations are concerned, since the start of the
1970s. On the one hand, the steady post-
war acceleration of inter-city trains was
cutting transit times to the extent that the
full-scale meal services to which a train
crew could be put during a tour of duty
were being seriously limited; at the same
time, though, inflation was driving wage
and material costs heavenward. The

same cost escalation, on the other hand,
was impelling the railway to exploit the
increasing speed of its trains by getting
more trips weekly from each train-set.
On the shorter inter-city runs that could
easily have a train-set making one journey over a main meal time a restaurant
service would possibly be justified, but
the next in late afternoon and early
evening certainly would not justify it
and a diner would be an intolerable

waste of money. The obvious solution on a great many routes was the self-service cafeteria car, microwave oven-equipped to produce at minimum crew cost and without risk of waste, a choice of entrées from pre-frozen and fabricated dishes so that reasonable meals could be structured for its customers as well as light snacks and, moreover, with the likelihood that its limited staff would be kept revenue-earning one way or another for most of every journey. After successful experiments with one or two converted restaurant cars, the French built a range of brand-new 'Gril-Express' self-service cafeteria cars which nowadays characterize train catering on the greater part of French Railways' internal intercity services.

The capital cost of new train catering vehicles was soaring as forbiddingly as every other overhead. Each successive post-war year's return from train catering was increasingly dwarfed by vehicle renewal costs. So in 1962 the Wagons-Lits company's client railways agreed that they should take over full responsibility for mechanical maintenance and renewal of the vehicles, leaving the Wagons-Lits company purely to provision and staff them. In 1973 the company's exclusive catering agreement with French Railways came to its term and French Railways further decided to end the company's monopoly on their system. Only about 15 percent of French train catering has in fact been passed to other concerns (Rail Service on routes from Paris–Montparnasse, Servair on those from Paris St Lazaire and Service Hôtelière et de la Restauration on the cross-country Turbo-trains operating out of Lyons) Wagon-Lits still rules the Eastern, Northern, South Western and South Eastern Regions of the French network and thus covers all the front-rank trains, including the 'Mistral.' The company still preserves its monopoly on the national railway systems of Italy, Spain, Austria, Belgium, the Netherlands, Portugal and Morocco, yet just over half its total train-meal business is done on French Railways.

The Wagons-Lits company aims at a high standard of French cuisine on the country's TEEs (and on the 'Train Bleu') and prices are similar: in the summer of 1978 the basic bill for a four-course *table d'hôte* lunch or dinner on the 'Mistral,' service included, was Fr65 or nearly £8/$16. For that, to quote the menu on my last 'Mistral' trip, you might be offered a cut of cold fresh salmon as a starter, then a choice of fillet of beef with artichoke hearts or chicken with savory prune stuffing, a cheese tray and finally the traditional Wagons-Lits *bombe glacée* or fresh fruit salad soaked in liqueur. Like DSG, Wagons-Lits maintains comprehensive cellars and you will have the choice, probably, of a score of wines, from an anonymous claret at Fr 11.50 the half-bottle to a Château Pontet Canet at Fr 21.00 for a half, or from a good Rhône or Beaujolais to a full bottle of champagne for Fr 75.00, if you are in the money. Outside the periods of main meal service the diner operates a *'brasserie'* card of dishes, but it is nowhere near as catholic as DSG's *à la carte* menu, with just a solitary hot *plat du jour* (dauntingly priced at Fr 43.00) and for the rest mostly all the changes it is possible to create on the staples of ham and eggs. If none of that appeals, then there is a range of cold dishes continuously available – for instance, cold meat, cold chicken, smoked salmon and *pâté* – as well as sandwiches and other snacks, at slightly less expense comparatively, in the 'Mistral's' bar car.

The 1969 'Mistral'-type coaching stock has since been extended to a number of French-equipped TEEs, among them, as already mentioned, the 'Cisalpin,' normally a nine-car train of these vehicles but occasionally loading up to 12 or even 13 in winter if ski traffic for Sion and Brigue and the nearby Valais Alps is heavy; in that event the six-axle French Railways multi-voltage CC21000 locomotive which customarily works the TEE throughout between Paris and the Swiss frontier at Vallorbe has to give place at Dijon to a pair of four-axle BB225500s for the grind up the 1 in 50 slopes of the route through the Jura mountains. Use of the French locomotive-hauled coaches has enabled the addition of a bar-car to the 'Cisalpin's' attractions; in summer the bar car is detached at Lausanne, but in winter it goes through to Milan, whereas the restaurant, conveyed all the way to Venice in summer, is conversely left at Lausanne.

One of the TEEs to employ 'Mistral' 1969-type was practically a replica of the 'Mistral,' featuring the same individualistic bar cars with secretarial service and hairdressing salon. This French Railways launched in the spring of 1971, persuaded that an early breakfast-time luxury train from Marseilles reaching Paris just in time for the afternoon reopening of business offices, with an early evening return from Paris and arrival in Marseilles

Modern 'Universal'-type sleepers of the German DSG tower above the platform. (Courtesy Deutsche Bundesbahn)

on the stroke of midnight, should have equal appeal to the 'Mistral' itself. Alas, it was a commercial misjudgment. The 'Rhodanien,' as it was titled, did passable business between Paris and Lyons, even as far as Avignon, but there were too many trips on which the expensive, 450 tonnes train was carrying only 20 or 30 passengers between Avignon and Marseilles. The Paris or Marseilles business executive taking the 'Mistral' to the other's city had clearly opted to take at least two days over his affairs and maybe relax over both lunch and dinner on the train: the 'Rhodanien,' on the other hand, seemed to compete with the out-and-home-in-a-day potential of air services. But whereas a Marseilles–Paris air journey, city center to center, usually absorbs no more than three hours, the 100mph 'Rhodanien' was over 6½ hours en route and its comforts were not enough to offset a very early start, an uncomfortably late return home and 13 hours of the day on the move. So, in 1978, the 'Rhodanien' was erased from the TEE tables and degraded to ordinary express status.

All of which reinforces my forebodings, talking of West Germany's ICs and TEEs, that the long-haul European luxury train, however tempting and varied its appointments, becomes steadily more vulnerable to our deplorable anxiety these days to get travel over and done with as quickly as possible. A maximum of three or at most four hours' journey time is becoming – maybe has already become – the planning base of prudent rail passenger service managers. One should add that the 'Rhodanien' was also one of a significant number of their TEEs which the French in recent years have decided draw insufficient business in the national holiday months of July and August to warrant high summer operation. Enforced idleness for two months of every year must turn the balance-sheets of such expensive equipment reddish around the edges, if nothing worse.

Of course, the French have tried harder than anyone in Western Europe to sustain luxury train appeal with ever-advancing speed. Having developed a satisfactory automatic train control and continuous cab signalling system, they were first in the continent to launch 125mph operation in regular daily service. The top-speed stretch was 31.1 miles of the Paris Austerlitz–Toulouse main line between Les Aubrais and Vierzon, near Orleans, and a refurbished first-class-only *rapide*, the 'Capitôle,' was put on to exploit it in the course of evening runs that reeled off the 443 miles between Paris and Toulouse in six hours flat each way. To power the 'Capitôle' the French specially modified and regeared four of its four-axle Class BB9200 locomotives.

The locomotives were repainted a distinctive red to match the train-set, which was distinguished more by technical refinement such as supplementary electro-magnetic track brakes than by any special new comfort. The ordinary seating coaches were the standard of the day in their appointments and devoid of air-conditioning, so that passengers used to be warned by train staff over the public address to shut all windows as the 125mph stretch approached, otherwise the noise and draughts could get insupportable.

It was another matter in the restaurant car, which was fully air-conditioned and one of a desperately-needed new series put in hand by French Railways after they had relieved Wagons-Lits of the equipment investment problem in 1962. The only excitement of top speed in its admirably sealed quietness was to watch the red band of a 'magic-eye' speedometer on each end wall of the saloon forge up to and hold 125mph. This was just as well for on my first 1967 summer's eve 'Capitôle' trip, the Wagons-Lits *cuisine* was an absorption in itself – a delicately-flavored *potage* with *croûtons*, cold lobster Cardinale, a well-varied selection of cold meat with an interesting salad (it was a sultry night) and a superb orange *soufflé*. Remarkably, the food was coolly fresh and perfectly presented even though we were on the third dinner sitting; the car had had to contrive to deal with more than 100 customers since leaving Toulouse.

The 'Capitôle' was a resounding commercial success almost at once, demonstrating the critical market importance of speed as well as luxury. A year later frequency was doubled to a morning and evening frequency each way. In more recent years the problem has been to maintain its overall schedule in face of the greatly increased loads which traffic has made imperative. They tax even today's mighty, six-axle 8000hp CC6500 class locomotives in the difficult terrain south of Limoges, where the Toulouse route winds and climbs to a high point of 1456ft above sea level as it cuts through the successive hill ranges lining the rivers sweeping down from the Massif Central to the Atlantic.

Today's 'Capitôle' is formed of French Railways' latest and quite possibly last generation of luxury day travel coaches, the *'Grand Confort'* series. Apart from its exterior livery – gray contrasted with horizontal bands of red and slender lines of orange – a *'Grand Confort'* is markedly different from a 1969 'Mistral'-type vehicle. You may not notice that it is slightly shorter but clearly perceptible is the marked outward taper of the body-side from its high domed roof almost to floor level. The reason for this is that the *'Grand Confort'* design was planned for easy adaptability to 'pendular suspen-

sion,' or automatic body-tilting on the move.

Few luxury train routes are free of speed-restricting curvature almost the whole way. Once a railway operator has pushed speed to the practical limit on the straight sections he can only gouge more time out of the end-to-end transit time by realigning some curves, or else by finding a way of taking those curves faster without distressing his passengers. Safety is not the problem; the speed limit set on a curve is always well below the risk area. It is fixed at the level beyond which passengers will be subjected to discomfort from centrifugal force effect. That level can be raised by increasing the superelevation of the curve but the degree of superelevation, or cant, must be function of the average speed of *all* trains using the curve, otherwise you will have the slowest exerting excessive wear on track and vehicles by bearing too heavily on the curve's inner rail. The only solution is to create an artificial extra superelevation for the trains of which acceleration is an urgent need, by building into their coaches a device that automatically senses the entry into and all the parameters of a curve, then smoothly imparts to the coach bodies as much exaggerated inward tilt as is necessary to compensate for the deficiency of cant in relation to the speed at which the train is moving. Thus a tilt-fitted *'Grand Confort'* coach is capable of negotiating at 125mph, in perfect passenger comfort, a curve which would restrict orthodox vehicles to 90mph. Having perfected an automatic body-tilt device, however, like most other major systems French Railways have balked at the considerable expense – and not inconsiderable extra train weight – involved in fitting it.

As yet, therefore, no *'Grand Confort'* coaches are tilt-fitted. But on straight or modestly curved track their riding is absolutely silent and serene at 125mph, as you can verify any day on the two fastest TEEs in Europe, the 'Aquitaine' and the 'Etendard.' Fortified by the 'Capitôle's' almost instantaneous success, the French prepared for considerably more extended 125mph operation on what is possibly the best-aligned route in all Europe for consistent speed, the 360-mile line from Paris to Bordeaux. So free of curves and junctions is its passage through the farmlands of Central France kept by its original builders that nearly two-thirds of the distance are practical 125mph ground. So, armed with its new 8000hp six-axle electrics and *'Grand Confort'* vehicles, the French bestowed on this route in the spring of 1971 the fastest long-haul train Europe had yet seen, the 'Aquitaine,' and later paired it with the 'Etendard' to provide a high-speed morning and evening service

This 1973 shot of the 'Train Bleu' headed by French Railways No BB25237 along the Côte D'Azur interestingly compares the size of two generations of Wagons-Lits equipment. The first vehicle is a P class duplex sleeper, then come three latter-day cars of either 'universal,' T2 or T2S type, but in the center of the consist – unusually – are two cars of inter-war style.   (Courtesy Yves Broncard)

each way. In one direction each of them makes intermediate stops, but the outward-bound 'Aquitaine' and return 'Etendard' cover the distance non-stop in 3 hours 50 minutes for an end-to-end average speed of close on 94mph start to stop. Besides these two trains and the 'Capitôle,' other French-equipped TEEs to employ *Grand Confort* stock at the time of writing are the 1971-introduced 'Kleber' and 'Stanislas' between Paris, Nancy and Strasbourg.

Influential in the French decision not to fit the *Grand Confort* stock with automatic body-tilting is the difficulty of timing an ultra-high-speed train through the ruck of conventional traffic without prodigal sacrifice of track capacity. In other words, if you devise a train that can negotiate a long, sinuous stretch of main line 25 percent faster than anything else, you will have to leave a considerable vacuum in your timetable both ahead of and behind it. Better, if there is sufficient inter-city passenger traffic volume (or environmental logic) to justify the investment, to build a brand-new railway, laid out *ab initio* for extreme pace.

And that is what the French are already doing between Paris and Lyons, and contemplate doing thereafter over at least part of the routes from Paris to Bordeaux and Toulouse. By the mid-1980s 160mph trains will be humming from Paris to Lyons over the new TGV Sud-Est at an end-to-end average speed of over 130mph. Technologically it will be a *tour de force*. But with uniform train-sets, seating shoehorned into low-slung, shallow-windowed coach bodies and catering reduced to galley service of airline-style tray meals it will degrade the express train to something of a long-haul Metro. No one with a right-minded sense of values who has ridden the 'Mistral' or the 'Cisalpin' between Paris and Lyons can accept that as pure gain.

'Trans Euro Night'
You might expect sleeping-car business to decline as rail speed technology progressively shrinks the day-travel distance between cities. It does not follow,

however. Even over such a comparatively short haul as that between London and Liverpool or Manchester British Rail were confounded when, having as they thought logically planned to discard sleeper service following electrification's dramatic speedup and intensification of the day service, the overnight demand persisted and enforced hurried reinstitution of the sleeper trains.

On the Continental mainland another factor sustaining a high level of domestic and international sleeping-car service has been the emergence since the 1960s of a substantial second-class market for good-quality overnight accommodation. That could only be satisfied, of course, by new construction, but sleeper-berth revenue was falling further and further short of contributing sufficient margin to meet the cost of new, fully-equipped sleeping cars.

In the summer of 1971, therefore, nine of Western Europe's national railway systems – the French, West German, Swiss, Italian, Belgian, Dutch, Austrian, Danish and Luxemburg – agreed to form a pool to take over the commercial and financial responsibility for both DSG and Wagons-Lits sleeper services operating across the frontier of two or more of the networks involved. Existing Wagons-Lits and DSG sleepers were leased to the pool organization (though the DSG cars were effectively owned by the German Federal Railway, as DSG's parent), but new construction would be wholly financed by the pool railways. Wagons-Lits and DSG would continue to staff the cars and undertake anything which could be broadly termed housekeeping within them. The two companies concluded a similar deal with French and Italian Railways over the latter's purely domestic sleeper workings, so that the 1971 negotiations finally left Wagons-Lits to fulfill all its historic obligations only for some of its sleepers running within Austria or from Austria into Eastern Europe. Disposition, routing and pricing of sleepers were now entirely the province of the pool members, who issued and pocketed the revenue from

the berth tickets. Remuneration of DSG and Wagons-Lits for their staffing and housekeeping within the cars was separately ordered.

With the TEE brandname usefully implanted in the European traveller's conscience the pool partners searched for a matching international sleeper tag. They came up with 'TEN,' a logo which could be expanded into an equivalent phrase in at least four different tongues – 'Trans Euro Nuit,' 'Trans Euro Notte,' 'Trans Euro Nacht' and 'Trans Euro Night.' Although the TEN logo has been gradually applied in standard bold italicized capitals to the lower body panels of most sleepers in the pool the participants have yet to accept a common livery; dark blue has been retained in ex-Wagons-Lits territory as the basic body color, though of late the delicate gold lining has been abandoned for bold white and the blue has taken on a purplish tinge, while DSG, after a spell in the early 1970s when a number of its cars were painted maroon above the waistline and light gray below in a tentative German Federal re-styling of all but its TEE vehicles, sticks to its traditional overall maroon.

Today's massive, high-domed-roof sleepers of the TEN network are easily the most awesome vehicles on European rails. They are much the heaviest, grossing nearly 55 tonnes each with full tanks of water, and also the most costly; the bill for a new, fully equipped sleeping car in the late 1970s will probably run out on the wrong side of half a million pounds sterling. But then the detail of their equipment and their comfort has been enhanced almost out of recognition compared with the largely pre-war fleet that supported most of the network until the 1960s. They are a revelation, I continually find, to Britons whose night journeys have previously been confined to the unhappily ageing, non-air-conditioned sleepers of more restricted dimensions (because of the more cramped British loading gauge) of their own system, or to the older Wagons-Lits cars which tend to be assigned to the car-

One of British Rail's self-contained 'Blue Pullman' diesel train-sets on the Western Region 'Birmingham Pullman' service. (Courtesy M Mensing)

sleeper trains from the French Channel ports to Southern France.

The first new sleepers in post-war Europe to be built to a distinctively new design were forty (Type WLAS 20) which the DSG acquired in 1950 with a unique arrangement of single-berth compartments on each side of a zig-zagging central corridor. These were the only European cars of modern times in which the beds were arranged longitudinally, in line with the track, not laterally. Half of them were originally operated by DSG for the American Army in West Germany, but as the USA ran down its military establishment these were sold to the Yugoslav Railways in 1967. The remaining score went into the TEN pool, but both Yugoslavs and Germans appear nowadays to maintain any surviving vehicles of this type purely as reserves.

Still in scheduled TEE use (and operating in Spain, to which 20 of the 1955–6 build of 80 were transferred as newer designs appeared) is a type for which I still have great affection, the stainless steel-bodied P with which the Wagons-Lits company adapted the American duplex roomette concept to the European mainland loading gauge. They are not air-conditioned, but the night ride in one of their upper compartments is as smooth and quiet as in any later breed of air-conditioned car. The duplex layout enabled Wagons-Lits to dovetail 20 single-berth compartments into each car and by some very ingenious design to leave the occupants very reasonable room for maneuver. In the upper-level berths the beds are too close to the roof to serve as daytime seats since they are laid along the ceiling of the interlocking lower-level compartment, and in each of the higher compartments you get a separate chair by the window. Maybe some find these high-perched little 'bedsits' somewhat claustrophobic, but to me there is a singular sense of privacy in the extra height above the rails, and I love the regal view of the landscape obtained from the throne-like elevation of the window chair. That a P berth is cheaper than a single in an orthodox first-class sleeper doubles the pleasure. Moreover, if my wife is with me a 'U' pair of upper compartments can be merged by having the conductor open a connecting door; that creates a modest little suite which would always be my preference to a single compartment with berths one above the other.

The *ne plus ultra* in overnight luxury if you are travelling *en famille* is to indulge in occupation of two adjoining compartments in one of the majestic, so-called 'Universal'-type air-conditioned sleepers which both DSG and Wagons-Lits introduced towards the end of the 1950s. The 'universal' tag derives from the *raison d'être* of the design: a sleeper in which each compartment would be adaptable to occupation by one, two or three passengers – ie, it would have room height sufficient for central and upper berths to be lowered from the compartment wall above a bed made up on the daytime seat – with the obvious economic aim of being able easily to adjust the

accommodation of such very costly vehicles to the categories of traffic offered from journey to journey. To allow room for three people to maneuver, each compartment clearly had to be made quite spacious; the coach bodies were some 12ft longer than those of the first post-war Wagons-Lits sleepers, yet the number of compartments was the same, 11 (in later series this was increased by one). The finish and fittings of both DSG and Wagons-Lits cars were – and still are – superb, with discreet fluorescent lighting and push-button controls wherever you might need them – at each berth level, inset in the washbasin mirror, and so on. The DSG cars have the bonus of a shower compartment, for use of which the DSG attendant holds a stock of bath towels, and an alarm buzzer and light for early morning calls by each berth; these are operated by the conductor from a control panel in his compartment.

High up my list of unforgettable journeys is one made with my wife from Paris to Venice and back when – courtesy of a benevolent Wagons-Lits company, which at the time had not yet surrendered full charge of the cars – we luxuriated in exclusive occupation of two adjoining compartments in a 'universal' sleeper. That was a trip when one could justifiably fall back on the 'hotel on wheels' cliché to epitomize the experience. Mind you, I would pause at footing the bill for such hedonism out of my own wallet. At the time of writing the supplement alone for that return journey would set me back £95.20/$200 per person on top of a not inconsiderable basic first-class ticket!

In terms of its original objective the 'universal' concept had one drawback: the comparatively small proportion of tourist-class sleeper berth customers who travel in trios. Married couples booking at the three-berth rate, therefore, were frequently faced with the Hobson's choice of separation overnight, so as to ensure all-male and all-female occupation of compartments, or of paying more for second-class, two-berth privacy. The problem was overcome, first by enlarging the duplex configuration of the P design into the 18-compartment T2 design, later by devising the 17-compartment T2S in an orthodox layout. The designers managed adroitly to find room for two berths in the lower compartments of the T2, so that both types of vehicle can accommodate two second-class occupants in every compartment. The lower compartments in the T2 and every compartment in a T2S are on first-class offer as a single berth, at approximately two-thirds of the supplementary rate for a single berth in a 'universal' car to compensate for their more restricted dimensions. In the T2S the compartment really is rather cramped and

the cars are unpopular in Germany.

The age of the exclusive, all first-class night sleeper, sadly, has passed. Even the Paris–Nice–Ventimiglia 'Train Bleu' is now a mix of 'universal' MU type and T2 cars, plus a P, and a multi-class train. In recent years the 'Train Bleu' has also been robbed of the lounge-bar car it conveyed in addition to the restaurant car which serves dinner in the southbound direction between Paris and Dijon, where it is detached (strangely there is no diner on the return, even though the 'Train Bleu' leaves Nice at precisely the same time as it departs from Paris outward bound, 20.45). Never mind, the 'Train Bleu' still lays on a dinner menu clearly aimed at the silkier pockets among its clientele. The *à la carte* bill of fare is the only one I know in Europe which leads off with caviar at Fr 40.00 or *medaillon d'or du Périgord* at Fr 32.00. Follow caviar with a *faux-filet garni*, a green salad, *fromage blanc*, and fruit salad, accompany it all with a half-bottle of white Burgundy and a half-bottle of good claret, then wind up with coffee and a Cognac, and the cost will be approximately $30/£15.

In the 1960s the finishing touch to a relaxed night in one of the stately new air-conditioned sleepers was still on most trips the tinkling bell of the restaurant car conductor, promenading the length of the train to announce breakfast service in the diner. You can still get breakfast and some, no doubt, count it progress to have it served in their berth. That is the spreading trend, as on more and more services the railways cut the cost of turning out a restaurant car and crew for early morning attachment to overnight trains and have each sleeping-car conductor serve plastic-tray breakfasts from his pantry. The coffee is freshly made and the Germans rise to an offer of boiled eggs. But orange juice and coffee out of Wagons-Lits' plastic cups and the rather tasteless rolls of their berth-served *petits déjeuners* are a philistine substitute for the glassware, solid breakfast cups and hot croissants in a restaurant car redolent of rich coffee and baking aromas which used to be the happily-anticipated pendant to most nights in the sleeper. A good many overnight trains have been deprived of their evening restaurant service, too, but on these Wagons-Lits have expanded the sleeper conductors' wares to include cold tray meals. The latter include a plate of cold meat, cheese, roll and dessert for Fr 25.60, a plate of assorted smoked fish, bread and butter for Fr 18.10 and *terrine* and a roll for Fr 5.90. DSG offers something similar.

Apart from immeasurably enhancing the comfort of overnight travel, Western European railways have substantially accelerated many of the longer-distance

left: A first-class compartment of a DSG 'universal'-type sleeper.   (Courtesy DSG)

right: The 'Trianon Bar' of the post-war 'Golden Arrow.'   (Courtesy British Rail)

bottom: The post-war 'Golden Arrow' headed by a 'Battle of Britain' class Pacific. (Courtesy Author's collection)

below: Two berths in an upper compartment of a duplex T2-type sleeper. (Courtesy Cie Internationale des Wagons-Lits et du Tourisme)

overnight trains to keep them highly competitive in the air age. Outstanding under this head is the 'Palatino,' which departs from Paris Gare de Lyon at 18.53 and is into Rome Termini no later than 9.20 next morning; a Florence section reaches Florence by 8.55. Departure from Florence and Rome in the reverse direction is slightly later in the evening, bringing the 'Palatino' into Paris at a minute past 10.00. The 'Palatino,' incidentally, is one of the crack overnight services which still observes the decencies by conveying a French restaurant car for dinner service from Paris to Chambéry, then attaching an Italian diner during its 4.32–4.35 call at Genoa for breakfast service en route to Rome.

Similar arrangements, happily, apply to another notable overnight train developed in recent years, the 'Puerta del Sol,' which lifts its clients out of Paris Austerlitz at 18.04 nightly and decants them in Madrid as early as 9.00 next day. Instrumental in achieving this striking contraction of transit times between the French and Spanish capitals was the invention of gantry devices by which the sleeping-cars are smoothly jacked up at Hendaye, the Franco-Spanish border station, so that their 4ft 8½in-gauge bogies can be exchanged for the wider-gauge bogies essential throughout the Iberian main lines (the same device serves through couchette coaches between Paris and Portugal on the 'Sud Express'). Passengers are left undisturbed in their berths during this nocturnal changeover.

Britain's Last Luxury Trains

After half a decade of war, rationing and drab austerity, Britons in 1946 were apt to salivate at anything which made eventual return to the remembered life of the 1930s less of a forlorn dream. A day to make the mouth water more than a little that year, then, was 15 April. For there, steaming out of London's Victoria in the aristrocratic umber and cream not glimpsed in public rail service since 1939, was the 'Golden Arrow.'

It was not quite the 'Arrow' of yore, not yet. On the plus side there was up front a new look in steam power, one of Bulleid's air-smoothed 'Merchant Navy' Pacifics; one of the train's cars had been converted into the 'Trianon Bar' and the whole was equipped with a public address system. There were a few years yet to endure, however, before the bonds of rationing were relaxed enough for the Pullman menu to regain all its old *à la carte* facilities – the smoked salmon, the Grilled Dover Sole *Maître d'Hôtel*, the toasted teatime crumpets, the prestigious option of Indian, Chinese or Russian tea, the wine list proudly headed by Mumm Cordon Rouge champagne (but tarnishing the image slightly by being non-vintage) and the tray of 'Cigars specially selected for the Pullman Car Company Limited. Within six years, however, the 'Arrow' was re-equipped with the brand-new train, including a new 'Pegasus Bar,' that had actually been ordered in 1938 but was then deferred by the war.

The early years of the nationalized British Railways, in fact, were high-season for Pullman services, with the gradual introduction of several new all-Pullman trains. The detail of most of them need not detain us, for they employed pre-war cars and little distinguished their amenities from those of the pre-war trains already described. One should, nevertheless, accord a mention to the 'Devon Belle' which the Southern Railway, oblivious to the Great Western's 'Torquay Pullman' fiasco of 1929, launched in 1947 between London Waterloo and, in seperate sections, Plymouth and the North Devon resort of Ilfracombe. For this service two 1918 Pullmans were converted into armchair observation cars with bars, but despite that inducement the train went the same commercial way as the 'Torquay Pullman.' Its death was a much more lingering affair, coming in 1954, whereupon all but the observation cars were diverted to a new – and this time successful – Western operation, the business market-oriented 'South Wales Pullman' between London and the heavy industrial area of the Principality.

Impressed with the European mainland's new-born TEE services and fastening on luxury as their best hope of tackling strengthening domestic air service bids for the business travel market, since speed was still checked by the massive job of making good wartime neglect, British Rail management decided in the late 1950s to go for a Pullman version of the streamlined TEE diesel multiple-unit train-set. It was a quite needlessly ill-judged decision. Internally the 'Blue Pullmans,' popularly so-called because of their new blue-and-white livery, were a delight both in design and comfort, not least because they were the first British train-sets to be fully air-conditioned. The trouble was that their deplorable riding took not just the edge but every bit of gloss off the rest of environmental advance. All the known problems of the day in obtaining a good ride from self-powered train-sets had been exacerbated by the mismatch of a justly reputed Continental European bogie design with shorter and lighter British coach bodies. And pointlessly: there were no quick turnrounds demanding double-ended reversibility.

The first 'Blue Pullman' sets took up 'Midland Pullman' service over the then through route from London St Pancras to Manchester in 1960, but when the principal trunk route from London to the northwest had been electrified in 1966, these units joined the other 'Blue Pullman' sets on the Western, which since 1960 had been deploying them on services from London Paddington to Birmingham, Bristol and South Wales. Exhaustive and prolonged research modified some of the 'Blue Pullman's' worst riding excesses in the course of time, but never brought them up to the standards

of BR's Mk II standard coaches.

In the 1960s new locomotive-hauled Pullmans were built both for the services over the one-time LNER network and to originate brand-new air-conditioned all-Pullman trains – and extremely fast, too – over the electrified main line from London Euston to Liverpool and Manchester. But although there was a brief period in this decade when British Rail policy tended to favor perpetuation of Pullmans and their extension to most front-rank inter-city trains as a de luxe option over and above ordinary first-class, at the same time the last rites were being practised for the British luxury train. Economic pressures for maximum weekly mileage from train-sets, in the context of Britain's comparatively short inter-city distances, were against main-tenance of special-purpose train-sets which were sensibly run at times only when there was a market for their pre-mium-priced comfort. Both marketing and operational considerations were dic-tating the evolution of standard time-tables, with regular-interval departures of standard train-sets at as near as pos-sible standard point-to-point speeds. Some Pullman services, too, could not

extreme left and left: Exterior and interior of the Pullman observation car built for Britain's short-lived 'Devon Belle.' (Courtesy British Rail)

extreme left below: Corner of a first-class saloon in the new series of locomotive-hauled Pullmans built for the former LNER services by Metro-Cammell in the 1960s. (Courtesy Author's collection)

below center: First-class saloon of a British Rail 'Blue Pullman' train-set. (Courtesy British Rail)

bottom: In 1967 British Rail rebuilt half of the bodies of three standard compartment coaches with ten-seater lounges modelled on the Italian 'Settebello.' Lounge accommodation was to be an extra-fare feature of top inter-city expresses but the idea was not pursued beyond the prototypes. (Courtesy British Rail)

left: The diesel-hauled, blue-and-white 'Midland Pullmans' introduced in 1960 between London St Pancreas and Manchester were known as the 'Blue Pullmans.' (Courtesy British Rail)

hold their premium-fare market against rival modes: that was the downfall, for instance, of the 'Golden Arrow,' the last Pullman rump of which disappeared in 1972.

So it is that the advent of British Rail's intensive 125mph 'Inter-City 125' services has done to death first the Western 'Blue Pullmans' and then, in 1978, the last survivors of the range of Pullman trains which developed from the LNER's 1920s enterprise. At the time of writing the last relic of Britain's specialized luxury trains is the electric 'Manchester Pullman.' But that is sure not to survive the hoped-for takeover of the electrified main lines from London Euston by 125mph, tilt-bodied Advanced Passenger Trains in the 1980s. If, of course, it lasts even that long.

CHAPTER 9
SOUTH AFRICA'S 'BLUE TRAIN'

The sort of rugged terrain which persuaded
the builders of South African Railways to
go for a narrow 3ft 6in gauge. Here, a class
15F 4-8-2 heads the Cape Town–Durban
'Orange Express' in Tulbagh Kloof, *circa*
1953. (Courtesy South African Railways)

It is a pedestrian train by the standards of the Japanese Shinkansen, Britain's 'Inter-City 125' or the majority of the Western European mainland's TEEs. The almost exactly 1000 miles of travel from Pretoria to Cape Town absorb 26 hours for an overall average of 38.5mph, nine calls en route included. But then you do not expect high speed on the 3ft 6in gauge which rules in South Africa, still less over a 3ft 6in-gauge line which climbs from near sea level at the Cape to 5735ft altitude at Johannesburg, sometimes as steeply as 1 in 40. Perhaps you would not expect, either, to find such a railway operating what is arguably the most luxurious train in the modern world – some might say the only true luxury train we have left – but that is what South African Railways have achieved, almost miraculously considering the limitations of track width, in their 'Blue Train.' Given its quality and the magnificent scenery it traverses, who worries about speed?

The tradition of a luxury service between Cape Town and Pretoria dates back to the 1903 creation of a train to connect with the Union-Castle liners from England. Titled 'United Limited' after formation of the Union of South Africa in 1910 and the consequent establishment by mergers of South African Railways, this express always vied with the most lavishly appointed and staffed on the world's standard gauge. In the 1930s its diner included a bar, there was an observation lounge at the rear, the roomy sleepers had shower-baths and there was continuous valet service on board.

The 'Union Limited' was transmuted into the 'Blue Train' in 1946. Striking new fully air-conditioned all-steel train-sets had been ordered from British builders Metropolitan-Cammell in the summer of 1937, but their delivery coincided with war's outbreak in 1939 and after a period of unsung service they were cocooned in 1942. Officially inaugurated four years later, these 'Blue Trains' were exciting enough, but even they have been quite outclassed by second-generation 'Blue Train' equipment, built in South Africa by Union Carriage & Wagon, which took over the operation in September 1972.

For a start, although the fare scale is a simpler choice from four categories, the 'Blue Train' offers eight different types of accommodation. The supreme luxury coach in the 16-car formation is designed for occupation by no more than six passengers. Its showpiece, nowadays without parallel on rails except in the few surviving royal trains, is a three-room suite for two which is of near-cruise-ship spaciousness and certainly of that standard in its furnishing. The fixed twin beds in the bedroom have a proper bedside table and bedhead reading lamps, and across the room are a wardrobe and a neat, mirrored dressing table. The adjoining lounge, with two free-standing armchairs and a settee, includes a drinks refrigerator and glass cabinet among its fittings. And beyond that is a full-scale private bathroom, with a generously-sized bath as well as another capacious wardrobe. Each of the other two sections in this de luxe coach is blessed with fully-equipped bathrooms of the same kind: one is a bed-sitting room with space for two or three occupants, the other a coupé for single occupation. Even in the two so-called 'Demi-luxe' cars each room has its own private shower and toilet; and here again the designed payload is only seven passengers per vehicle. One of the three rooms in each car is a single, the other two arranged for use by two or three occupants with ample floor space which can accommodate a loose table and two armchairs to complement the bench settee into which the lower berth converts. In category A accommodation, less roomy than that of the top two grades, you have to make do with a common-user shower at one end of the car; at the bottom of the scale, category B, you have to be content with the washbasin in your berth. Single-berth compartments are available in both the lower-priced categories, however, as well as rooms for two or three.

Whatever level of comfort your wallet will run to – at the time of writing a Cape Town–Pretoria single will set you back around £125/$250 in a de luxe suite as against £80/$160 in Category B, inclusive of meals – you will have equal benefit from a host of the 'Blue Train's' superb amenities. An old-style prodigality of train-board service, for instance. To minister to a capacity payload of 107 passengers the 'Blue Train' deploys a staff of 26 including its locomotive crews and technical equipment supervisors. A touch of a button on the control panel in every compartment, whatever its price-tag, brings a steward who will ferry to your compartment any drinks or snacks you might like from diner or bar: he has inter-train phone communication with both from his quarters. He is at your disposal, too, for old-fashioned valet service: put your shoes in an appointed locker by your berth door at night and they will be quietly removed, cleaned and returned to you shining by morning. If the sun bothers you, another knob on your compartment control panel easily adjusts power-operated venetian blinds between the tinted panes of the double-glazed window. There is a control, too, by which you can vary the air-conditioning temperature of the compartment to your own taste. Every compartment has

A first-class compartment (above) and the observation car lounge (right) of the pre-World War II 'Union Limited.' (Courtesy South African Railways)

South African's luxurious 'Blue Train' and the remarkable spaciousness of the bedroom in its de luxe suite. (Courtesy South African Railways)

ice-cold drinking water on tap from a separate third faucet at the washbasin. And every compartment also has its own push-button radio with a choice of three programs: Radio South Africa, the national system; Springbok, the commercial channel; or taped music. If you are not a gregarious type, payment of a modest surcharge will even buy full meal service in your compartment. Finally, every room is supplied with a guidebook – bi-lingual in Afrikaans and English, as you might expect – to the train's facilities and the highpoints of its route. I have always admired the Austrian and German gatefold *Zugbegleiter* leaflets they lay on every seat of their principal trains, helpfully setting out not only the schedule of the train concerned but also the times and destinations of connecting services at every stop on the way. The *Zugbegleiter*, however, is as a broadsheet to the *New York Times* set against the handsome, cloth-covered and spiralbound 40-page 'Blue Train' companion, splendidly illustrated in full color at every opening.

With all this pampering there is little inducement to leave your compartment the whole way. So far as the South Africans themselves are concerned, in fact, one notices significantly less movement up and down the 'Blue Train's' corridors than on a European *train de luxe*. But there is steady traffic to and from the beautiful lounge car, with its stool-fronted bar at one end and saloon of easy armchairs and occasional tables at the other.

Making your way to the lounge, you are at once impressed that the sound insulation and air-conditioning is as impeccable in the corridors as within your room. Riding on the vehicle's air-cushion bogies, too, is immaculate – a not inconsiderable accomplishment even though speed is unlikely to exceed 65–70mph, given the narrow gauge and the curvature of the route.

The very first step into the 'Blue Train's' diner will have grayer-haired American or European visitors sighing for their Pullmans of yore. But that first reaction to the original decor and the gleaming ware of laden tables each crowned with a bowl of Cape fruit is likely to intensify to searing nostalgia once they are seated and take the measure of 'Blue Train' diner service, menus and cuisine.

To begin at the beginning, consider the breakfast menu for a typical spring day in 1978. After the usual starters, there are not many other diners on the world's rails these days where you are offered a choice of poached haddock, sautéed kidneys, bacon, sausages and eggs to any fashion you may wish. Lunch that day opened with a tropical fruit cocktail, continued with an option of Cape salmon or lobster, then fillet of beef or roast leg

The present-day 'Blue Train,' hauled by a trio of electric locomotives. (Courtesy South African Railways)

of mutton and culminated in Diplomat Pudding, cheese, fresh fruit and coffee. The evening's dinner card led off with a grapefruit cocktail and cream soup, then proposed a fried sole with sauce tartare, lamb cutlet with Sauce Réforme, asparagus with mayonnaise, roast stuffed turkey and salad or beef sirloin and spring vegetables, Bavarian chocolate cream pudding, pear melba, cheese, fresh fruit and coffee. And to complement the main meals, of course, the knowing traveller would pick some of the train cellar's admirable Cape wines ('très honnête,' I have heard one discriminating Frenchman acknowledge them).

Alcohol apart, none of this prodigious bill of fare adds so much as a coin to what you have already paid to ride the 'Blue Train,' since South African Railways package all main meals into the 'Blue Train' basic fare. Would that many other railways copied this, to my mind, eminently sensible practice: from the railway catering manager's angle it makes economic provisioning easier, and from the passenger's it usefully finalizes the journey budget as soon as the ticket is bought. You will have deduced already that the full sleeping berth charge is also incorporated in the rounded 'Blue Train' prices.

It is not so long since the 'Blue Train' was steam-hauled over part of its journey. A substantial mid-section of the route, between Beaufort West and Kimberley, is not yet electrified and until as recently as 1972 this was steam territory for the 'Blue Train.' That was deemed an intolerable anachronism for the second generation equipment, however, and over this stretch it is now powered by specially blue-liveried diesel locomotives.

The British-built luxury train-sets on 'Blue Train' service between 1946 and 1972, now repainted green externally, today cover South Africa's other de luxe service, the Durban–Johannesburg 'Drakensberg.' The range of 'Drakensberg' accommodation and amenities is consequently on a par with that of the 'Blue Train,' except that the decor is of an earlier period. Wrote one American traveller, stepping into its diner for the first time on a 1977 visit to South Africa:

'What I saw was an incarnation of my dreams of what a dining car in the great age of rail travel must have been. Soft incandescent lighting glimmered off dark wood panelling. In the center of the car, on a service buffet, stood an astounding bouquet of fresh flowers – lavish in size, color and variety. Tablecloths and napkins were a satiny ecru. . . . Pedestalled silver bowls teemed with fresh fruit on each table for four. All tables, large or small, were filled to overflowing with a great variety of flatware and hollow ware: silver seemingly sufficient for two or three meals. . . . Everything was served from silver: tureen, platter or pot.'

One curious custom distinguishes the 'Drakensberg' from the 'Blue Train.' The 'Blue Train' is in fact unique among South African trains in supplying full bedding within the inclusive price of its tickets. On every other express, including the 'Drakensberg,' the passenger has to rent mattress, sheets and blankets separately – an unfathomable irritation to the European visitor, accustomed always to be supplied with full bedding in his sleeper compartment, even though the latter is also a convertible day-night room like those on South African trains.

At the exceptional levels of staffing and equipment refinement in relation to payload I have outlined, you might doubt that the 'Blue Train' is an economic proposition. Moreover, its abundant staff is all-white, a conspicuous contrast to the workforces of even top-grade hotels on the ground. Doubt is magnified by the fact that from April right through to November the 'Blue Train' runs just once weekly each way. For the rest of the year it functions only twice weekly, except for a peak season from early December to late January when operation is intensified to three times weekly. So much grounded time every year for such capital-intensive equipment would have some European rail finance directors gulping tranquillizers by the fistful.

Skepticism is justified: the 'Blue Train' is not viable. Since South African Railways these days sound no less cost-conscious than most, is the 'Blue Train's' future then at risk? Happily not, it seems. National prestige and the country's tourist trade count for more than the red ink of the 'Blue Train's' balance-sheet. Such a handsome train, built in South Africa, is a rolling advertisement for domestic industry. And the panorama from its windows is a never-ending tourist trade commercial. No need to worry that even a first-class fare on the state-owned domestic air service between Cape Town and Johannesburg costs about 10 percent less than the cheapest Category B 'Blue Train' ticket, and that the flight takes two hours as against the train's 23½ hours. No tourist comes to South Africa for just a craned-neck, bird's-eye glimpse of the Veld, the mountains and their wild life. The 'Blue Train,' thank heavens, is one above all in which scarcely anyone travels just to arrive.

Scenes inside the modern 'Blue Train': room service in the luxury three-room suite (top left); a standard single-berth coupé (note the switch panel for radio, waiter service, etc at the bottom of the window) (top right);cocktails in the lounge bar (center left); dinner in the diner (center right); a train crewman removes shoes for cleaning from the corridor side of a compartment's locker (bottom right). Other South African expresses have attractive amenities too as witnessed by the lounge bar in the 'Drakensberg' (bottom left). (Courtesy South African Railways)

CHAPTER 10
AUSTRALIA'S GREAT TRANSCONTINENTAL

Australia's transcontinental, the 'Indian-Pacific,' eastbound near Port Pirie after its crossing of the desert from Western Australia. (Courtesy Australian National Railways)

Travel Australia's 'Indian-Pacific' and you will ride the newest transcontinental route in the world. It was not finished until 1969. Until then it was impossible to make a rail journey from New South Wales to Western Australia without change of trains because of the gauge-breaks inherited from the short-sighted State administrations of the 19th century. While New South Wales accepted the standard 4ft 8½in gauge. Victoria and South Australia preferred the Irish 5ft 3in width. and Queensland and Western Australia went for the narrow 3ft 6in gauge. as the most economic medium for the substantial mileage they needed to open up their far-flung terrains.

There was no rail at all between Western Australia and the east until this century. when the 1901 federation of the six states into a commonwealth prompted an attack on one of the most formidable construction jobs in all rail history. It was not a case of engineering complexity. but of logistics. Practically all the 1051-mile standard-gauge line from Port Augusta in South Australia. to Kalgoorlie in Western Australia had to be laid through desperately arid. totally uninhabited country totally devoid of natural running water. and where ambient temperatures ranged from sub-zero in winter to over 120°F/50°C in summer. At the center of the route stretched 450 miles of the absolutely featureless Nullarbor Plain – 'the plain of no trees.' thus named with full justification – where the engineers put down the longest stretch of continuous straight track in the world: 297 miles (cynical historians claim it might have been longer still had the line's surveyors not been paid an enhanced rate for plotting curvature). Begun in the autumn of 1912 under the aegis of the 1901-formed Commonwealth Railways. the enterprise was completed after unimaginable privations for the workforce in October 1917.

It was a great step for Australian mankind. but sailing from Europe to Australia in pre-jumbo-jet years and disembarking in Western Australia at Fremantle near Perth. the rail journey on to the eastern states was still laborious. In the 1950s you would have taken the 3ft 6in-gauge 'Westland' of the Western Australian Government Railways over the Darling mountains from Perth to Kalgoorlie. a 15-hour journey in no mean train. for despite the narrow gauge its stainless steel sleepers were built out to a width of nearly 9ft and housed shower-baths. At Kalgoorlie you would change to Commonwealth Railways' 'Trans-Australian Express' for the extraordinary run through 1000 miles of desert to Port Pirie. In the 1950s that train would still be steam-hauled by 4-6-0s dwarfed by tenders nearly half as heavy again as the engines themselves because of the shortage of fuel and water replenishing points en route. The 'Trans-Australian' would be your home for nearly two whole days – as yet not a train to rank among the world's finest for luxury, but with air-conditioned diner and lounge car. The latter included in its furniture the piano which invariably featured in photographic reporting of this express from its debut in 1917 onwards.

At Port Pirie you would have to switch to the 5ft 3in-gauge 'East-West Express' of the South Australian Government for the 4¾-hour run on to Adelaide behind a streamlined green-and-gold 4-8-4; then at Adelaide to Victorian Railways' 'Overland' to continue to Melbourne behind another breed of massive 4-8-4, a superb spectacle as it hoisted its train up the 1 in 37 gradients through the Mount Lofty range east of Adelaide. Another Victorian Railways train, the fully air-conditioned, observation-car-tailed 'Spirit of Progress,' resplendent in royal blue-and-gold external livery, would ferry you the 191 miles from Adelaide to the New South Wales border. But there, assuming your ultimate goal was Sydney, break of gauge would enforce yet another change, to the care of a bullet-nosed New South Wales Pacific and the comfort,

maybe, of one of the two drawing-room suites with separate bedroom and lounge in its first-class, all-sleeping car 'Melbourne Limited.'

Today the whole 2462-mile trip from Perth to Sydney is possible without any transhipment and in supreme luxury, in just over 2¾ days. Four evenings a week the 'Indian Pacific' pulls out of Perth at 21.00 and on the third day it rolls into Sydney at 15.50.

The barrier to through travel was unlocked by the decision to build a new standard-gauge line in Western Australia for bulk movement of ore in 9000-ton trains from huge deposits at Koolyanobbing, 37 miles west of Kalgoorlie, to the Australian Iron & Steel complex at Kwinana on the Indian Ocean coastline south of Perth. Thereupon decisions were taken to reduce to standard gauge the 216 miles of South Australian 5ft 3in-gauge to Cockburn, the border with New South Wales, and to upgrade the existing 4ft 8½in-gauge in New South Wales, which extended reconstruction or fettling up to the whole transcontinental route apart from the desert section of Commonwealth Railways. The huge enterprise was completed throughout by the end of 1969; and in February 1970 the

impressive 'Indian-Pacific' took up revenue-earning service, under the joint ownership and operating management of the railways constituting the through Sydney-Perth route – New South Wales, South Australian, Commonwealth and Western Australian. Since March 1978 the Commonwealth Railways, Tasmanian Railways and all but the urban sections of South Australian Railways have been reconstituted as the Australian National Railways.

The Commonwealth Railways' 'Trans-Australian' set high accommodation standards for the rest of the country before World War II. It was equipped with shower-baths in its first-class sleepers as early as 1918 and took in its air-conditioned restaurant and lounge cars well ahead of the majority of world railways in 1936. The 13-car 'Indian Pacific' amply sustains the tradition in modern times. One says 13-car, but there are peak seasonal dates when the service is duplicated and then, once each part has negotiated the exit from Sydney, with its fearsome 1 in 33 gradients on the ascent to a 3503ft summit in the Blue Mountains, the two parts are combined as a gargantuan 26-car train for the whole of the remaining mileage from Broken Hill to

left: The world's most extraordinary luxury train route: the record 297 miles, straight across Western Australian's vast Nullarbor Plain. (Courtesy Australian News and Information Bureau)

left: Another splendid steam-age giant, a South Australian class 520 streamlined 4-8-4, seen at Mount Lofty on the 'South Coast Limited' from Adelaide. (Courtesy Author's collection)

far left: Final steam-age power for the great trains of New South Wales was the class C38 Pacific. Here one crosses the old Hawkesbury River Bridge between Newcastle and Sydney with the 'Inter-City Express.' (Courtesy NSW Railways)

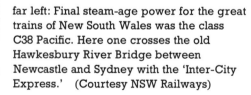

left: One of the class C 4-6-0s, dwarfed by a huge tender, which used to haul the 'Trans-Australian Express' across the desert from Kalgoorlie to Port Pirie. (Courtesy Author's collection)

The simplicity of British Rail's new 1978 cars for Royal travel, employing the system's standard Mk III car bodies, contrasts strongly with the floridity of earlier vehicles illustrated in this book. The pictures show the Queen's saloon (above) and the Duke of Edinburgh's saloon (right). (Courtesy British Rail)

above: Lounge car – with piano – of the 'Trans-Australian Express' in the 1930s. (Courtesy Author's collection)

top right (all four): Aboard the modern 'Indian-Pacific' showing: (top two) two views of a de luxe two-berth compartment or twinette; (bottom left) the first-class lounge; and (bottom right) the cafeteria club car. (Courtesy Public Transport Commission of NSW)

right: Today's transcontinental, the 'Indian-Pacific,' runs in two parts on some peak seasonal dates and for most of the distance the two sections are combined into one gigantic train, here made up of no fewer than 36 cars and a van. (Courtesy Western Australian Government Railways)

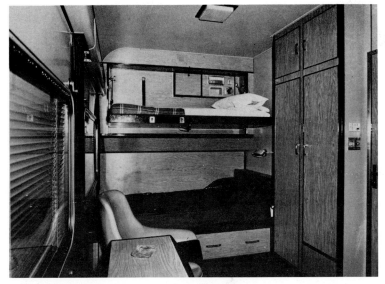

Perth. It is electrically hauled for the first 97 miles from Sydney to Lithgow and nowadays, naturally, diesel-hauled by locomotives of the appropriate systems the rest of the way.

Of all the luxury trains described in this book, the 'Indian-Pacific' probably demands the most of its air-conditioning, for in the extreme heat of the central desert sector – where dust is also an extreme irritant – the surface of its stainless steel cars can reach a temperature of nearly 140° F/60° C. At the other end of the climatic scale, in winter the 'Indian-Pacific' is quite likely to find its tracks mantled with snow on the upper slopes of the climb through the Blue Mountains west of Sydney, before it begins its night run through the increasingly monotonous scrubland plain of western New South Wales to Broken Hill.

'Indian-Pacific' rooms have similar refinements to those of South Africa's 'Blue Train,' though not quite the same range of accommodation. There are no drawing-room suites, but in the de-luxe first-class carriage of very roomy, wardrobe-fitted two-berth compartments, or 'twinettes'

as the Australians term them in unwarranted understatement, there are adjacent rooms which can be opened up via a connecting door for family travel. Each first-class twinette has its own enclosed shower-bath and toilet, but single first-class roomettes have only a private toilet. Both first-class roomette and economy-class passengers have free use of shower-bath rooms at the ends of every sleeping-car in the train, however. Every compartment, too, has iced drinking water on tap as well as a hot and cold washing supply, its own built-in radio with choice of programs, and power-operated venetian blinds between the double panes of the window.

The second day of a westbound 'Indian-Pacific' journey from Sydney begins with compartment service of early morning tea and biscuits, compliments of Australian National Railways (afternoon tea also comes free of charge). After breakfast there is a chance to stretch legs at Broken Hill, where the train pauses for 25 minutes to change traction for an ex-South Australian diesel and to replenish its train water reserves. You will have

got a thumbnail briefing on the character of this mining city from the admirable 12-page, large-format full-color brochure on the train's facilities and route which is issued to every passenger.

The scenery is pretty desolate on to Port Pirie, the landscape of arid speargrass plain enlivened only by the occasional dust storm that comes blasting down from the north, blotting out the scorching sun with its swirling black clouds. If you are travelling *en famille*, now maybe will be the time for personal laundry: by prior arrangement your conductor will have arranged an iron and ironing board for use in your compartment, as well as a bassinette for your youngest. But take time off at the midday Peterborough and Gladstone stops to catch the flavor of Australian rail history, for these are transhipment junctions between the new standard-gauge route you are on and the broad-gauge systems of South Australia and Victoria, and hence with the big cities of Adelaide and Melbourne. At Peterborough and in mid-afternoon at Port Pirie where 'Indian-Pacific' halts for 1½ hours to undergo a

161

complete change of train crew as well as locomotive, you will notice the comprehensive arrangements for exchange of bogies beneath freight wagons to allow through running between the transcontinental and broad-gauge systems. Passengers are encouraged to leave the train and prospect the Spencer Gulf port during the long stop.

Around the dinner hour on its second day out the 'Indian-Pacific' enters the historic Trans-Australia line at Port Augusta, operational headquarters of the former Commonwealth Railways and junction of the 761-mile line northwards to the heart of the country at Alice Springs. Railway staff and their families manning the railway on the desert ground are totally reliant on Port Augusta for the means to live. Once a week a so-called 'Tea and Sugar' train makes a round trip to Kalgoorlie and back, loaded not only with everything from food to clothing and household goods, but also with drinking and domestic water for some settlements far from any natural supply; also in its format are a welfare car, manned by medical staff, dentists and ministers of religion, and a cinema car for showings of the latest movies.

You will have got the measure of the 'Indian-Pacific's' diner at breakfast, typically Australian in the meat options of the menu – a choice of grilled lamb chops or sirloin minute steak and mushrooms as well as the traditional English bacon, eggs and sausages. A likely lunch menu will have been soup, then a choice of Chicken Mornay or fish fillet, followed by salads – eggs and asparagus, roast turkey and ham, or a collation of cold meats – a range of desserts from baked lemon rice pudding to fruit sundae, and ending with cheese and biscuits. Now your dinner menu may well read soup or fruit cocktail as a starter, a baked fillet of fish with anchovy sauce, a choice of grilled fillet steak with *sauce Béarnaise*, roast turkey and ham, or roast leg of pork, for dessert a Dutch apple tart with cream, apricot trifle or a Neapolitan ice, and to round off the card a cheese savory. As accompaniment you will naturally go for the car's Australian wines. Drinks apart, you have no worry about the impact of all this on your travelling budget: all set meals are packaged in the fare.

En passant, the tradition of meal stops on a rail journey rather than trainboard catering was longer dying on the Australian continent than anywhere else in the industrialized world. Not until the early 1970s, for instance, did Queensland Railways equip its long-distance air-conditioned Brisbane–Cairns streamliner, the 'Sunlander,' with a buffet-diner and eliminate intermediate meal stops aggregating around four hours of journey time: nor did the overnight Mel-

bourne–Adelaide 'Overland Express' take on a buffet-lounge to supersede the highly-reputed, station-prepared breakfasts put aboard during its Tailem Bend call and served to its passengers in their beds. New Zealand had no train refreshment cars of any kind until early 1972.

The westbound 'Indian-Pacific' begins the world record length of straight track just after 7.00 on the second morning. For hours on end only an occasional emu, kangaroo, dingo or camel briefly breaks into a vista of flat, sun-scorched plain reaching to the horizon on both sides of the train. At night a train's headlight hereabouts can be seen 50 miles away. It is almost a shock when your coach leans to the ordinarily insignificant curve which ends the straight just before 12.30. Your watch will have come almost to 16.00 before you catch faint sight to the west of the belt of trees marking the rim of the plain, which signifies that the famous gold-mining town of Kalgoorlie is only some 200 miles further on.

Departure from Kalgoorlie is at 20.30 and after dinner you will be taking your last drink in the 'Indian-Pacific's' bars. For the train as a whole, there is an attractive cafeteria-club car providing a comprehensive snack and hot drink service as well as liquor, but first-class passengers have their own exclusive cocktail bar-lounge car, with writing tables and – perpetuating the Trans-Australian tradition – a piano. At 7.00 next morning an unforgettable luxury journey ends, after negotiation of the sinuous and pretty Avon valley, in Perth.

Despite chronic shortage of investment capital and keen domestic air competition, Australian railways have in modern times established a number of

excellent trains between the country's principal cities. They cannot challenge Europe's finest for speed, but the best of them are not all that much out-distanced in the luxury ratings. For example, following 1962 completion of the through standard-gauge line between Melbourne and Albury, the Victorian and New South Wales Government Railways combined to create the 'Southern Aurora,' an all first-class, all-air-conditioned-sleeper overnight train between Sydney and Melbourne. Like the 'Indian-Pacific,' it affords every twinette berth its own enclosed toilet and shower-bath and also has a de luxe suite for one or two occupants on offer. A club car is carried as well as a diner, which serves full dinner, remains open for lighter fare until 23.00, and returns to action soon after 6.00 next morning for full breakfast, Australian style, though if that daunts you Continental breakfast and a morning paper can be served in your berth, plus a complimentary, fast shoeshine service. Another well-equipped overnight train is the Adelaide–Melbourne 'Overland,' and Queensland's air-conditioned 'Sunlander,' 'Midlander' and 'Weetlander' merit mention.

Until recently even Tasmania offered saloons with rotating, reclining chairs for a leisurely prospect of its lush, green countryside from the 'Tasman Limited.' Not a luxury train to compare with Dalziel's, Nagelmackers' or Pullman's finest, granted. But their gilded brochures never came up with an invitation half as compelling as this simple, homely advice from the 'Tasman Limited' promotion sheet:

'The home-made scones and jam at morning tea shouldn't be missed.'

top left and right: The Melbourne–Adelaide
'Overland' of the 1950s in the Mount Lofty
ranges near Adelaide, hauled by a South
Australian class 500B 4-8-4 (left) and (right)
today, re-equipped with air-conditioned
sleepers and hauled by a pair of Victorian
Government Railway's class S diesels.
(Courtesy Author's collection)

left: The club car of the Sydney–Melbourne
'Southern Aurora.'   (Courtesy Australian
News and Information Bureau)

A Shinkansen train speeds through Tokyo.
The two 4ft 8½in-gauge Shinkansen tracks
are alongside the original 3ft 6in-gauge
approach to Tokyo's main station.
(Courtesy Japanese National Tourist Office)

A transportation service for one of the most densely-packed nations on earth has little scope for the same sort of luxury travel ambience as a North American or even a Western European rail system. The ratio of Japanese to the country's total land area masks the transport operator's critical problem: the islands' mountainous spine ranges so widely that only about 15 percent of the Japanese land surface is flat enough to allow full industrial and population development.

The effect is seen most starkly along 350 miles or so of the southern coast of Honshu island, between Tokyo and Osaka. This littoral belt packs some 40 percent of the whole Japanese population into a mere one percent of the country's land surface. That helps to explain why Japanese National Railways move ten times more passengers annually than British Rail, over 7000 million compared with 700 million, on a rail network that is little bigger in terms of route-miles: just over 13,100 as against slightly more than 8200 (counting only the British track open to passenger trains). Naturally the emphasis of Japanese National Railways passenger policy since World War II has been on speed, frequency and equipment capacity. Comfort has necessarily had to be subordinated to these overriding preoccupations – the more so because the Government kept rail fares pegged at woefully uneconomic levels until the spring of 1977, when rates were abruptly jacked up by 50 percent at a stroke as one counter to JNR's disastrously deteriorating financial situation.

Nevertheless, by the end of the 1950s JNR were producing some handsome new streamlined multiple-unit train-sets for the front-rank services of their then exclusively 3ft 6in-gauge system. These electric train-sets appeared first on the 3ft 6in-gauge main line between Tokyo and Osaka. Fully air-conditioned, each 12-car 1500V DC train-set accommodated 598 passengers. Most of the first-class accommodation was in open saloons, with every seat semi-reclining and rotatable. Every seat, too, was wired for sound, with a socket into which the passenger could plug earphones and pick up national radio programs, and one corner of the saloon was set up with a small writing-room. In addition the first-class accommodation featured a parlor car with individual, revolving armchairs, by each of which was a point into which train staff could fix telephones enabling passengers to be connected with the national network along the route. This car also included a small shop vending magazines and light refreshment. In 1960 Japanese National Railways introduced similarly furnished diesel train-sets for its non-electrified lines.

In recent years JNR have abolished

first-class. In theory at least the whole system operates on a basic one-class tariff, to which supplements are added according to the class of train used – 'Super Express,' 'Limited Express,' 'Ordinary Express' and stopping passenger, or local service. In fact, first-class survives in the form of so-called 'Green Cars,' the former first-class vehicles, which command a surcharge on the basic fare and in which seat reservation is *de rigueur*. The only word for the reasoning behind this change in denomination of the superior-category accommodation is inscrutable.

The 'Super-Expresses' are the 'Hikari' and 'Kodama' of Japan's remarkable Shinkansen, or new railways. The latter were born in the late 1950s when the Japanese recognized that there was no way they could adapt the existing 3ft 6in-gauge railway in the Tokaido belt to the demands of the exploding industrial economy. Quite apart from the operational constraints imposed by the narrow gauge, the line was quite sharply graded and curved, and intersected by more than a thousand level crossings. In 1958 the Government decreed that a new railway be built between Tokyo and Osaka.

From the start it was accepted that the new line should be predominantly passenger; before long, however, it was assigned *exclusively* to passenger traffic. That greatly simplified the route's engineering for high speed, which was another key objective, and in furtherance of which 4ft 8½in gauge was selected, even though that would completely divorce the new railway from the rest of the JNR system. Another Shinkansen distinction from the rest of JNR was its electrification at 25kv AC 60HZ, instead of 1.5kv DC.

This is not the place to describe the extraordinary effort of design and civil engineering which had 320 miles of new railway carved through the teeming Tokaido belt in five years, or to expand on the technology which created for the Tokyo–Osaka Shinkansen (often called the New Tokaido Line) what is still the world's fastest inter-city rail service and one of the two most intensive on earth (the other is British Rail's).

Today the New Tokaido runs at least six trains each way every hour between Tokyo and Osaka between 06.00 and midnight (the railway is shut for maintenance throughout the small hours – and also of late for the whole of eight days spread through the year, for the same reason). There are only five intermediate stations, of which the superior 'Hikari,' four times hourly, call only at Nagoya and Kyoto and cover the whole distance in 3 hours 12–13 minutes for an overall end-to-end average speed of 100mph or marginally under. The route's fastest

timing is one of 110.3mph start-to-stop for the 108.5 miles from Nagoya to Shizuoka.

Top speed of the 'Bullet Trains,' as the world popularly knows them by reason of their projectile-shaped ends, is 130mpn. The Japanese have been aiming for 155mph and have engineered later Shinkansen for that maximum, but its attainment in day-to-day operational practice is now improbable for a decade and more. JNR have encountered too many problems from track wear and tear under an intensive very high-speed service on the one hand, and from virulent environmentalist campaigning against Shinkansen noise on the other.

In the 1970s the New Tokaido Line was gradually projected beyond Osaka to Hakata via the New Sanyo Shinkansen. That meant crossing from Honshu to Kyushu islands in a new 11.6-mile tunnel (longest in the world after the Swiss Simplon) under Kanmon Strait. A good deal of the New Sanyo Line is restricted to 100mph or even less because of geological conditions. Nevertheless from early morning to early evening one of two trains every hour from Tokyo to Hakata, calling at six of the eleven stations en route, reels off the whole 664 mile journey in four minutes under seven hours at an end-to-end average speed of 95.8mph.

In the early 1970s the Japanese Government envisaged quite rapid expansion of the Shinkansen system (the length and breadth of the country) to a total of some 4350 route-miles. By the middle of the decade, however, the oil crisis, economic depression, inflation (which has trebled Shinkansen land acquisition and construction costs since the New Tokaido Line) and environmental protest had muted ambition. JNR management itself was not enthusiastic. Although the New Tokaido Line's enormous business – it has carried over half a million people on a single day – has amply remunerated the heavy investment in it, JNR fears being saddled with some Shinkansen built largely as instruments of social policy to help disperse population, which have no hope of paying off their cost out of revenue. Only two new Shinkansen, the Joetsu and Tohoku, are therefore building at the time of writing.

As opposed to sheer speed, the most significant contribution of Shinkansen to the subject of this book is the achievement of Japanese technology in cocooning passengers from the sensations of such a pace. For instance they are completely insulated from the effects of two trains passing at a combined speed of 260mph within the confined space of a tunnel. Each train-set is fitted with power-operated devices, actuated automatically at the approach to a tunnel, which press all vestibule and entrance doors so

tightly against their frames that the air-conditioned train interior is almost hermetically sealed while it is underground. That shields sensitive ears very effectively from the unnerving effects that would otherwise be caused by the abrupt changes of air pressure set up by passing trains.

'Bullet train' riding is splendidly silent and stable, but although the seating is relaxing, the character of the Shinkansen operation demands a three-and-two lay-out across the central gangway of each open saloon. Consequently each car's seating capacity is as high as 110. At first on-train catering establishments were restricted to buffets, but with the opening of the New Sanyo Line and the lengthening of journeys, restaurant cars were added to Shinkansen equipment.

If you cannot find a place at the buffet-bar or in the diner, however, you will not starve. Packed meals are a long-standing tradition of Japanese rail travel. Before World War II Japanese restaurant cars were among the most poorly patronized in the world. The majority opted for *o bento*. A sonic hallmark of most Japanese main-line stations was the sing-song cry of the *bento*-boy, parading his neat wooden boxes sectored with portions of hot boiled rice and its accompaniments – fish or an omelette, vegetables, soya beans and tough pickles, plus a serviette, chopsticks and tooth-pick. Vying vocally for attention would be the sellers of *o cha* – tea, as you might suppose – and *o chichi*, which is milk. Some stations had the same treasured reputation for their *o bento* as the famous British refreshment rooms had for their luncheon baskets in the 19th century, before the emergence of dining cars.

On Shinkansen you do not buy your *o bento* on the platform. Often coming these days as stewed eels in a wine and soya sauce, it is one of the main wares of the hostesses who incessantly patrol the trains with light refreshments.

top right: One of the electric train-sets which provided Japan's finest inter-city service on the 3ft 6in-gauge before the coming of Shinkansen. (Courtesy Author's collection)

right: The luxury parlor car of a Japanese National Railways 3ft 6in-gauge electric inter-city train-set. (Courtesy Author's collection)

Candle-lit gala dinner in a vintage Pullman
on the 'Nostalgic Orient Express'; second
from the right is Albert Glatt, genius behind
the revival of the train.   (Courtesy
Intraflug)

The European inter-city train of the 1980s, I have been grumbling intermittently in this book, is at risk of degeneration into as characterless a conveyor-belt-with-seats as most international airlines. But some, thank heaven, are bucking the trend to turn rail into another medium for blinkered Gadarenes like the *autobahnen* and the air lanes. Standard-bearers are the concerns which are keeping the luxury train handsomely alive, both as a pleasurable living experience but also as the most relaxing vantage-point for a panorama of the continent, by resurrecting the cruise-train concept. Also encouraging is the demand from businesses and private individuals for special-purpose vehicles which they can charter for conferences or parties on the move, instead of in the static, soporific confines of an hotel.

Cruising by train was no novelty by the end of the 19th century. In the early 1880s, for instance, the Boston travel agents Raymond & Whitcomb of the Eastern US hit on the idea to introduce New Englanders to the splendors of the West and of Mexico. Pullman built them special equipment which in the mid-1920s included, as well as some elegant all-room sleepers with fixed lower beds in every apartment and private shower-baths in two of them, a recreation car with a fully-equipped gymnasium – punch-bag, weights, mechanical horse and all – and a 38ft-long room for dancing or movie shows. The firm's Land Cruise Liners foundered in the 1931 Wall Street crash aftermath and never resurfaced.

Across the Atlantic, in the mid-1930s Polish Railways had what they called a 'train-hotel' ranging from Warsaw through Germany, Belgium, France, Italy and Austria then back to the Polish capital on a continuous 13-day itinerary. The rail travel was all nocturnal, to leave each day free for detailed sightseeing by road or on foot, but they seem to have lived it up on those night rides. After dinner in the diner, you had the choice of a bar car or another coach gutted internally to make a dance hall, with resident band. Both bathrooms and a hairdressing saloon also figured in the accommodation make-up.

From 1933 to 1939 you could also make the round of a good deal of Britain in the 'Northern Belle,' a week-long cruise train which the London North Eastern Railway ran four times annually in June and July. Operation had to be confined to that short season because some of the train's consist were specialist cars borrowed from normal year-round services: for instance, the hair-dressing saloon and cocktail bar from the 'Flying Scotsman' and some of the LNER's pioneering – for Britain, that is – shower-fitted sleeping cars, which also had a movable bed in one center compartment so that the latter could be converted into a private lounge for the adjoining berth. Another vehicle in the train was an antique Great Northern family saloon, the separate sections of which served as writing room, smoking room and ladies' room. Centerpiece of the 'Northern Belle's' itinerary and occupying the greater part of the week was a round of the Scottish Highlands lines within the LNER's domain. Only Royal trains have ever approached the 'Northern Belle' for prodigality of staffing on a British train; a crew of 27, some female, was rostered to minister to just 60 passengers – each of whom, incidentally, had paid only £20 for the inclusive cruise package, including side-trips by road from various halts en route.

In agonizing contrast, it will set you back £400/$800 to spend three days and nights on the star of present-day cruise trains, the 'Nostalgie-Orient Express,' the enterprise of a Swiss travel executive, Albert Glatt of the Zurich firm Intraflug AG. As a farewell gesture to the fading 'Simplon-Orient Express,' the Swiss Federal Railway had in the autumn of 1976 mobilized as many Wagons-Lits antiques as they could muster to form a vintage special train from Zurich to Istanbul and back. The venture pulled in enthusiastic business, but neither the railway nor Wagons-Lits was inclined to repeat it. Although Glatt had hitherto chiefly operated airline charters, he sensed an opportunity going begging and stepped in. At the start, however, railway managements were not merely edgy about the whole idea of regular operation, but decidedly reluctant to have it exercise a continuous lien on their museum-piece cars. Since Glatt was insistent that the train must be formed as near completely of period pieces as possible, his only option was to go to market with his own money. He quickly bought whatever was available – and went on buying, notably at a highly-publicized and celebrity-studded auction staged by Sothebys at Monte Carlo in October 1977.

By 1978 Glatt's company, Intraflug AG, had enough vintage vehicles of its own to cover practically all accommodation needs. For diners it owns an ex-'Sud Express' Pullman kitchen car, featuring coupés as well as a main saloon, and an ex-'Côte d'Azur' Pullman; to accompany these he can now hire from their railway owners two more ex-'Côte d'Azur' Pullmans, one of them the vehicle that was late in its career converted into a bar car for the 'Train Bleu.' Intraflug also disposes of seven sleepers from the interwar period, six of them 1929-built Type 'LX16' cars each with the roominess of a 16-compartment layout (four of them singles and the remainder doubles), instead of the more general 17 rooms, and the last an 'LX20' of the same year with double berths throughout.

This fleet Intraflug supplements with hired vehicles to fulfill all functional requirements. One of them is a unique

Intraflug's 'Nostalgic Orient Express' crosses Switzerland headed by a Swiss Federal Class Re 4/4 electric; the first car is the staff sleeper, then come the stores van and next a Wagons-Lits diner followed by two Pullmans. (Courtesy Swiss Federal Railways)

'Douche car,' which apart from staff quarters and a storage room is given over entirely to eight shower baths; normally held in Italy, it was fashioned by Wagons-Lits out of a British-built 'Golden Arrow' Pullman of 1926 to solace Milan's La Scala opera company when on tour. A modern sleeper is marshalled at the front of the train to house the 20 train staff mustered to look after the cruise train's complement of 75 passengers. Behind that and next to the diner comes a baggage car, the whole of which is pre-empted as a larder and household store, since the cruise train has to set out fully victualled for a week's round trip: amongst other things, that means setting out with some six tons of ice.

Glatt has been meticulous in the restoration of his charges to pristine state, even down to commissioning precise replicas of the traditional Pullman table lamps, since these were erased from

left: Class A4 Pacific No 4489 *Dominion of Canada* heads the LNER's land-cruise train, the 'Northern Belle,' out of London Kings Cross on 18 June 1937. (Courtesy British Rail)

bottom left: The vintage Wagons-Lits diner of the 'Nostalgic Orient Express' which retains its original chairs and panelling of the 1930s (as can be seen in the bottom picture on page 63). (Courtesy Intraflug)

below: The 'Northern Belle' included a prototype LNER sleeper of 1932, equipped with a shower-bath (left) and in which adjoining compartments could be opened up to form a suite (center and right). (Courtesy Author's collection)

bottom right: Canapés for the pre-lunch aperitif in one of the restored Pullmans of the 'Nostalgic Orient Express.' (Courtesy Intraflug)

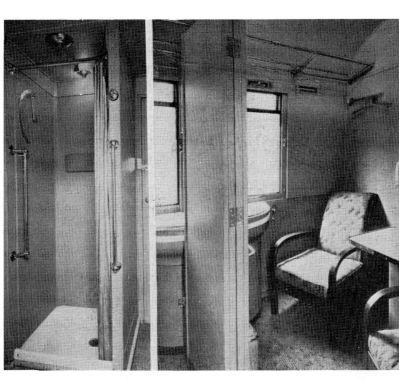

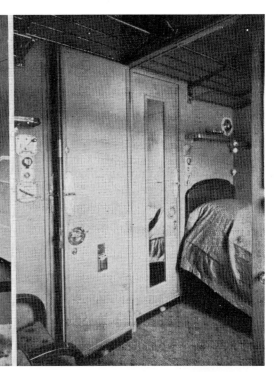

Wagons-Lits warehouse inventories years ago. Only in one vintage car, the borrowed Douche, is the venerated Pullman image of rich wood panelling and delicate marquetry effaced by latter-day plastic.

Intraflug is currently running its 'Nostalgie-Orient Express' five or six times a year. The most frequently followed route is that of the one-time 'Arlberg-Orient Express,' from Zurich to Istanbul and back vïa Buchs, the Arlberg Tunnel, Innsbruck, the Tauern route through Austria, Ljubliana, Belgrade and Sofia, but the tour has also been started from Stuttgart and from Lausanne, in the latter case tracing the 'Simplon-Orient' path via Milan, Venice, Ljubliana, Belgrade and Thessalonika to Athens and back. In 1978 a more ambitious itinerary was projected as far as Baghdad and in 1979 the train was to be taken from Central Europe for a round tour of Scandinavia. It has also been exploited for a luxury gourmets' outing to Bordeaux. Recently some Zurich-Istanbul trips have been run to the charter order of the American pioneers already mentioned, Raymond & Whitcomb, who now operate from New York.

To sustain the ambience of nostalgia Intraflug contrives haulage by vintage steam power wherever it is still available (and allowed to function, which it is not, for instance, anywhere on the German Federal). The Yugoslavs fire up an ex-German 'Kriegslok' 2-10-0 for about two hours of the 'Arlberg-Orient' route journey from the end of the catenary at Nis through the Dragoman pass to the Bulgarian border, and the Turks turn out steam for the final approach to Istanbul, though all the surrounding traffic is electrified.

On its 'Arlberg-Orient' itinerary the cruise train pulls out of Zurich around 10.00 and reaches Istanbul at around 17.00 on the third day, having paused at cities like Innsbruck, Belgrade and Sofia for stopovers each of about three hours for sightseeing. The Intraflug package offers options of either a two-day stay in an Istanbul hotel, then a return to base by air; the air-hotel-cruise train round in that order; or return in the train after one night in Istanbul. The third is the most expensive, running out at well over £800 per person if you go for a top-bracket hotel in Istanbul.

The inclusive price covers everything but drinks and tips on the train – and a consultation of the doctor who always travels with it, should you be luckless enough to need him. It takes in the pre-arranged bus trips round the stopover cities as well as all meals, and they include two five-course marathons billed as a 'Capitain's Dinner' and a candlelit 'Gala Dinner,' at which evening dress is virtually *de rigueur*. The cuisine, en-

trusted to a picked *maître d'hôtel* and diner and kitchen staff of nine from Wagons-Lits' Milan base, is spoken of reverentially by fortunates who have ridden the cruise-train.

Despite the daunting fares, after one or two early disappointments Intraflug's cruise trains have been drawing full and enthusiastic houses. And that, despite the formidable investment and operational costs, has fired others to imitate Glatt's enterprise. Intraflug is said to have spent nearly £250,000/$500,000 on the vehicles and to be paying out 30 percent of the trains' revenue on just the railways' bill for running it, never mind the hotel service on board. Glatt was not the only bidder for period Wagons-Lits vehicles at the Monte Carlo auction. As I write there is talk of other successful purchasers planning a vintage de luxe service from London to Venice, with Pullman links on both sides of the English Channel or North Sea (which connecting port on the European mainland might be used is as yet vague).

The Wagons-Lits antiques owned and prized by the railways are exploited by the latter for their own special train events, and also hired out to other entrepreneurs. Significant among the latter are the big travel agencies which, especially in West Germany, have latterly been agglomerating quite large fleets of their own branded rolling stock for charter train services to and from the continent's most popular holiday areas. In an earlier chapter I mentioned the purchase by the German concern Apfelgold of the former 'Rheingold' and 'Rheinpfeil' dome observation cars, which are now decked out in Apfelgold's bright orange and green livery to match the rest of its equipment which is contemporary and not vintage.

In France two ex-'Côte d'Azur' Pullmans, including the 'Train Bleu' bar car, are frequently to be seen in the 'Azur 2000' charter trains which Vacances 2000 have been running overnight since the late 1960s from Paris to winter sports areas and of more recent years from the French capital to the Riviera coast in summer. The Vacances 2000 specials are train-cruising in a modern idiom. Arguably they are not quite in the luxury class, since they include couchette as well as the most modern sleeping-cars, but they challenge strongly for inclusion when you assess the package as a whole. The kitchens, Pullman and bar, function practically the whole night, as does a newspaper/tobacconist's kiosk in the bar, which is tape-equipped for dancing. If you want the quieter life, the rear of the train is brought up by French Railways' custom-built cinema car, which screens a feature film twice or even three times through the night. You can safely pack your family off to bed and make the gay round of the train with a clear conscience,

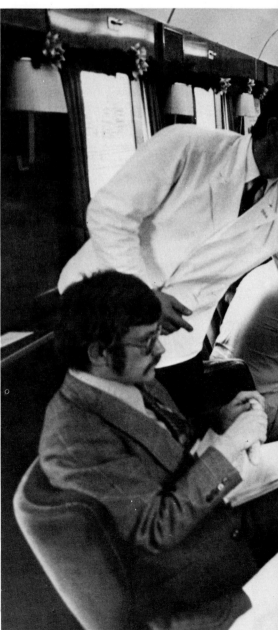

left: A German Federal charter comprises (from the rear) a new business car, the West German Chancellor's special saloon, four diners and two bar cars. (Courtesy DSG)

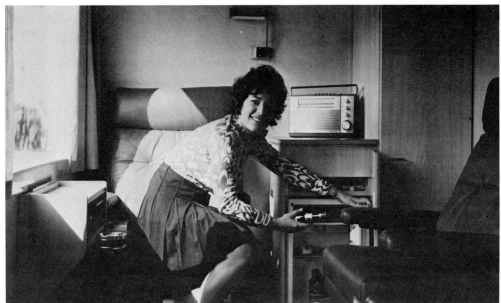

below: A corner of the special compartment for conferences on Australian Federal Railways' premium-fare 'Komfortwagen.' (Courtesy Austrian Federal Railways)

as the Vacances 2000 package comes with benefit of a brigade of train hostesses geared to mount guard on the children and deliver them next morning properly washed, brushed and (if the parents have been living it up) no doubt obscenely alive the following morning.

To court the younger, automobile-oriented travel market especially, several mainland European railways have since World War II gutted and refitted coaches as mobile dance-halls for charter trains. The German Federal has had particular success in every sector of the party travel market, setting itself out to cultivate use of the train for business conferences as well as purely social outings, and in the late 1970s has been building up a fleet of vehicles easily adaptable to a variety of customer demands. The latest are conversions from former self-service buffet cars, from which the adequate kitchen has been retained. The main body of the car is a saloon which can be set up with mobile furniture as needed – with long table and suitable chairs for business sessions perhaps, or more sparsely for dancing – and which has a bar at one corner. There is a control room for the vehicles' range of sound equipment, an office for the chairman or party leader, and a full cloakroom suite.

left: Continuous refreshment for the guests in a German Federal bar car during a press conference on wheels. (Courtesy DSG)

CHAPTER 13
ROYAL TRAINS

A particularly florid example of
locomotive decoration for Royal Train duty
is seen on this London Tilbury & Southend
Railway 4-4-2 tank No 80 *Thundersley*,
decked out for a trip in the early 1900s.
(Courtesy Author's collection)

'The Great Western Railway,' proclaimed a London newspaper one morning in 1840, 'anticipating the Patronage of the Queen and her illustrious Consort, Prince Albert, and the Members of the Royal Family, have just built a splendid Royal carriage for their accommodation. . . . The interior has been most magnificently fitted up by Mr Webb, upholsterer, Old Bond Street. The saloon is handsomely arranged with hanging sofas of carved wood in the rich style of Louis XIV and the walls are panelled out in the same elegant manner, and fitted up with rich crimson and white silk and exquisitely executed paintings representing the four elements, by Parris. The end compartments are also fitted up in the same style, each apartment having in the center a useful and ornamental rosewood table; and the floors of the whole are covered with chequered India matting.'

One doubts the vehicle was quite as palatial as this florid period description suggests. Such data as survives show it to have been four-wheeled (the wheels had wooden tires in the hope of protecting royal ears from the noise of travel) with a sharply tapering body below the waistline of the kind which characterized the road posting carriages of the age. That would account for the 'hanging sofas': the floor space would have been too constricted for them to stand.

Nevertheless, it was an historic vehicle, the first custom-built royal coach. The Great Western had built it speculatively but with ample cause for optimism of royal patronage. The royal residence on

the western fringes of London, Windsor Castle, was so close to the new Bristol railway as to be clearly visible from the latter's trains. Better yet, those trains had been enthusiastically sampled by Her Majesty's intended, Prince Albert of Saxe-Coburg-Gotha, on his missions to Windsor to advance his suit in the closing months of 1839. The first monarch actually to use the coach was King Frederick William IV of Prussia, accepting an invitation to the Prince of Wales' christening on 24 January 1842. Not until the following June did the Great Western get the first return on its promotional investment, when word was transmitted from the castle one Saturday afternoon that Queen Victoria, Prince Albert and family were graciously minded to take train from nearby Slough to London at noon the following Monday.

The following Monday! In the century of its succeeding life the Great Western may not have passed a more frenetic weekend. But there was contretemps neither in the hectic planning nor in the execution. A suitable six-coach train including the royal saloon was assembled, one of Locomotive Superintendent Daniel Gooch's latest engines, newly run in, was mobilized, the Queen and her entourage embarked, and on the stroke of noon, 13 June 1842, the world's first exclusive royal train steamed out of Slough, Gooch at the regulator and Engineer Isambard Kingdom Brunel at his side in the cab, to draw up alongside the red carpet at Paddington's arrival platform 25 minutes later amid what one newspaper breathlessly reported as 'the most deafening demonstrations of loyalty and affection we have ever experienced.'

Some of Victoria's subjects were less enthusiastic about the adventure. Alarmed that royal approval had thus sealed rail travel, the landed gentry who were fighting the spread of railways tooth and nail had their brethren in Parliament denounce the affair as wantonly submitting Her Majesty to untold perils. Had not the world's first rail disaster just been reported from France – to a train conveying back from Versailles to Paris the guests at a royal party, 57 of whom had perished in their locked coaches as they were consumed by fire? That had dissuaded the King of France from taking a train on good advice. Queen Victoria was unmoved. She had been 'quite charmed' by her first rail journey, she confided to her uncle, King Leopold of the Belgians. And from that day forward she was an inveterate rail traveller.

The first royal sleeping carriage was built in 1842 for Victoria's aunt, the Dowager Queen Adelaide, by the London & Birmingham Railways. A four-wheeler of the same road coachwork pattern as Victoria's first saloon, it was an ennobling of the superior 'bed-carriage' which some of the earliest British railways had been offering the travelling gentry from the late 1830s. The bed was formed by inserting a cushion-covered stretcher between the facing seats, then lifting a flap in the end wall of the body to open up a cushioned 'boot' built on to the bodywork: only that way, since the compartment was only 5ft 6in between lateral walls, could decent room be secured for the royal matriarch to recline at full pillowed and cushioned ease. Queen Adelaide's coach is still lovingly preserved in Britain's National Railway Museum.

By the mid-1840s the railway had proved itself to the conviction of the Establishment throughout Europe and Victoria's peers on the mainland were not afraid and were even eager to follow her lead. The first really elaborate royal vehicle was probably that commissioned by Emperor Ferdinand I of Austria from his State Railways in 1845. It was an American-style bogie car with five rooms: a state saloon with four heavy armchairs, a retiring room with *chaise-longues*, a two-berth bedroom, a small room with settees for the royal equerries, and an ante-room with two chairs one of which, contemporary documents hint, may have discreetly concealed a lavatory bowl.

The London & Birmingham Railway's four-wheeled coach of 1842 for Queen Adelaide, with the seats arranged for night-time use. Note (on the right) the lifted cover of the 'boot' allowing Her Majesty to stretch her legs beyond the width of the compartment itself. (Courtesy British Rail)

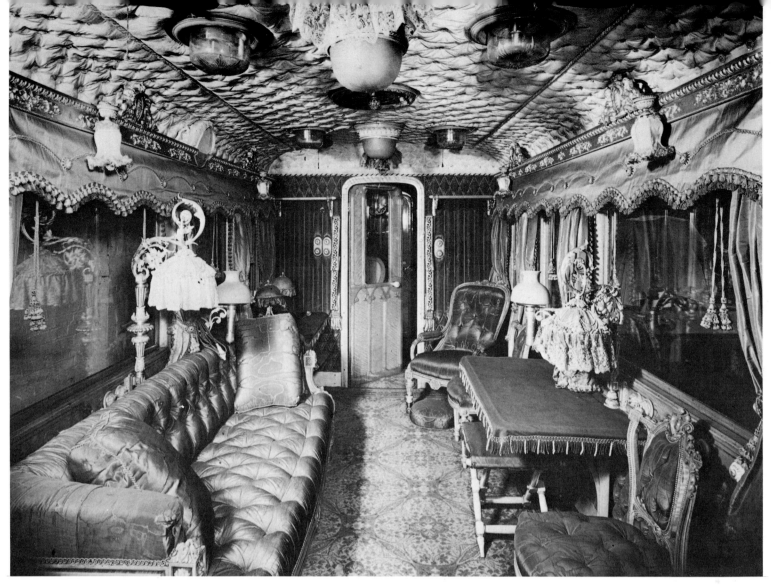

above: The day saloon of the LNWR twin six-wheeled Royal coaches built for Queen Victoria in 1869.   (Courtesy British Rail)

extreme right, top: The LNWR Royal Train poses behind 'Precedent' 2-4-0 No 1684 *Speke*. The two 1903-built saloons are the fourth and fifth cars from the left. (Courtesy British Rail)

extreme right, bottom: The LNWR Royal Train is seen here en route to Ballater from London Euston behind LMS streamlined Pacific No 6225 *Duchess of Devonshire*. (Courtesy C R L Coles)

below: The two six-wheeled Royal saloons of 1869, rebuilt as one bogie twelve-wheeler in 1897.   (Courtesy Author's collection)

Victoria's first eight-wheeled saloon was provided for her by the Great Western a few years later. That may or may not have also had one of the first portable water-closets seen in a European train – historians are not positive – but it certainly had one novel fixture which deserves mention. That was a roof-mounted disk-and-crossbar signal by which the Queen could have her minions warn the engine crew that they were going too fast for her comfort. The visual message was passed to the footplate by a wretched individual, known as the 'travelling carriage porter,' who was made to ride in fair weather and foul perched on the rear of the locomotive's tender, his back to the elements and the

locomotive's exhaust. On two of Victoria's most frequented rail routes this purgatorial sentry duty was still a canon of royal train operating practice until the end of her many days in 1901, even though the visual transmission of royal commands to the cab had long since lapsed.

Once British rail coach design had settled into established patterns a royal train externally was not markedly dissimilar to other expresses on the same railway. Of course, the royal coaches would stand out for their immaculate finish, maybe a flourish or two by way of ornamental door handles and grips, a royal cipher on the bodywork and the regal curtaining of Her Majesty's win-

dows. The locomotive, too, might be embellished with fabrications of the royal coat or arms or crowns, but rare was such flamboyance as the North British Railway's, when Victoria inaugurated the London–Edinburgh route's Royal Border Bridge over the River Tweed at Berwick in 1850, in having the locomotive of her train painted overall in Royal Stewart Tartan. Other potentates, however, demanded rococo magnificence outside as well as inside their rail vehicles.

There was, for instance, Egypt's Turkish Viceroy in the third quarter of the 19th century, Said Pasha, who not only had built an extraordinary 16-wheel car housing his own apartments at one end and those of his harem at the other with a

Inside the two superb LNWR Royal saloons of 1903 showing: (far left) the King's day saloon with his smoking-room beyond (note the array of bell-pushes by the communicating door); (left) the Queen's bedroom; (top) the Queen's bathroom; and (above) a view from the King's bathroom – with the bath decently covered under the left-hand window – to his bedroom. (Courtesy Author's collection)

below: The LNER Royal Train was mostly used for journeys between London Kings Cross and the Royal residence at Sandringham. For this Royal duty, Cambridge depot in the 1930s maintained two immaculate, green-liveried ex-Great Eastern 4-4-0s, known popularly as the 'Royal Clauds' (the first of the class had been named *Claud Hamilton* after the GER chairman). One of the pair, No 8787, heads the train away from Cambridge for London. (Courtesy Author's collection)

right and center: Exterior and interior of a South Eastern & Chatham Railway Royal saloon of 1903. (Courtesy British Rail)

extreme right: An extravagant state saloon built by the US Pullman company for the Mexican government in 1897. The chair coverings and curtains were of costly satin. (Courtesy Arthur Dubin collection)

central loggia decently separating the two, but insisted that the locomotive to go with it be unmistakably viceregal in its appointments. Instead of a conventional cab, this 2-2-4 well tank had a sort of semi-coach body, open above the waist but fitted with elegant curtains; its chimney was fluted, its dome of polished brass shaped to represent a Grecian pedestal and its livery a dazzling purple and silver with elaborate decorations of gold and vermilion.

Even more staggering was the saloon built in 1859 for Pope Pius XI, the last Vatican hierarch to exercise temporal as well as spiritual rule, by one of Rome's first two railways, the Pio Latin. The inside was gorgeous enough. An ornately bronze-gated verandah at one end led via a small reception room to His Holiness' throne room, which was dominated by a massive, heavily cushioned chair on a prayer cushion-fronted dais at one end, and nobly curtained and furnished elsewhere, predominantly in white velvet. Besides being spectacularly windowed, the throne room had a raised roof section deliberately shaped to create the look of a papal dome crowning the center of the car; on the inside the dome was rich with painted frescoes. Beyond the throne room were the private papal rooms – an oratory, a reading-room and a retiring-room. Externally the car was an incredible confection of wood carving or *papier-mâché* molding. As if the roof dome alone were not conceit enough, the designers contrived for its 'support' ornamented external pillars, extending from floor to cantrail, which were fronted by life-sized representations, crowned and haloed, of Faith, Hope and Charity. The vehicle, presented to the Pope as an earnest of its piety by the Pio Latina Railway (or possibly one should say by its French financiers) is said to have cost £5500/$11,000 in the money values of the day, a prodigious outlay for the times. One should add that Rome's other early railway, the Pio Centrale, not to be outdone in fealty, also bestowed suitable rail conveyance upon Pius IX, in this case two four-wheelers, one enclosed and the other semi-open but hung with rich purple drapes, from which His Holiness might pronounce a benediction upon the

faithful wherever his train paused.

The most extraordinary royal train of this period, happily, is preserved intact in West Germany's Transport Museum at Nuremberg. It was begun by King Maximilian of Bavaria in 1860 and completed in 1865 by his successor, the capricious Ludwig II, creator of the fantastic fairyland castles which still mark his domain. Ludwig added to an already fabulous equipage, an eight-wheeled saloon which compressed within a rail vehicle all the rich fantasy of his castle-building. But he was as eccentric about his train as everything else. He cherished it and was constantly enhancing it (in a train whose fancies included a pure swansdown cushion topping to the lavatory seat that must have been work of

supererogation). But as a functional conveyance, he normally preferred horse and carriage for his journeying, the train as a peripatetic royal residence to which he could repair at journey's end. At times he would proudly dispatch the empty train around his domain just to parade his opulent aestheticism before his mightily impressed subjects.

The several British railways which built royal saloons or whole royal trains for Queen Victoria had to contend with her extreme conservatism. Thus the London & North Western, faced at the end of the 19th century with the obsolescence of two saloons it had built for the Queen and her retinue in 1869, felt it was best advised to preserve the coach bodies and their interiors unaltered by

remounting them, joined as one, on a unitary frame with twelve-wheel bogies. Even after electric lighting had become practical she insisted on the retention of foul-smelling oil lamps in her own apartments, claiming that they gave her a softer light for reading. When the Great Western proposed construction of a new six-coach train for her Jubilee year travels in 1897 Victoria strictly enjoined not only that oil-lighting illuminate her coach, even though the rest of the train would be electrically lit, but also that her favorite quarters in the previous Great Western royal saloon of 1873 build be precisely reproduced, as she doted on them. Dutifully, the Great Western did even better: by dint of most dextrous coachbuilding they inserted the 1873

compartment bodily in a coach of the new train.

The accompanying illustration of the London & North Western 1869 saloon typifies the character of vehicles built for Queen Victoria's use during the last thirty years or so of her reign. Notice-able is an obsession with many British royal coach furnishers of the period, the heavy padding with buttoned upholstery. The Great Western covered the walls with it, but the London & North Western even applied it to the ceiling. The most absurd expression of this style was per-pretrated by the Great Eastern, which in 1897 turned out for the Prince of Wales and four years later when he had suc-ceeded to the throne, for his Queen Alexandra, paired saloons which were padded from floor to ceiling in buttoned morocco leather, with matching arm-chairs and settees. The *tout ensemble* looked more like a stockbrokers' gin palace than royal apartments.

Elsewhere in Europe late 19th century royal train designers and builders did not have to work under the same inhibi-tions. In the case of the two Emperors, William II of Germany and Franz Joseph I

of Austria-Hungary, moreover, the trains had to be structured for journeys of far greater length and complexity than Vic-toria's. This was especially so for the Austro-Hungarian Emperor, whose rule stretched from Poland to much of what is now Czechoslovakia and to the Adriatic. For him in 1891 the Prague coachbuilding firm of Ringhoffer built what was un-doubtedly the most ramified royal coach fleet of any 19th century monarch's and by all accounts the most splendid train to run on European rails in the 19th century. At the end of the day the Emperor had no fewer than a score of cars from which to form his train, one of them a mobile steam generating station with a vertical boiler to feed the train with heat and light.

The Imperial Saloon itself embodied a full-width bedroom, nearly 11ft long, with an imposing bed and a regally furnished saloon with armchairs, *chaise-longue*, table, office desk and chair, plus small adjoining staff compartments. For the elite of the Imperial court there was a cross between a Pullman and a Wagons-Lits sleeper, with sleeping compart-ments flanking a full-width lounge in the

center of the car. The diner housed at one-end a Pullman-style smoking room and at the other a state dining-room, with a long central table, seven chairs each side backs to the window and at each end one more. Beyond that was what must surely have been the most lavish culinary provision yet seen on rails: a car with first a serving room 12ft long, then a huge kitchen no less than $22\frac{1}{2}$ft long, and at the far end sleeping berths for the head chef and his deputy. The rest of the train would be made up of staff vehicles.

Presidents were just as concerned as monarchs to ride in the state befitting their station and some remarkable vehicles were built in both Britain and America for the South Americans. Par-ticularly worth mention are some British-built cars of the early 1890s for the head of the Argentine state, in one of which the drawing room boasted an open fire-place surmounted by a heavy overmantel that bore, in true Victorian style, a pon-derous parlor clock. The Argentinians evidently fancied this caprice, as they had it repeated in subsequent Presi-dential vehicles.

extreme left: One of the last duties of the LNER Royal Train was to serve at a Royal wedding at York on 8 June 1961. It is seen here leaving London Kings Cross behind class A4 Pacific No 60028 *Walter K Whigham*. (Courtesy British Rail)

left and below: A day saloon and the King's bathroom in the 1926 saloons of the LNER Royal Train. (Courtesy British Rail)

Canadian provision for Royal travel in the 1930s: the lounge (above), dining-room (center) and observation lounge (above right) of a specially refurnished car. (Courtesy Author's collection)

bottom, extreme right: Canadian Pacific 'Royal Hudson' 4-6-4 No 2850 heads the Royal Train on the Canadian tour of King George VI and Queen Elizabeth in May 1939. (Courtesy Author's collection)

A marked change came over British royal train equipment with the accession of King Edward VII in 1901. And, for that matter, over British royal train operation. Victoria was nothing like so paranoic about undue speed as a visiting Shah of Persia who, having been conveyed from Dover to London in a royal train at a gross excess of, in his view, the safe limit of 10mph, demanded that the delinquent driver be put forthwith to the sword. But she was insistent that progress be at all times sedate. In 1850 her private secretary had been bidden straightly to inform the Great Western Railway 'that the speed of the Royal Train should on no account be increased at any one point on the line to make up for the time lost by an unforseen delay at another.' The command, the equerry added, had 'probably arisen from one of the Directors telling Her Majesty that they had been driving the train at the rate of sixty miles an hour, a gratuitous piece of information which, very naturally, alarmed Her Majesty.'

Her Majesty's bones must have shuddered and turned unconscionably on their final journey. That was in her coffin, en route from her Isle of Wight residence at Osborne to London. There had been a last-minute change of route which got the working off to a nail-biting start. Then the departure of the funeral train from the mainland port, Gosport, was delayed by

problems in platforming the vehicles and marshalling the visiting royal mourners and other dignitaries to their appointed seats. By the time they got on to the main line to London Victoria at Fareham the proceedings were ten minutes adrift with only 88 miles to go.

Edward VII was a martinet where punctuality was concerned, so the engine crew of 4-4-0 No 54 *Empress* were told to forget the decorum of the occasion and make up as much time as they could. In the event they pulled into Victoria two minutes early, having roared through the cathedral city of Chichester at 80mph, taken some curves more daringly than the rubrics allowed ordinary service trains and at one point – so officials blenching at the roughness of the ride swore later – hitting 90mph. This was only the first of his kingly rail journeys on which Edward VII, wittingly or unwittingly, set up a record performance for the times.

Edward VII was a man of the sea. Consequently, when the royal opinion was sought of the style to be applied to new vehicles for his use, the answer was a simple 'Make it like a yacht.' Hence the abrupt change from the claustrophobic interior padding of Victoria's coaches to the clean white walls of the London & North Western's two magnificent twelve-wheeled saloons of 1903, seen in the accompanying illustrations. The full royal

The Queen's saloon (far left), the King's bedroom (center above) and the dining hall (above) of the extraordinary Italian Royal Train of 1929. (Courtesy Author's collection)

left: The French Railways streamlined Nord Pacific No 3.1280 is appropriately decorated for the British King and Queen's rail trip to Paris in 1938. (Courtesy Author's collection)

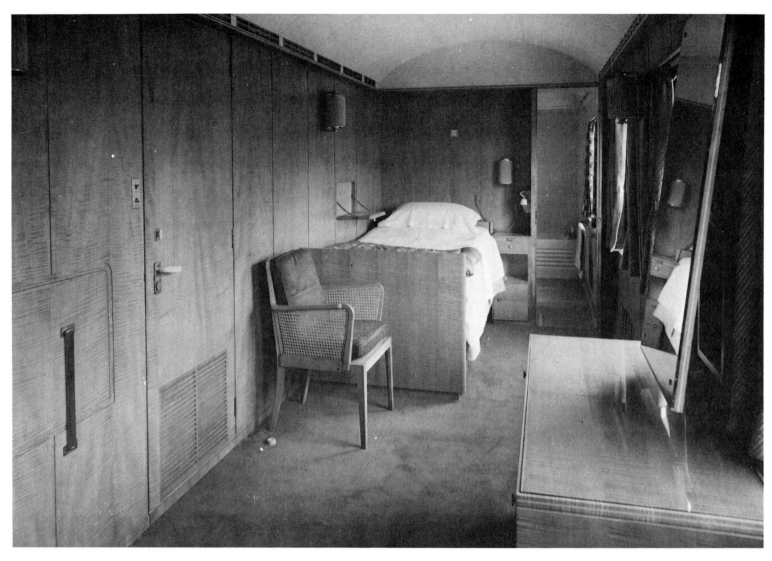

train of which these were the centerpieces
was remarkably long-lived, retaining its
original chocolate-and-white LNWR livery long after the company's 1923 absorption into the LMS; this was at the
behest of King George V, who was
adamantly opposed to repainting in LMS
red. Not until 1941 were the royal saloons
superseded by new LMS-style twelve-
wheelers with handsomely updated internal decor and furniture. These, too,
are illustrated.

In the 20th century the preferred royal
residences outside London have been
Balmoral on Scotland's Dees-side, and
Sandringham, much nearer London in
Norfolk. Until the mid-century the LMS
train was mostly used to the former
destination, the LNER to the latter (each,
of course, was frequently turned out for
one-off royal visits elsewhere). Almost as
durable as the 1903 LNWR saloons were
the LNER train's two twelve-wheelers
assembled in 1908, one by the Great
Northern at Doncaster, the other by the
North Eastern at York. Some of their
detail was decidedly advanced for the
day: cooking as well as lighting was in
part electric, they had an early form of
air-conditioning, and concealed electric
lighting in the wall cornices. The 17½ft-
long rooms in the center of the car were

almost devoid of fixed furniture, so that
they could be set up either as bedrooms,
as lounges or as dining rooms according
to length of journey.

Royalty went very much out of fashion
with World War I, but in 1929 the king who
clung to his throne by grace of Mussolini
was presented with three coaches of 19th
century imperial extravagance to add
to his compensations. There was little
externally to distinguish these cars which
Fiat, themselves grateful and relieved to
discover Fascism counted capitalism its
handmaiden not its ogre, built for Victor
Emmanuel III. They were of similar outline to Italian State Railways cars of the
period though painted a distinctive dark
blue. But within the designer, one Pro-
fessor Giulio Casanova who gained the
job in national competition, had been
given *carte blanche*. There he conjured
up, seemingly quite regardless of cost,
an incredible miniature of a Renaissance
palace, complete with a banqueting hall
of a dining room.

Even pictured in monochrome the
results look more like fantasy than reality,
but imagine what the banqueting hall
must have been like seen in its full glory
of red and gold, and the other rooms with
their finery of Genoa velvet, tooled and
gilded leather, brocades, silks, tapestries

and exotic woods. Of the carpets, created
by expatriate Armenians on the Adriatic coast, Fiat boasted in its official
brochure that there were no fewer than
38,000 knots in every square foot of the
banqueting hall's floor covering. The
cars were designed and technically
fitted out to run throughout Western
Europe so that, as Fiat proclaimed, it
would be not only a travelling royal
palace but a showpiece of Italian arts and
crafts. 'It will show the foreign Sovereigns,
Princes, Ministers and Diplomats who
may be received as guests of the King of
Italy how the ancient artistic genius of the
Italians is able to co-operate with the
most modern of industrial products. In
this train can be seen the close collaboration of engineer and artist, steel and gold,
pencil and pneumatic hammer, art gallery
and workshop.'

It was the last of the really indulgent
royal trains. A beautiful and superlatively-
equipped train was built by the British
firm, Metropolitan-Cammell, in 1946 for
King George V's last great overland tour
in the distant reaches of his Empire, his
spring 1947 circuit of South Africa. But its
beauty lay in its excellently-achieved
ambience of domestic comfort, a haven to
which the royal family would be eager to
retire after a day's wearing ceremonial,

above and left: Royal travel on the 3ft 6in-gauge: (above) coaches of the last Royal Train to be built for South Africa, constructed in Britain by Metro-Cammell for the Royal tour of 1947; and (left) a view of its lounge car.   (Courtesy Metro-Cammell)

extreme left, top: The more austere style of the King's bedroom in one of the two new saloons built in 1941 by the LMS is conspicuous.   (Courtesy British Rail)

not in any striving for grandiose effect.

A royal train survives in Britain, refreshed with a couple of new royal saloons as recently as 1977. The new cars' interiors, though, are restrained, soberly but comfortably furnished executive suites compared with the saloons of old. Economically, they have been created within the shells of standard British Rail Mk III coaches, and the rest of the train nowadays consists largely of adapted and refined nationalization era coaches (though one has the body of a 1920 London & North Western chairmen's business car mounted on a new 1967 underframe and modern bogies). Elsewhere Presidents and Premiers, on the rare occasions they are not airborne, make do with a train of the latest business cars, diners and sleepers their railroads have to offer.

Of all luxury trains, royalty's were the crowning jewels. Sadly, we shall never see the likes of these again.

The dressing room (below) and bedroom (right) of a car prepared for Queen Elizabeth and the Queen Mother's travels on the meter-gauge Kenyan Railways in 1959. (Courtesy East African Railways & Harbours)